W9-CSL-694

THE CLASSIC ASIAN COOKBOOK

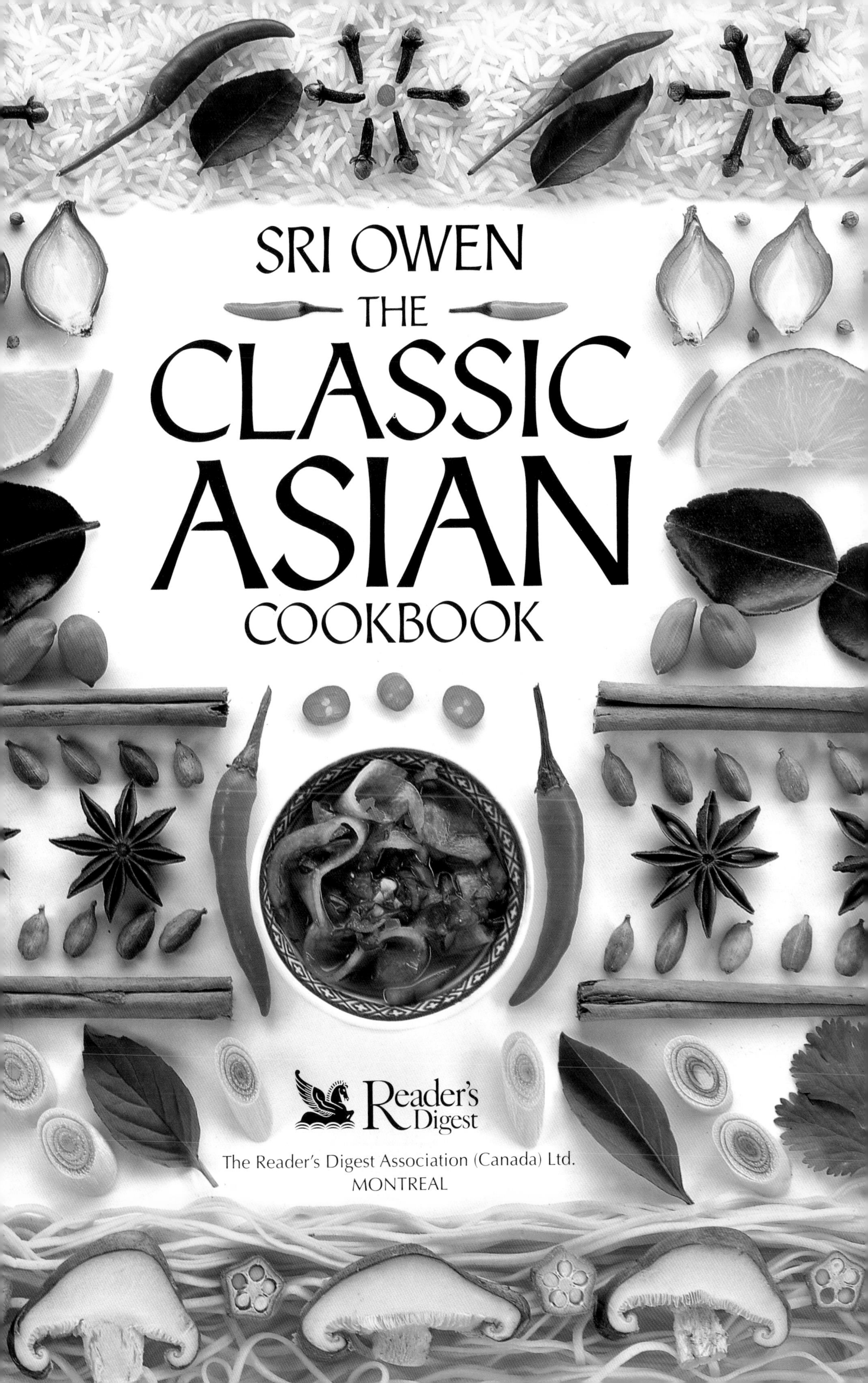

SRI OWEN

THE CLASSIC ASIAN COOKBOOK

Reader's Digest

The Reader's Digest Association (Canada) Ltd.
MONTREAL

A DK PUBLISHING BOOK

Project Editor *Kate Scott*
Senior Editor *Nicola Graimes*
Art Editor *Sue Storey at Patrick McLeavey & Partners*
Senior Art Editor *Tracey Clarke*
DTP Design *Karen Ruane*
Managing Editor *Susannah Marriott*
Managing Art Editor *Toni Kay*
Photography *Clive Streeter*, *Patrick McLeavey*
Food Stylist *Oona van den Berg*
Production Controller *Patricia Harrington*

To the memory of my mother Dianah Poeradidjaja Djamil

All nutritional-information figures are approximate and are based on figures from food composition tables with additional data for manufactured products, where appropriate, not on direct analysis of prepared dishes. Nutritional information is given per serving based on the number of servings in parentheses. Use these figures as a guide only.
Please note that KCal is an abbreviation for kilocalories, sometimes inaccurately called calories. (TF = total fat, SF = saturated fat, and UF = unsaturated fat.)

Published in Canada in 1998 by
The Reader's Digest Association (Canada) Ltd.
215 Redfern Avenue, Westmount, Quebec H3Z 2V9

For information on this and other Reader's Digest products or to request a catalogue, please call our 24-hour Customer Service hotline at 1-800-465-0780.

You can also visit us on the World Wide Web at http://www.readersdigest.ca

Canadian Cataloguing in Publication Data

Owen, Sri
Classic Asian cookbook

Includes index.
ISBN 0-88850-550-7

1. Cookery, Oriental. I. Title

TX724.5.A1094 1996 641.595 C900906-2

Reproduced by Scanner Services SRL
Printed and bound in Italy by A. Mondadori, Verona

98 99 00 01 / 5 4 3 2 1

CONTENTS

INTRODUCTION

I was born among the mountains of Sumatra and spent the first part of my life there. My grandmother had rice fields, a vegetable garden, a hectare or two of coffee bushes. I accompanied her on her rounds of inspection, gathered wild herbs at the edge of fields, and watched her cook. Then the whole household would eat together, sitting cross-legged on straw mats, eating with our fingers as the grown-ups exchanged the gossip of the day. It was perhaps the best possible education for a small child in the appreciation of good food and convivial good manners.

As a high-school student and then an undergraduate in Java, I knew every street-food vendor in town and could bargain with anyone for the freshest vegetables in the market. I took for granted my familiarity with the dishes of Central Sumatra and West and Central Java, and of West Malaysia as well. In every city there were eating houses that specialized in the food of other regions and islands, and I got to know most of them. One of my friends was a Chinese student who loved Cantonese cooking and taught me the basic techniques and recipes. As a young university lecturer I went on trips to Jakarta and was invited to some of the fine Chinese restaurants in Glodok, the old commercial center, where the food was as good as the best I have eaten since in Singapore and Hong Kong.

In 1964 I moved to London, the wife of a young English teacher. Then I broadcast topical talks for the BBC Indonesian Service, and in my spare time hunted for spices and chilies to re-create some of the flavors my cooking and my palate demanded. Shopping trips to the Netherlands kept me going in those early years, but soon all sorts of new foods were appearing in Britain. My dinner party menus became more and more adventurous, and seemed to be well received. My first book, *The Home Book of Indonesian Cookery*, was published in 1976, and I set myself to the serious enjoyment of learning and cooking everything I could, first from Indonesia, then from a widening circle of Asian countries and traditions. And not for the world would I have missed the food of Europe, the Middle East, Mexico and North America, and of course the cuisines of the countries I keep going back to, Australia and New Zealand.

With the food came the history of how ingredients and recipes have traveled the trade routes of the world. I had always known that Indonesian cooking was deeply influenced by Persian, Indian, Chinese, and even Dutch cuisine, but I then found out how the classic dishes of each country can absorb all kinds of novelties and still keep their own essential character. It was a turning point; from then on I thought of myself as a creative professional cook. For a while I ran a delicatessen in South London, cooked for Harrods as well as for my own local customers, and gave Indonesian and Thai cooking classes and dinners. This was fun and it went

well enough, but I knew I still had to travel to many countries in Asia, and to many islands of my own country, that I had never seen. This book is one of the results of this time of travel that has taken up so much of my life and that of my husband in the past ten years.

Much as I like to write about food, frankly, I love eating and I love cooking much more; so I have included only the recipes that I have enjoyed cooking and eating several times at least during the period in which this book was researched and written. It is always hard to choose what to include, but obviously I had to strike a balance between all 14 different countries featured and the various chapter headings of the book – meat, vegetables, and so on. Knowing what to leave out is even harder, but I have not selected dishes that require an unreasonably long time to prepare. With unfamiliar food we all need a little help planning the whole meal, so I have offered four Indian menus and three menus each from China, Indonesia/Malaysia, Thailand, and Japan. There are also menus suitable for entertaining and for vegetarian meals. I hope you will enjoy all these, but do, once you are familiar with the flavors and techniques, start experimenting, especially with combinations of Eastern and Western dishes in the same meal and indeed the same course; this can be very rewarding.

Sri Owen

THE CUISINES OF ASIA

This map of Asia is spread like a huge table, its cloth embroidered with rice fields, coconut groves, gardens of fruit trees, spice and coffee plantations, and oceans teeming with fish. Regional cuisines have always flourished in this great expanse, each area using local resources and flavors to the fullest, but at the same time trading ideas and ingredients with its neighbors. The greatest dishes have long been recognized as classics, and have been carried from the countryside to the cities and then far beyond their original borders. On this tablecloth are set some of those dishes that have been brought to perfection over centuries, in palaces and farmhouses, by chefs and home cooks, street traders and philosophers.

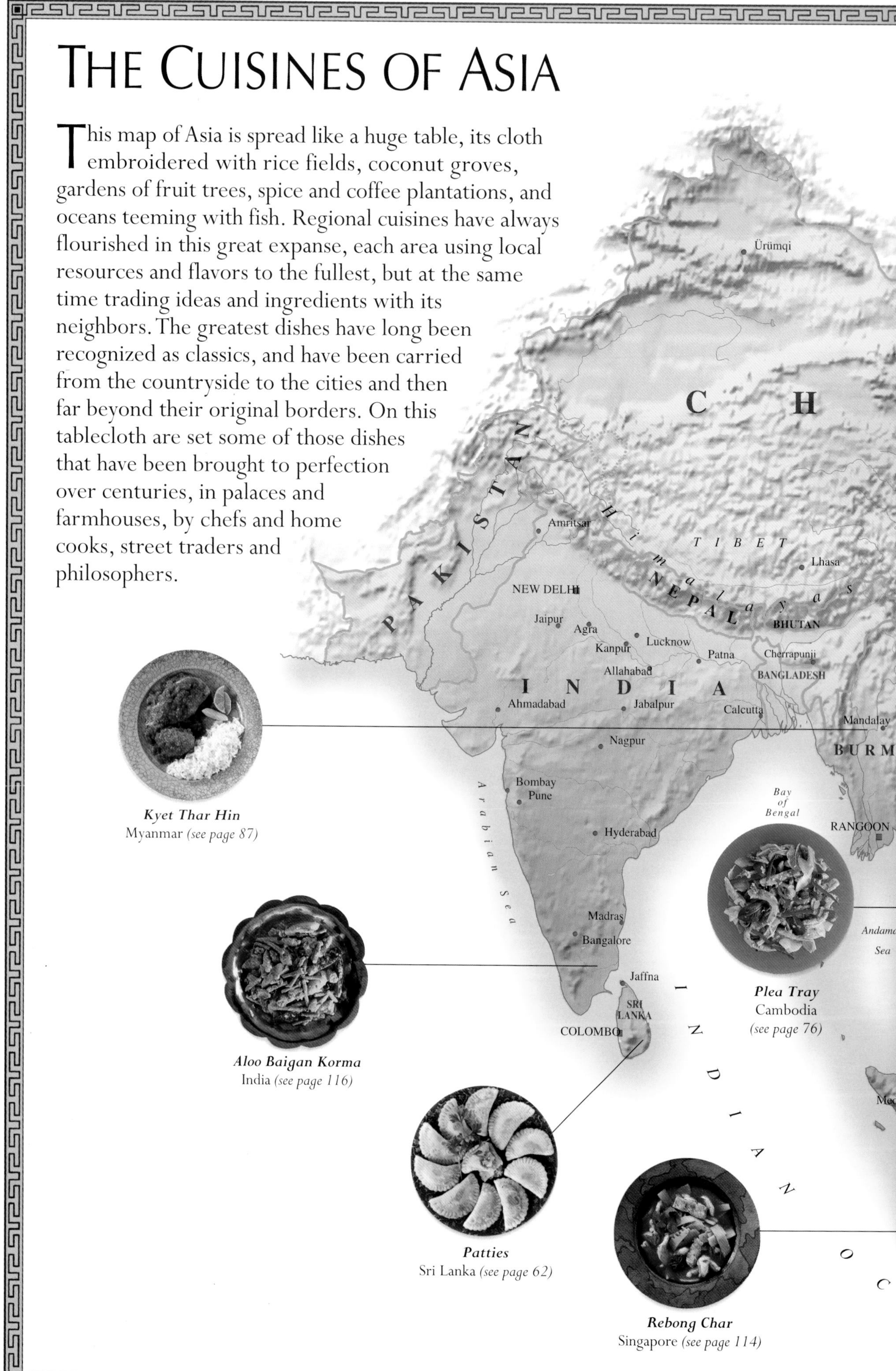

Kyet Thar Hin
Myanmar *(see page 87)*

Plea Tray
Cambodia
(see page 76)

Aloo Baigan Korma
India *(see page 116)*

Patties
Sri Lanka *(see page 62)*

Rebong Char
Singapore *(see page 114)*

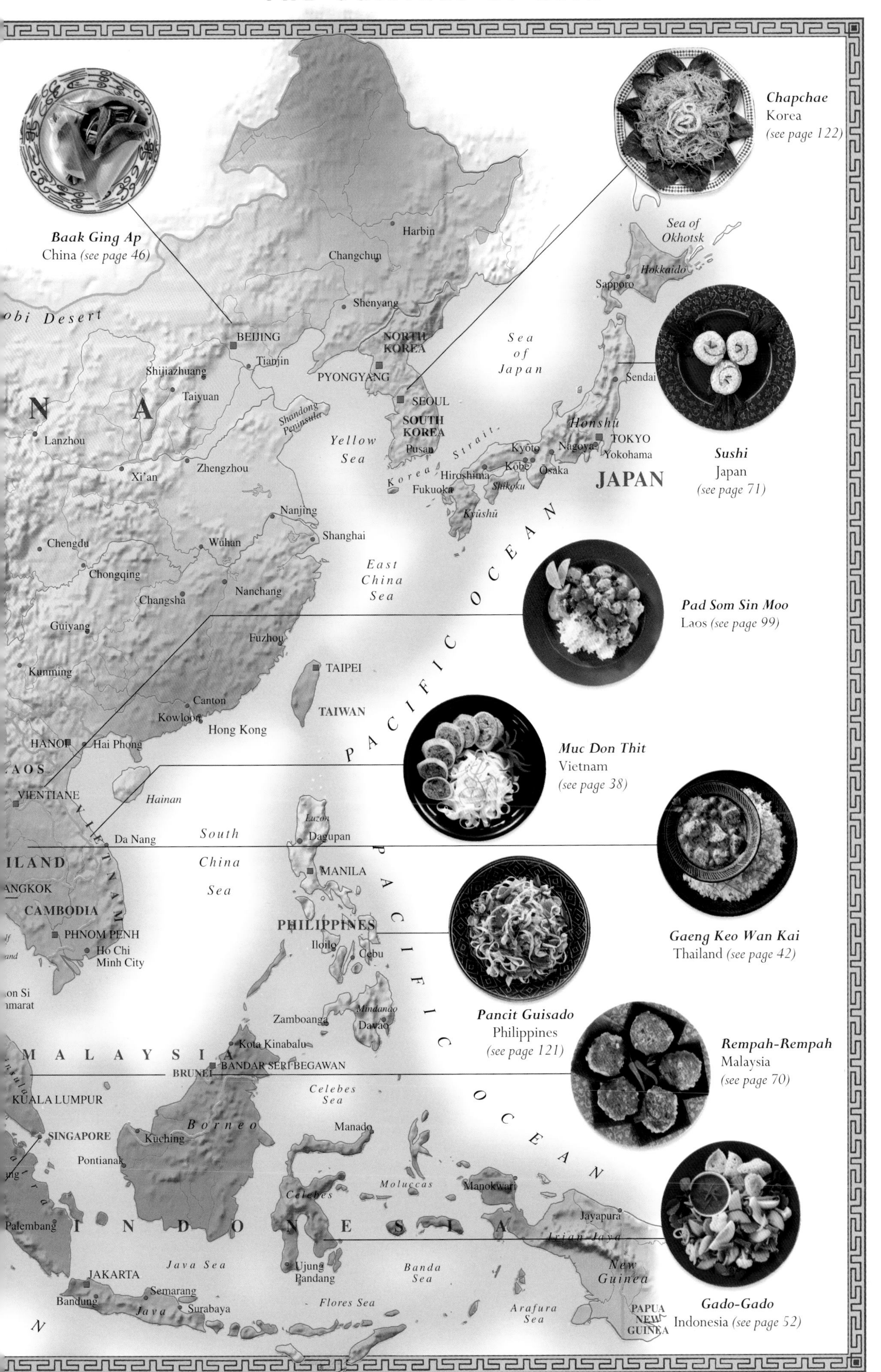
Baak Ging Ap
China (see page 46)
Chapchae
Korea
(see page 122)
Sushi
Japan
(see page 71)
Pad Som Sin Moo
Laos (see page 99)
Muc Don Thit
Vietnam
(see page 38)
Gaeng Keo Wan Kai
Thailand (see page 42)
Pancit Guisado
Philippines
(see page 121)
Rempah-Rempah
Malaysia
(see page 70)
Gado-Gado
Indonesia (see page 52)
Gobi Desert
Harbin
Changchun
Shenyang
BEIJING
Tianjin
NORTH KOREA
PYONGYANG
SEOUL
SOUTH KOREA
Pusan
Shijiazhuang
Taiyuan
Lanzhou
Xi'an
Zhengzhou
Shandong Peninsula
Yellow Sea
Sea of Japan
Sea of Okhotsk
Hokkaido
Sapporo
Sendai
Honshū
TOKYO
Yokohama
Nagoya
Kyoto
Kobe
Osaka
Hiroshima
Fukuoka
Shikoku
Kyūshū
Korea Strait
JAPAN
Nanjing
Shanghai
Wuhan
Chengdu
Chongqing
Nanchang
Changsha
Guiyang
Fuzhou
Kunming
East China Sea
PACIFIC OCEAN
TAIPEI
TAIWAN
Canton
Kowloon
Hong Kong
HANOI
Hai Phong
LAOS
VIENTIANE
Hainan
VIETNAM
Da Nang
South China Sea
Luzon
Dagupan
MANILA
THAILAND
BANGKOK
CAMBODIA
PHNOM PENH
Ho Chi Minh City
PHILIPPINES
Iloilo
Cebu
Mindanao
Zamboanga
Davao
MALAYSIA
Kota Kinabalu
BRUNEI
BANDAR SERI BEGAWAN
KUALA LUMPUR
SINGAPORE
Celebes Sea
Borneo
Kuching
Pontianak
Manado
Moluccas
Manokwari
Celebes
Jayapura
Irian Jaya
INDONESIA
Palembang
Java Sea
Ujung Pandang
Banda Sea
New Guinea
JAKARTA
Semarang
Bandung
Java
Surabaya
Flores Sea
Arafura Sea
PAPUA NEW GUINEA

India

Aloo Baigan Korma
(see page 116)

This vast land-mass must surely be, culturally, the richest and most complex area of the world. Over the centuries every great power, friendly or not, sooner or later "discovered" India, introducing new food habits and customs and exchanging them for recipes, spices, and exotic fruits. From the cook's point of view, however, India has always given more than it has received. Almost every ingredient required for an Indian meal is native to the country, and the cooking of each region has developed around its own produce. In India, Pakistan, or Bangladesh, as in my own country of Indonesia, I am always aware of the differences among regional cuisines; yet these cannot hide the family likeness that all the regions share.

FAMILIAR INGREDIENTS

Many ingredients are familiar to other parts of Asia: spices, herbs, and other aromatic flavors; tamarind; palm sugar, or jaggery; coriander leaves (cilantro) and seeds; cumin, cardamom, ginger, turmeric, and chili – these, along with rice or wheat bread and fish, are much the same as in neighboring lands. The main difference in Indian cuisine is the use of milk and dairy products, which until recently were almost unknown in most other parts of Asia. These are made into *paneer* and other soft cheeses and ghee, or clarified butter, which is the cooking medium of the north as coconut milk is of the south. And while most Asians consume large amounts of fruit and vegetables, only India has a true vegetarian tradition. *Dhal,* or lentils, are a major source of protein for everyone. At a family meal, besides lentils, there are at least two vegetable dishes, and unlike a typical Thai salad, an Indian lentil or bean salad is without meat. Meat dishes, on the other hand, usually contain vegetables, and curry normally has plenty of sauce, enriched with spices and thickened with well-ground chilies and plenty of sliced onions softened in ghee or oil. In the recipes for this book I have included enough meat to satisfy Western appetites, but an Indian family might have equal satisfaction from dunking chapatis in the curry sauce, or pouring the sauce over a plateful of basmati rice.

Samosa *(see page 65)*

CULINARY RULES

The Indian subcontinent has nurtured two major religious faiths, Hinduism and Buddhism, and has embraced a third, Islam. Muslim food originally came from the Ottoman Empire and from Persia, and was the basis of what we now know as Mogul cooking. Hindus and Muslims observe dietary rules that prohibit the consumption of beef or pork, appoint times for feasting or fasting, and favor milk products and vegetables. There is an understanding that the soul has to be nourished as well as the body, for fasting, or abstaining from meat, feeds the spirit; milk products provide the body with the nutrients it requires. Rules bring order to the world and help us make the best use of limited resources. They do not prevent people from enjoying food. Indeed, the rules have challenged Indian cooks over the centuries to greater heights of invention. It is no wonder that from these three nations – India, Pakistan, and Bangladesh – have come some of the most brilliant cooks, and the most passionate gourmets, that I have ever met.

Sri Lanka

Patties (see page 62)

Sri Lanka has perfect beaches, high hills in the center, fertile plains for growing rice, and a huge variety of tropical and subtropical vegetables and fruit, all in a remarkably small area. One of this island's many wonders is that the tourist business has not yet overwhelmed it. Though it has suffered political troubles in recent years, in the long term I am optimistic about the Sri Lankan people, as I am about the Balinese; their personalities and cultures are strong enough to adapt and reassert themselves. In the past, Sri Lanka, though close to southern India, has remained culturally independent, and its food reflects this. True, it bears the traces of many invaders and colonists – Tamils, Portuguese, and the Dutch left their marks, and though the British left little behind in the way of cooking, their tea plantations among the hills are still productive. Cakes, sweet dishes, and snacks still popular around the coastline of the Indian Ocean show Dutch and Portuguese influences. The patties on page 62, for example, are found not only here but 3,000 miles away in Menado on the northern tip of Sulawesi, where they are still called by the Portuguese name, *panada*. Sri Lankan *sambol* is also very similar to the *sambal* of Malaysia and Indonesia. There is a distinctive Sri Lankan culinary style and flavor, however, which I have tried to bring out in the recipes that follow. Curries use characteristically dark-roasted spices or are colored red with chilies. Coconut milk and ghee (clarified butter) are both used as a cooking medium. And, as in Southeast Asia, a great quantity of intensely flavored, savory, sharp-tasting, sweet, or hot accompaniments allow everyone at the table to create a dish to his or her own taste.

Myanmar (Burma)

Kyet Thar Hin (see page 87)

The recent history of Burma – or Myanmar, as its rulers now wish it to be called – has to a great extent cut it off from the outside world. Like Indonesia, Burma has never been a great place for restaurants, and the best Burmese food has always been found in family homes. Traditions of hospitality are as strong in Burma as they are anywhere else in Asia, and no guest ever goes hungry. Large families and frequent Buddhist celebrations mean big, elaborate meals, shared with the extended family and a wide circle of friends. The atmosphere of such a gathering is festive but informal, a celebration of the bounty of nature. Traditionally, the hostess and her daughters, having supervised many hours of work in the kitchen, would have their meal first before dressing in their finest clothes and coming out to greet their guests and look after them throughout the meal. The rice and curries are displayed for everyone to help themselves, flanked by what an old Burmese friend of mine used to call the "toly-molies" – sauces, relishes, pickles and chutneys, and chopped raw vegetables and herbs – for the guests to decorate and flavor their food just the way they like it. These complement fine cooking behind the scenes, where the basic flavors of Burma – onion, ginger, garlic, chili, and dried shrimp paste – are blended in curry pastes.

Thailand

Gaeng Keo Wan Kai (see page 42)

Thai food has had a big impact in the West during the past 20 years. There are several reasons for this, but the key has been Thai self-confidence and flair for opening small restaurants, where the staff are friendly and the cooking is usually good. Ingredients are often flown in from Bangkok – lemongrass, kaffir limes, basil, galangal, dried shrimp, pea eggplants, small white eggplants, green vegetables – and the dishes are cooked to more or less authentic recipes; even in the takeout places, customers seem to like Thai food as it is, and there has been no compromising of flavors as there has been in too many Indian and Chinese restaurants. The basis of much Thai food is an aromatic sourness and the delicate heat of chilies, flavors that blend well with meat, vegetables, and seafood. A marriage between Thai and French or other Western cooking has produced "fusion cuisine," which has passed beyond being merely trendy and is now well established – though it can work well only if the cook is equally familiar with both traditions. In Thailand itself, food commands respect and much attention, and I love to spend a morning walking through a small-town marketplace, watching street-food vendors, and then having a long lunch in an open-sided restaurant with a shady verandah. But even better is to be invited for the evening to a friend's house, especially if it is a very old friend who will first take me shopping with her and then give me the run of the kitchen as dinner is being prepared.

Cambodia

Plea Tray (see page 76)

Laos, Vietnam, and Cambodia make up what used to be called Indochina – a name that, for a lover of Asian food, sounds like a paradox, for you could hardly find two cultures more distinct than those of China and India. But this region has had plenty of contact with both, and still has preserved its own character. Its complex history even includes almost a century under French rule, and a few French restaurants are still in business there today, although French and local food are regarded as two quite different things. Cambodia, focused on the mouth of the Mekong River, shares in the Vietnamese "rice bowl" of the delta, with its rich soil and plentiful water for irrigation; the huge artificial lakes near the Angkor temples were probably built to control its flow. Like Laos to the north, it has (or had until recently) enough forest to provide game, particularly deer. Cambodian cooks use salty fish sauce, coconut milk, and aromatic herbs such as lemongrass and kaffir lime leaves. Chilies are added sparingly, but chili addicts will demand raw chilies or extra-hot cooked side dishes.

Laos

Pad Som Sin Moo
(see page 99)

I once introduced a Lao friend to the Thai chef of a famous London restaurant, and they were delighted to find that, although they were from opposite sides of the Mekong River and spoke different dialects, they could understand each other. Landlocked as it is, this country – almost as big as Vietnam but with a much smaller population – has had a stormy history that shows little sign of lapsing into calm. Its southern portion occupies the fertile valley of the Mekong, while in the north are high mountains thinly populated by a number of tribes. Its food traditions have much in common with those of its Thai and Vietnamese neighbors, but the *Montagnards*, or northern mountain-dwellers, have given it a taste for "sticky" rice (often called glutinous or sweet rice). My Lao and Thai friends found they could understand each other's cooking, too, despite differences mainly in the proportions of spices used in mixes that were otherwise basically similar. There are very few Lao cookbooks; the only one I possess is a transcript, with an English translation, of a collection of traditional recipes dictated by an old man who had been *maître chef des cuisines* in the royal palace at Luang Prabang. They were published by Alan Davidson, the British ambassador to Laos in the early 1970s. The old chef's instructions, as printed, are difficult to interpret and impossible to follow exactly, but I have tested and developed a few of them with excellent results. Naturally, there is a strong southern Chinese influence: coconut milk is often used, and many dishes are deep-fried, stir-fried, or steamed.

Vietnam

Muc Don Thit
(see page 38)

Like its neighbors, Laos and Cambodia, Vietnam uses a lot of *nuoc mam*, fish sauce, to give its food the sharp savory tang that is one of its principal traits. The country's most popular sauce, *nuoc cham*, is based on it. There is, of course, Chinese influence, but I suspect that few Chinese would approve of the quantity of garlic that goes into an authentic Vietnamese meal, especially in the south of the country. People here are what I call "wet eaters" – many soup dishes contain enough meat, fish, and vegetables to be eaten as one-dish meals, though of course with plenty of rice. They also like to cool down in hot weather with salads and have adopted the Chinese classification of foods into *yin* and *yang*, those that cool the body and those that heat it. Vietnamese food has a special appeal to health-conscious eaters because so many dishes are cooked in water, not oil, and many vegetables are served raw or very lightly cooked. More important, however, is the balance between *yin* and *yang*, and between the different textures of the meal: wet and dry, soft and chewy, smooth and crunchy.

Malaysia

Rempah-Rempah
(see page 70)

Malaysian food is as varied as the origins of its people, many of whose ancestors came from neighboring countries and islands. The climate, soils, and natural resources are similar to those of western Indonesia and the islands of Java and Sumatra, so it is not surprising that many favorite Malaysian dishes have an Indonesian flavor. Often it is difficult to tell on which side of the water a recipe originated. But Malaysians also have numerous links with China, Indochina, India, and southern Thailand, and all these have contributed to the use of spices, herbs, and aromatics in cooking. Pungent shrimp paste and fiery chilies are as popular here as in any part of Southeast Asia, and at the right time of year the air is full of the bewitching scent of ripe durian fruit. Over the course of two or three centuries, a great number of merchants and craftsmen left their homes in south China and settled in the towns along the Malay Peninsula and the northern coastline of Borneo. They prospered and married local women, who were thereafter addressed by the polite title of *nyonya* or *nonya*, "lady." Their cooking combined recipes and tastes from both sides of the family, so that Nonya food is now recognized and written about as a tradition in its own right, and Nonya restaurants are found not only in Malaysia and Singapore but in Europe, Australia, and North America.

Satay Daging
(see page 67)

Singapore

Rebong Char
(see page 114)

Singapore is one of the great gastronomic centers of the world, where cooks and restaurants represent the finest cuisines from all over Asia and beyond. Food could almost be said to be modern Singapore's only link with the past, and even food has been affected by the speed of economic growth. The colorful street-food stands that once thronged the city have long since been tidied into covered food courts. However, this has the advantage that you can eat well, at low cost, and be confident that what you are eating was prepared in clean conditions. In 1981 I took my two young sons to Singapore as part of their first visit to Southeast Asia. In the evenings we ate Malaysian food in the open air at Newton Circus and hoped it would not rain, or we ate satay in a food court near the waterfront. Then we fed the younger boy at McDonald's, and the whole family ended up with ice cream at the Raffles Hotel. That, I think, is pretty typical of the Singaporean food scene today, though the city's tastes continue to develop apace in all directions. The closest thing to a local cuisine is Nonya cooking, which has continued to develop among Singapore's predominantly Chinese community: a combination of Chinese techniques (such as stir-frying) and ingredients (soy sauce, five-spice powder) with the tropical flavors of chili, coconut, and peanut sauce.

INDONESIA

Gado-Gado (see page 52)

The classic Indonesian landscape is one of terraced rice fields mounting from the river valley to the foothills of the local volcano. Yet this is typical only of Java and Bali, parts of Sumatra and Sulawesi, and a few other islands. Millions of Indonesians depend more on sago or cassava than on rice. The real staple food of Indonesia is fish, from the sea and from lakes and rivers, as well as from the flooded rice fields. Indonesians, living among their 15,000-odd islands, have always been sailors, traders, and fishermen. When fish could not be eaten fresh, they had to be dried in the sun and salted, and fish spread out to dry are still a common sight.

BALANCING TASTES

The basic diet of many Indonesians is plain boiled white rice, with fish, *lalab* (raw or plainly cooked vegetables), and a few hot chilies. Mere hotness, however, is not all that people demand of food. Most Indonesian cooking is inspired by a love of sourness delicately balanced by sweetness. The sweetness comes largely from coconut milk, often used as a cooking medium, or coconut palm sugar. Many agree that sour notes offer more subtlety and greater range, and tamarind, lemongrass, fruit, and galangal are among the sources. The other contrast to sweetness, saltiness, is provided not only by salt but by fermented products, particularly soy sauce, introduced by the Chinese, and *terasi*, a pungent shrimp paste.

Sate Pusut (see page 66)

TYPICAL MEALS

The usual family meal, in a reasonably well-off household, consists of rice with one or two meat or fish dishes, vegetables, and soup to wash everything down – many people will not drink even water with a meal. Many savory dishes are variants on a few basic ideas: There are innumerable versions of *sambal goreng*, for example, in which spices, onions, garlic, shrimp paste, and chili are fried in a little oil, then added to the main ingredient to flavor it while it cooks. There are many recipes for stuffings and marinades, and for meat or fish wrapped in leaves (usually banana leaves) or cooked in a segment of a large bamboo stalk, or in the hard sheath of a coconut flower. These retain juices, nutritional value, and flavor. Cooking times are often very short, because much time has been spent preparing and cutting up the ingredients. No one expects to cut up meat at the table, and knives are rarely provided. Many Indonesians prefer to eat with their fingers, of the right hand only. A whole chicken may be torn in pieces and shredded by hand, but any chopping or carving must be done in the kitchen. Most dishes are boiled, steamed, fried, broiled, or barbecued over charcoal. In the past, the only way to bake food was to wrap it in leaves and put it for several hours in a trench lined with hot embers. Dessert is usually fresh fruit, while sweets and cakes are eaten in the afternoon, especially when visitors call. Ninety percent of the population is Muslim (making this the largest Islamic nation in the world), and the end of Ramadan, the fasting month, is marked by at least two days of social visiting, when junior family members (or employees) visit senior ones (or employers) to ask forgiveness for the year's trespasses, drink sweet black tea, and eat cakes of steamed glutinous rice flour and coconut.

PHILIPPINES

Pancit Guisado
(see page 121)

The scenery, the people, even the languages of the Philippines seem familiar to visitors who arrive from Indonesia, but culturally the nations are very different. The Filipinos were converted centuries ago to Catholicism by their Spanish overlords, whereas Indonesia is predominantly Muslim. Almost a century after the Spanish left Manila, their language, culture, and food still have great prestige. It was Spanish ships that brought new foodstuffs from Central and South America – tomatoes, potatoes, corn, and above all the ever-present chili and its milder relatives. Some popular Spanish dishes have been adopted and have evolved over two or three hundred years into luxury feast-day dishes – for example, *paella* has become *bringhe* (cooked with coconut milk instead of olive oil) and *adobo*, originally a Spanish relish, has become a party dish of pork or chicken. Chinese influence is also strong, but Filipino food would be unimaginable without rice, fish, and the tropical fruit that grows on every patch of cultivated land.

CHINA

Baak Ging Ap
(see page 46)

A country as big as China, with at least a fifth of the world's people and scarcely a fifteenth of its arable land, with every climate from cool temperate to monsoon tropical, inevitably has many different regions, each with its own style of cooking. Most people outside China will be familiar with the big four, based on Beijing in the wheat-growing north, Shanghai on the coast, Canton in the south, and Szechwan in the landlocked west. The last is the favorite of those who like food to be strongly flavored and peppery. But China remains one country, and this variety is underpinned by a common philosophy of food and a general agreement on the principles of cooking and its relation to life. Every activity tries to achieve a balance between the forces of *yin* and *yang*, and in the kitchen this means between foods that cool the body and those that heat it. *Yin* foods include sugar, salt, scallions, soy sauce, many vegetables, and much seafood; *yang* include vinegar, ginger, pepper, wine, and fat, oily, or fried food generally. Rice is usually regarded as *yin*. Equally important is the balance between *fan*, the basic or staple food, and *ts'ai*, the secondary but more flavorful part of the meal. Food, in other words, is medicine as well as nourishment for the body. It is no wonder that cooking, at the highest gourmet level, has always been a highly esteemed profession in China. A restaurant culture developed in Chinese cities a thousand years ago and has never looked back. However, there is plenty of good food that can be made easily at home. My own favorite Chinese recipes are those that I learned from Chinese friends, some of them professional chefs, others housewives or students. The dishes I most enjoy eating are the ones I remember from my own youth in Indonesia and Singapore. They may not be classics of the high Imperial past, but the cooking methods (stir-frying, deep-frying, steaming, or slow-cooking), combined with fresh ingredients and spices, give them the zest and appeal of real food.

Korea

Chapchae (see page 122)

My recollections of a train journey across Korea are of low cloud and cool air among the hills, something like the north of England but with rice farmers. The people we met were warmly hospitable but tough and outspoken. For many centuries Korea was like the nut caught in the nutcracker between China and Japan; its people suffered greatly, but they have retained many good things gleaned from so much foreign contact. Korean food shows plenty of Chinese and Japanese influence but has kept its own delicate but unpretentious character. At first sight, Korean cooking may seem rather fussy. The elaborate presentation, however, is achieved by simple methods, such as the precise arrangement of different-colored vegetables, or the use of one ingredient to stuff another. Koreans, perhaps more than any of their neighbors, like to steam their food: soups and steamed fish and vegetable dishes with tofu are plentiful. Seasonings and spices are positive but discreet, based on the "five flavors" considered essential in Asian cooking – sour, sweet, salty, bitter, and hot. Sourness comes from vinegar and from preserves such as *kimchi*; sweetness from rice wine, *mirin*, or strawberry or cherry wine. Saltiness is from soy sauce, bitter flavors mostly from roots such as ginseng, and hotness from black pepper and chilies.

Japan

Sushi (see page 71)

Japanese cooking has been called "a simple art," but its simplicity, the result of centuries of refinement, is exquisite, breathtaking, and not easily combined with other styles and traditions. Japanese food is more appreciated in the world at large as it becomes better known, and its savoriness and freshness are particularly appealing. Though I cook many Japanese dishes with confidence, I admit I am not yet sufficiently sure of myself to serve a complete Japanese meal in traditional style. To do this, you need to have your roots in Japanese life, to sense the importance of the sequence of dishes throughout the meal. Eating becomes a kind of theater, and the play must have a beginning, a middle, and an end. That sounds simple enough: appetizer, main course, dessert. But the first course usually consists of three items: an appetizer, perhaps a morsel of beautifully cut fish or shrimp with one or two ginkgo nuts or chestnuts, then a small bowl of clear soup, followed by *sashimi*, a delicacy of raw seafood. An elaborate main course will be a sequence of dishes: grilled, steamed, simmered, and deep-fried, and one either cooked or dressed in vinegar. For a family meal, all these may be replaced by a one-pot dish, the equivalent of a stew or casserole. The meal ends not with a sweet, but with a small bowl of gleaming white boiled rice, a bowl of miso soup and some pickles, then green tea served with fresh fruit, beautifully sliced. At the end everyone, guests and host, feels satisfied but never uncomfortably full; the meal has been a feast for the eyes, the mind, and the spirit, as well as for the palate.

創製
瀬戸風味
mishima
てあずき
涼茶大王

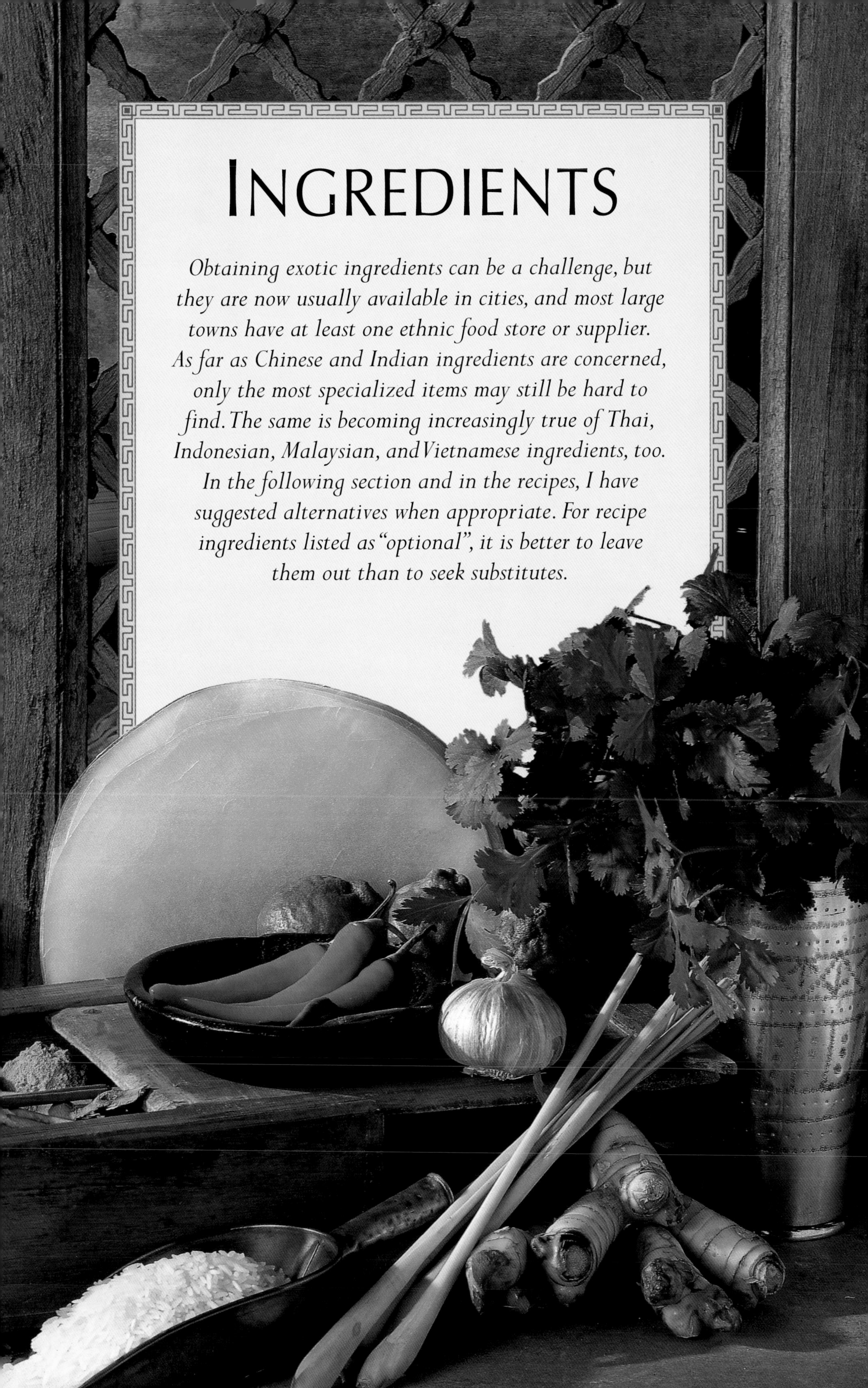

INGREDIENTS

Obtaining exotic ingredients can be a challenge, but they are now usually available in cities, and most large towns have at least one ethnic food store or supplier. As far as Chinese and Indian ingredients are concerned, only the most specialized items may still be hard to find. The same is becoming increasingly true of Thai, Indonesian, Malaysian, and Vietnamese ingredients, too. In the following section and in the recipes, I have suggested alternatives when appropriate. For recipe ingredients listed as "optional", it is better to leave them out than to seek substitutes.

VEGETABLES

Asians have always had a high regard for vegetables; for hundreds of years they have recognized the therapeutic properties of many cultivated and wild plants and their importance to a healthy diet. Much of tropical Asia is very fertile and can produce several crops a year. Vegetables are often intercropped with rice, and even the tiniest patch of land can support a few bean plants or squash, or a banana tree. So almost everyone has a supply of fresh, healthy food.

EGGPLANTS
Purple eggplants are readily available. Choose ones that are firm and shiny; those with wrinkled skins are no longer fresh. Most recipes in this book use medium-sized eggplants, though a few specify baby purple eggplants, which can usually be found at Indian specialty stores. Round, greenish eggplants, also called "apple" eggplants, and very small pea eggplants can be bought in Thai stores – they are commonly used in Thai curries.

DAIKON
This giant white radish, also known as mooli, has a peppery and slightly bitter flavor. Most Asian food stores and some supermarkets sell daikon. It can grow longer than 12in (30cm), but smaller ones are available. For salads, peel the mooli, then cut into tiny strips and soak in cold water for 30 minutes to make it crisper. It is also good added to soups or stir-fried.

Baby purple eggplant

Apple eggplants

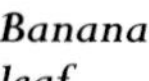

Banana leaf

Plantain

Pea eggplants

Banana flower

BANANA LEAF
Wash before use, then cut into shapes to line serving plates or use to wrap food for cooking. If frozen, use within a few hours of defrosting.

PLANTAIN
Ripe yellow plantains make the best fried plantains. Use unripe green ones for chips.

BANANA FLOWER
Discard the hard outer petals and slice the tender center. Boil for several minutes, and add to soups or salads.

OKRA

These are called bandakka *in Sri Lanka and* bindhi *in India. The texture is a little slimy, but they are delicious when sliced and fried until crisp.*

YARD-LONG BEANS

Available from Thai and Indian food stores, these should be fresh and firm. They are excellent eaten raw, though they are usually lightly cooked until tender but crisp.

ASIAN RED ONIONS

I use these for making Crisp-Fried Onions (see page 132 for recipe) because of their low water content. Buy them from Chinese and Thai food stores.

Fresh shiitake

Dried shiitake

SHIITAKE MUSHROOMS

Fresh shiitake have a delicate texture and are excellent added to stir-fries. Dried ones must be rehydrated in hot water (see page 155). The hard stalks and soaking water are ideal for making stock. Fresh and dried varieties are available from Asian food stores and some supermarkets.

WATER SPINACH

In Southeast Asia this grows as abundantly as watercress and is also known as swamp cabbage. The flavor is between that of watercress and spinach, and the stalk remains crunchy even when cooked. Buy it from Asian food stores or, if unobtainable, use watercress or spinach as a substitute.

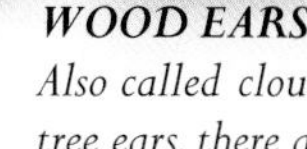

WOOD EARS

Also called cloud ears or tree ears, there are in fact several varieties of this mushroom – the smallest ones have the most delicate flavor. When rehydrated in hot water (see page 155), they have a pleasant crunchy texture.

WATER CHESTNUTS

You can buy these in cans from most supermarkets, or fresh from Chinese food stores. If using fresh, however, choose firm, unblemished ones, rinse off the mud, then carefully peel with a sharp knife.

BAMBOO SHOOTS

Use prepared shoots in cans or glass jars; fresh ones are not worth the trouble. Leftover shoots can be stored in a glass bowl, covered with water; they will keep refrigerated for up to one week.

STRAW MUSHROOMS

These are popular in many Asian countries, where they are cultivated on rice straw. In the West they are available only in cans and have lost much of their flavor, so I usually suggest fresh mushrooms as an alternative.

Fruit, Nuts & Seeds

With the exception of pot marigolds perhaps, the following ingredients are not usually found growing wild, even in their countries of origin. Most have been propagated and cultivated for centuries; many have traveled and have been introduced to new homes. Even the humble peanut has become a highly sophisticated commercial product. The reason is simple – raw or cooked, these are some of the world's best-tasting and most versatile plant foods.

QUINCE
Usually available in fall, these fragrant fruits may be the size of an apple, or larger. In Asia they are used as vegetables and either filled with meat, or diced and added to stuffing mixtures for poultry and seafood.

KAFFIR LIME
The juice of this fruit adds piquancy to chili sauce. The peel, which is rather bumpy, is usually sliced and added to curries and similar dishes to make them more fragrant. Dried peel can be bought packaged.

POMELO
Larger than grapefruit, with a thick yellow-green skin, pomelo is good eaten by itself or added to almost any salad.

POT MARIGOLD
Fresh pot marigold petals from the garden give color and flavor to Moo Wan (see page 98 for recipe) and to salads. Some Asian food stores sell the dried petals.

CANDLENUTS
These come from Indonesia and Malaysia. Always cook them; raw ones are mildly toxic. Use almonds or macadamias as substitutes.

GINKGO NUTS
These small, pale nuts are used in Japanese and Chinese cooking. They are available only canned in the West from Chinese food stores.

CASHEW NUTS
In Asian cooking these are used whole, roughly chopped, or made into a paste. Frying them first imparts extra flavor.

ALMONDS
In this book almonds are used in several Indian recipes; they are also a suitable alternative to candlenuts.

MANGOES

The finest mangoes are Indian, Thai, and the "Manila" mangoes of the Philippines. Ripe ones are firm but not hard, and should have sweet, orange-colored, fragrant flesh, without any trace of fibers. Small green mangoes, available from Indian food stores, are refreshingly sour and good for pickles and chutneys.

GUAVA

Guavas vary in size and are usually pear shaped with pink or cream-colored flesh. They can be eaten like apples, or peeled and thinly sliced. The seeds are edible, if you like them. For cooking, only the flesh is used, and the skin and seeds are discarded.

COCONUT

Before buying a fresh coconut, shake it – you should hear the liquid inside. Dried and grated coconut flesh is the most convenient for making coconut milk, the white liquid extracted from soaking grated coconut flesh in hot water. Coconut cream is the thick white "top" that separates from the milk when refrigerated.

MACADAMIA NUTS

Asian food shops and many supermarkets sell these roasted or fried. They make a good substitute for candlenuts.

PEANUTS

Used widely in Asian cooking, peanuts are also called groundnuts. Buy shelled raw nuts and roast them yourself for the best flavor.

POPPY SEEDS

The gray-blue seeds are used mostly in bread; the cream-colored ones are added to curry sauces as a thickening agent.

SESAME SEEDS

Important in all Far Eastern cooking, these seeds are rich in aromatic oil and are used whole or crushed into a paste.

RICE, NOODLES & WRAPPERS

Beans and grains – basically starches – are the most versatile foods available, and these pages are a tribute to the ingenuity of farmers, cooks, and food manufacturers. Most natural starches can be ground to a flour, then formed into a dough to make noodles, bread, or pastry. Rice, too, depends on starch for its stickiness. Soybeans are amazingly nourishing and adaptable, forming the basis of tofu, as well as flavoring ingredients such as soy sauce, essential in authentic Asian cuisine.

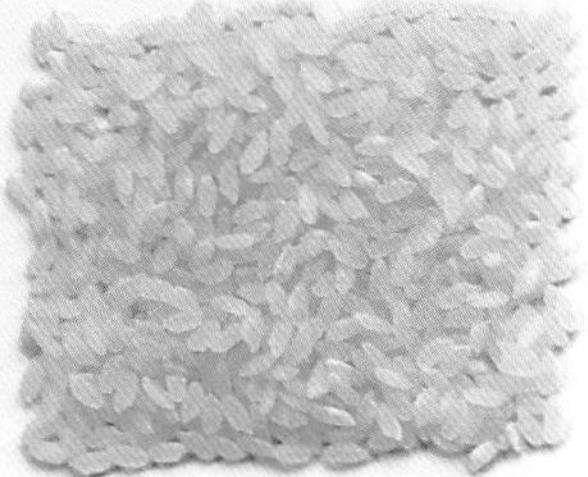

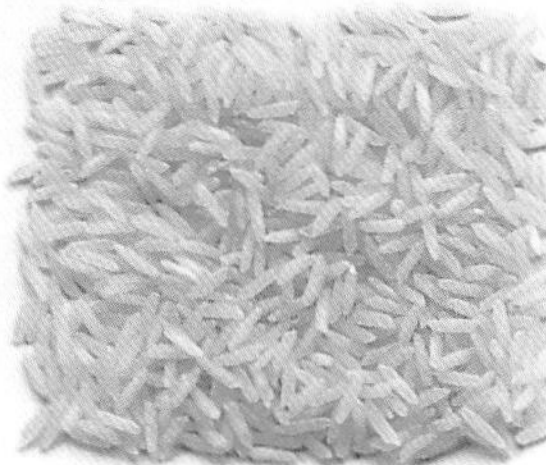

JAPANESE RICE
Japan does not export rice, and almost all the Japanese-style rice available in the West is grown in California. There are many varieties, all short-grained "japonica" rices.

BASMATI RICE
The world's longest-grained rice, basmati is grown in the foothills of the Himalayas. The best is exported to Europe. Basmati-type varieties are also grown in the United States.

JASMINE RICE
The finest rice from the world's largest rice-exporting country, Thailand, is widely available, and often called Thai fragrant rice. The grains are long, softer than basmati, and slightly sticky.

GLUTINOUS RICE
When cooked the grains are soft and sticky, hence the name. White glutinous rice is grown all over Southeast Asia, but black varieties are rare and are more difficult to find in shops.

Japanese silken tofu

Chinese tofu

Fried tofu

TOFU
Japanese soybean curd, "silken" tofu, is very soft, while Chinese tofu is firmer. They are sold in sealed plastic boxes filled with water in Asian food stores and health-food stores. Fried bean curd absorbs sauce during cooking and can also be stuffed.

YIFU OR YI NOODLES
These are deep-fried egg noodles that have been dried and are available from Chinese food stores. Soak in hot water for 3–4 minutes before using. If unobtainable, use fresh or dried egg noodles instead.

UDON NOODLES
Available from Japanese food stores, these round or flat noodles are made of wheat flour. They are usually served in broth, hot or cold, with chopped scallions, flavored with seven-spice powder.

SHIRATAKI
These thin strands are made from a plant known as elephant's foot or devil's tongue. They are added to sukiyaki, a Japanese hot pot, and are also sold as a gelatinous paste called konnyaku*, used in soups.*

SPRING ROLL WRAPPERS

These can be bought in three sizes from most Asian supermarkets. The smallest, about 5in (12cm) square, are used to make mini spring rolls. For standard-sized spring rolls (see page 64 for recipe), use the wrappers that are 9in (24cm) square. The largest, 12in (30cm) square, can be cut into strips and used to make samosa (see page 65 for recipe).

WONTON WRAPPERS

Made from a flour-and-egg dough, these are available fresh or frozen from Chinese food stores, sold in two thicknesses – very thin for stuffing and frying, and thick for steaming.

Bean curd sheet

BEAN CURD SHEET

Also sold as bean curd skins, these sheets are quite large and very brittle. Buy them from Chinese food stores wrapped in waxed paper and packed in clear plastic bags. To use, soak in cold water until pliable, and then cut with scissors. In this book, they are used for Vegetarian Goose (see page 118 for recipe).

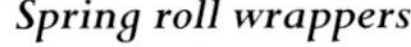

Spring roll wrappers

CHINESE PANCAKES

Essential for serving Peking Duck (see page 46 for recipe), these pancakes are made with plain flour, water, and a little sesame oil. They are available, usually frozen, from Chinese food stores. Defrost completely, then steam for 8–10 minutes. Keep the steamed pancakes in a covered dish or wrapped in a dish towel or napkin as they dry out very quickly.

Wonton wrappers

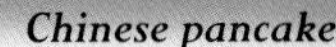

Chinese pancakes

RICE NOODLES

Manufactured from rice flour, then dried, these are sold as very thin strands (rice vermicelli) or ribbons of various widths (also called rice sticks). Rice sticks are popular in Vietnam, Singapore, and Malaysia, while Thais and Indonesians prefer the thinner rice vermicelli.

CELLOPHANE NOODLES

These are also sold as mung bean-flour noodles and bean threads (they are made from mung bean starch), and as glass vermicelli, because they look like spun glass. Cellophane noodles do not need to be boiled, merely soaked in hot water for 10–15 minutes.

Rice vermicelli ***Ribbon rice noodles*** ***Cellophane noodles*** ***Cellophane vermicelli***

HERBS & SPICES

Herbs and spices are at the heart of Asian cooking. Many of them were once luxuries in Asia, just as they were in Europe, while those that were cheaper were often undervalued. One flavoring that is almost universally used in Asia is the chili pepper – and this did not arrive from Central America until the sixteenth century.

THAI BASIL
In Thailand there are at least three kinds of basil: Anise basil (illustrated), Thai basil and holy basil all taste different, so buy the one specified in the recipe if you can.

TURMERIC
This adds a warm yellow color and distinctive flavor to Asian festival dishes. It is definitely not a substitute for saffron.

CHINESE CHIVES
This herb is more pungent than the European chive. Chop the chives, flowers and all, and use in spring rolls and stir-fries. The opened flowers make an attractive edible garnish.

CLOVES
Used in most parts of Asia in both savory and sweet dishes. Remember to remove whole cloves before serving.

FENUGREEK SEEDS
Very popular in Southern India, where they are always an essential ingredient in curry pastes.

FENUGREEK
Fresh fenugreek leaves, used extensively in India, can be bought from Indian food shops. Dried leaves, often called methi, *are also available.*

CORIANDER
Dry-roast the seeds before using; this gives a more aromatic result. Ground coriander loses its fragrance if stored for too long.

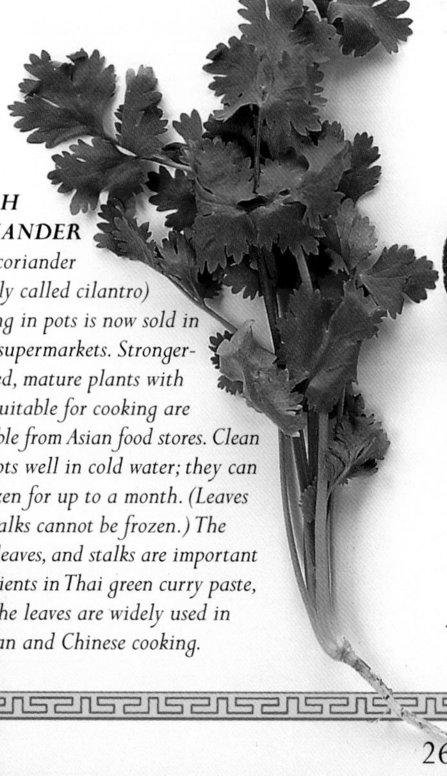

FRESH CORIANDER
Fresh coriander (usually called cilantro) growing in pots is now sold in many supermarkets. Stronger-flavored, mature plants with roots suitable for cooking are available from Asian food stores. Clean the roots well in cold water; they can be frozen for up to a month. (Leaves and stalks cannot be frozen.) The roots, leaves, and stalks are important ingredients in Thai green curry paste, and the leaves are widely used in Indian and Chinese cooking.

KAFFIR LIME LEAVES
Found in Thai food stores, these fragrant leaves are used whole, shredded, or mixed into a paste.

CURRY LEAVES
Can be bought, fresh or dried, from Indian food stores; there is no substitute for their flavor.

Large chilies

Medium chilies

GOLDEN NEEDLES
These are the dried buds of the tiger lily. Available from Chinese food stores, they need to be soaked in hot water before use.

STAR ANISE
The dried star-shaped fruit of a member of the magnolia family is native to China and has a pronounced aniseed flavor. Use whole or ground.

CHILIES
What is pleasantly warm in one person's mouth may be searingly hot in another's. The hotness is mainly in the pepper's inner tissues, so by cutting out the seeds you remove most of the heat but retain the flavor. Generally, small chilies are hotter than large, and dried hotter than fresh. If a mild dish is preferred, reduce the number of chilies specified in the recipe.

Bird's-eye chilies

Dried bird's-eye chilies

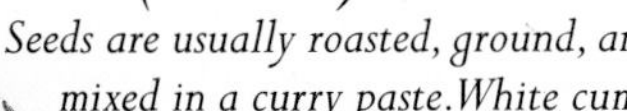

NIGELLA (CENTER) & CUMIN
Seeds are usually roasted, ground, and mixed in a curry paste. White cumin is used in Southeast Asia; Indian cooks usually prefer Nigella, *or black cumin.*

SEVEN-SPICE
Japanese shichimi *is a blend of fragrant spices, including tangerine peel, sesame seeds, poppy seeds, and seaweed flakes. Hot blends usually include sansho pepper and ginger.*

GINGER
This rhizome scarcely needs an introduction, it has become so familiar. Be sure to cook with fresh ginger rather than dried – the flavor is well worth a little extra trouble. Break or cut off a piece, then peel before slicing, chopping, or crushing.

CINNAMON
Buy rolled-up quills rather than ground cinnamon – they have more flavor and keep fresh for much longer.

FIVE-SPICE
The usual ingredients of this aromatic rather than hot mix are cassia, fennel seeds, star anise, cloves, and anise pepper – better known as Szechwan pepper.

GREEN CARDAMOMS
Native to Southern India, these are now grown throughout the tropics. They give a more subtle flavor to a dish if the pods are removed before serving.

GALANGAL
A rhizome that gives an aromatic bitterness to savory dishes, fresh galangal is sold in most Thai stores (the Thai name is ka*), but dried or powdered galangal will do. Use ¼ teaspoon of powder for ½ in (1 cm) of fresh. Do not put dried pieces into a blender – they are hard enough to damage the blades.*

CASSIA BARK
This is related to cinnamon, but the bark is thicker. It is used in large pieces to flavor pilafs and similar savory dishes. The pieces can be picked out easily and discarded before serving. For sweet dishes, cinnamon is preferred.

LEMONGRASS
Unknown in the West a few years ago, this has shot to favor as the essential ingredient in Thai cooking and is now sold in supermarkets. As the name suggests, it adds a pleasant citruslike sourness to a dish.

THE PANTRY

These distinctive-tasting products have long shelf lives while they remain unopened (take note of any expiration dates). Once opened, soy sauce and fish sauce, wines, and vinegars will keep almost indefinitely, but oils should be used within a few months. Bean sauces last for up to a month, refrigerated in a screw-top jar, but other ingredients should be used within a month or so. They may not go bad but they will gradually lose flavor – and flavor, after all, is what you buy them for.

HOISIN SAUCE
The classic sauce for Peking Duck (see page 46 for recipe), made from soybeans, wheat flour, vinegar, garlic, and sesame oil.

YELLOW BEAN SAUCE
Also known as fermented yellow beans, these processed puréed soybeans are sold in jars or cans – with the addition of chilies it is called chili bean sauce.

BLACK BEAN SAUCE
This is made from black soybeans, usually dried after fermentation. The sauce is more widely available than the dried beans and is especially good with fish and shellfish.

CHILI SAUCE
Buy a plain sauce, containing only chilies, salt, and a little vinegar. With most brands 1 teaspoon is the equivalent of one fresh red chili.

SOY SAUCE
Light soy sauce is salty and does not change the color of food, unlike the sweeter dark version. Tamari *is a dark, mild Japanese soy.*

OYSTER SAUCE
Make sure you buy real oyster sauce made with oyster juice – many brands are simply "oyster-flavored" sauce.

FISH SAUCE
Pungent fish sauces are popular all over Southeast Asia. Nam pla *is the Thai version, while* nuoc mam *is Vietnamese. Use the one specified in the recipe.*

WINES

Cooks all over Asia use wine made from glutinous rice. In China, the most famous is Shaohsing wine, made with mineral water. It can be bought in Chinese food stores, and the only substitute is good dry sherry. Mirin is a sweet rice wine from Japan; when combined with soy sauce, it adds flavor to simmered dishes and gives a gloss to teriyaki. Sake, Japan's national drink, is also used in cooking, in a tenderizing marinade for meat, for example.

VINEGARS

White distilled vinegar is used in small quantities in Asia, but most Asian vinegars are brewed from rice. These have a low acid content and are mostly used as flavorings. Ordinary Japanese rice vinegar (e.g., Mitsukan*) is pale and mild. The brown rice vinegar (togazu), made by traditional methods, is best, but is not always available. Chinese "red" vinegar (usually brown or black in color) is made from millet or sorghum.*

CHILI OIL

Although widely available ready-made, chili oil can be made at home by steeping chilies in peanut oil. Add to salad dressings or dishes needing a mild chili flavor.

GHEE

The Indian cooking medium is similar to clarified butter but has a stronger flavor. Buy from Indian food stores in cans or tubs.

SESAME OIL

Use sparingly in Chinese, Japanese, and Korean cooking to add flavor. Not suitable for frying.

PEANUT OIL

Ideal for frying because it can be heated to high temperatures and does not flavor the food.

Sesame oil

Chili oil

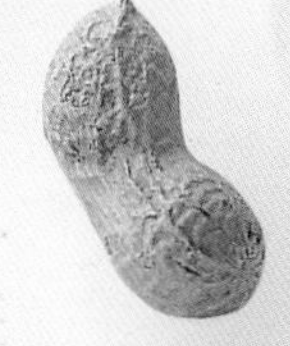

Peanut oil

Ghee

BONITO STOCK

Bonito stock, called dashi, *is made from kelp* (kombu) *and dried bonito flakes* (katsuobushi). *It is used as a soup and a stock in Japanese cooking. Instant dashi is available from Japanese stores, but it is better to make your own (see page 156).*

Bonito flakes

Kelp

Dashi

White miso

Red miso

Yellow miso

MISO

A Japanese flavoring made by fermenting soybean paste with rice, salt, and water. White miso (shiromiso) *is used mostly in sweet dishes. Red miso* (akamiso) *is high in protein and salt. All-purpose miso, called yellow miso* (shinshu-miso), *is not sweet and it has a higher salt content.*

TAMARIND

The pulp and seeds of the tamarind fruit are compressed and sold in blocks. A piece is soaked in warm water to give a sour-tasting paste or liquid (see page 101).

ASAFETIDA

This is sold in Indian stores as a powder called hing. *Store in an airtight container and use sparingly. Its powerful odor disappears during cooking, and you will find that it enhances the flavor of the cooked food.*

SUGARS & TREACLE

Palm sugar is often called by its Anglo-Burmese name, jaggery. It is a brown sugar, made from the sap of the coconut palm flower. If unavailable, use dark brown sugar. Kitul treacle is available from Sri Lankan food shops, but a substitute can be made at home (see page 156).

Grated palm sugar

Palm sugar

Kitul treacle

Tamarind

DRIED ANCHOVIES

Called ikan bilis *in Malaysia and* ikan teri *in Indonesia, these are sold in packages – with or without their heads. Before using, the heads should be broken off and discarded, then the dried fish should be fried in oil or baked in the oven until crisp and crunchy.*

RICE POWDER

Some of the best brands of rice powder are Chinese. (Do not confuse rice powder with glutinous rice powder.) Rice flour cannot be used as a substitute as it is not fine enough.

RICE FLOUR

This is often obtainable in supermarkets, as is glutinous rice flour. Read the label carefully when buying – they are quite different when cooked.

AGAR AGAR

A vegetarian gelatin, made from seaweed, that gels without the need for refrigeration. It is sold in strips or sticks in Asian supermarkets.

Red split lentils ***Green lentils***

LENTILS

Lentils are sold split or whole. Red ones are used in soups and to thicken sauces. Green lentils, which look brown when you buy them, are used mainly in Indian dishes.

Whole mung beans ***Split mung beans***

MUNG BEANS

Whole mung beans are good for sprouting (commercial bean sprouts are grown from mung beans), while the split beans are cooked and eaten like lentils.

CRISP-FRIED ONIONS

Made from small Asian red onions or shallots, these are available in supermarkets and food stores everywhere, packed in sealed containers. To make your own, see page 132.

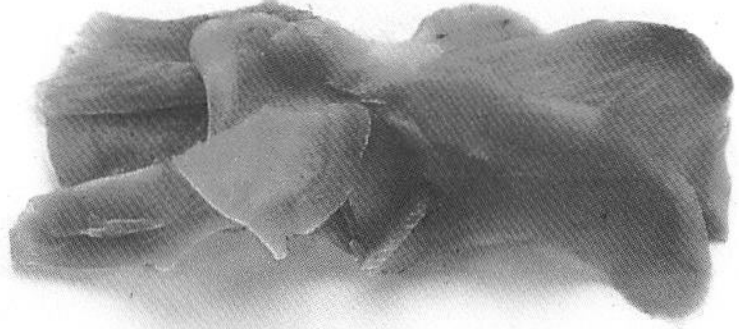

PICKLED GINGER

Only young root ginger is pickled, because it is soft and not at all fibrous. Japanese pickled ginger is often pink, because the pickling vinegar contains red shiso leaves.

PICKLED CHILIES

Buy a good brand as some can taste too much of vinegar. Add a small quantity to spice mixtures or curry pastes.

WASABI PASTE

Fresh wasabi (Wasabi japonica) *is rarely available outside Japan, but wasabi paste is available in tubes. Wasabi powder, sold in small cans, is made from horseradish with a little green coloring. The flavor is not as good.*

SHRIMP CRACKERS

Chinese shrimp crackers are sold, dried, in packages; but Indonesian krupuk *are tastier.*

Uncooked shrimp crackers

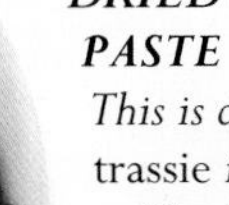

DRIED SHRIMP PASTE

This is called terasi *or* trassie *in Indonesia,* kapi *in Thailand, and* balachan *in Malaysia. Before using it in a spice paste or sambal, grill, fry, or roast it for 5–10 minutes, until dry and crumbly (unless the paste itself is sautéed as the first stage of cooking).*

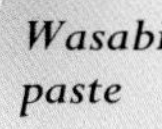

Wasabi paste

DRIED SHRIMP

Use as a condiment, crushed with chili or garlic.

Dried shrimp paste

Dried shrimp

Cooked shrimp crackers

Classic Dishes

Here is a selection of 18 dishes that most people will have heard of and perhaps tasted, either in restaurants or during travels. They are simple to cook, and are just as much at home on the family dinner table as they are at a chic dinner party or an informal buffet. Two or three dishes can be combined successfully to create an exotic and original meal.

All dishes serve 4, unless otherwise indicated.

Snacks & Appetizers

Today we call it "grazing" – the habit of snacking at any time of the day. In Asia it is a long-established art, brought to perfection in the towns where street-food vendors supply refreshment to passersby. In large modern cities, where traffic makes pavement life less attractive, trading has now transferred to big food centers, but the cooking should be just as good.

Rempah-Rempah

Shrimp and bean sprout fritters (Malaysia)

Popular throughout most of Southeast Asia, wherever shrimp are plentiful and cheap, these fritters combine bean sprouts with whole and chopped shrimp. They are equally delicious hot or cold, at a dinner party or for a picnic.

See page 70 for recipe.

Shuen Guen

Spring rolls (China)

These are said to date from the days of the Tang dynasty (6th–9th centuries AD). Then, they were stuffed with the first green vegetables of spring, which must have been welcome after the preserved foods of winter. The name and the concept have not changed, but fillings have evolved to suit the resources and tastes of different countries.

See page 64 for recipe.

Pergedel Jagung

Corn fritters (Indonesia)

Corn was brought to Asia by Portuguese and Spanish settlers in the 16th century and is now grown almost everywhere. Equally popular at that time was another newcomer, the chili pepper – these fritters have just enough to give them a kick.

See page 64 for recipe.

Patties

Small filled pies (Sri Lanka)

The Sri Lankan equivalent of a spring roll, these little pies are loved by children as much as adults. You can use regular pie pastry or make real Sri Lankan pastry with coconut milk.

See page 62 for recipe.

Sushi

Rice rolls (Japan)

This sophisticated snack comes from one Asian country where you hardly ever see anyone eating in the street. Instead, Japan has developed the sushi bar, the equivalent of the European cafe. There is a vast range of sushi, but this kind is easy to make and will appeal to everyone's taste.

See page 71 for recipe.

Ikan Masak Molek

Fish curry (Malaysia)

Malaysians consider fish heads a great delicacy, and fish-head curry is a popular classic. This milder version is made with whole fish so that the fish head can be offered to an honored guest, a compliment to be gracefully accepted. Serve with Bandakka Curry (see page 115 for recipe).

INGREDIENTS

5 cups (1.25 liters) thick coconut milk (see page 141)
salt and freshly ground black pepper, to taste
2 medium red snapper or tilapia, cleaned and scaled, or 4 medium trout, cleaned
2 tbsp Crisp-Fried Onions (see page 132 for recipe), to garnish
2 tbsp chopped fresh flat-leaf parsley, to garnish

For the paste

3 large fresh red chilies, seeded and chopped
4 shallots, chopped
1in (2.5cm) piece of fresh ginger, peeled and chopped
1in (2.5cm) piece of fresh galangal (see page 27), peeled and chopped
4 candlenuts (see page 22) or 8 blanched almonds, chopped
2in (5cm) piece of fresh lemongrass, outer leaves removed, center chopped
1 tsp ground turmeric
2 tbsp tamarind water (see page 101)
1 tsp salt

PREPARATION

1 Put all the paste ingredients, plus 4 tablespoons of the coconut milk, in a blender and blend until as smooth as possible.

2 Transfer the paste mixture to a wok or a large shallow pan. Cook for about 5 minutes, until the oil separates from the coconut milk. Stir for a few seconds, then add the remaining coconut milk.

3 Cook, stirring frequently, for 30 minutes, or until it has reduced by half its volume. Season to taste, then place the fish, head-to-tail, in the sauce. Simmer for about 7 minutes on either side for snapper and tilapia, or about 5 minutes for trout.

4 Transfer the curry to a warm platter and sprinkle with the Crisp-Fried Onions and parsley to garnish.

5 Alternatively, the fish can be served off the bone. Remove the fish from the sauce and keep the sauce warm over low heat. Carefully peel the skin off the fish, separate the fillets from the backbone, and remove any remaining bones. Place each fillet on a warm dinner plate, pour the sauce over, and garnish.

KCal 492 P 30g C 21g S 0.9g TF 33g SF 24g UF 6g (4)

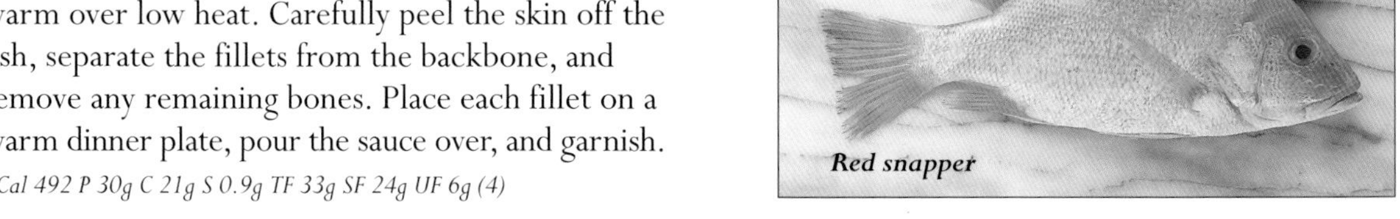

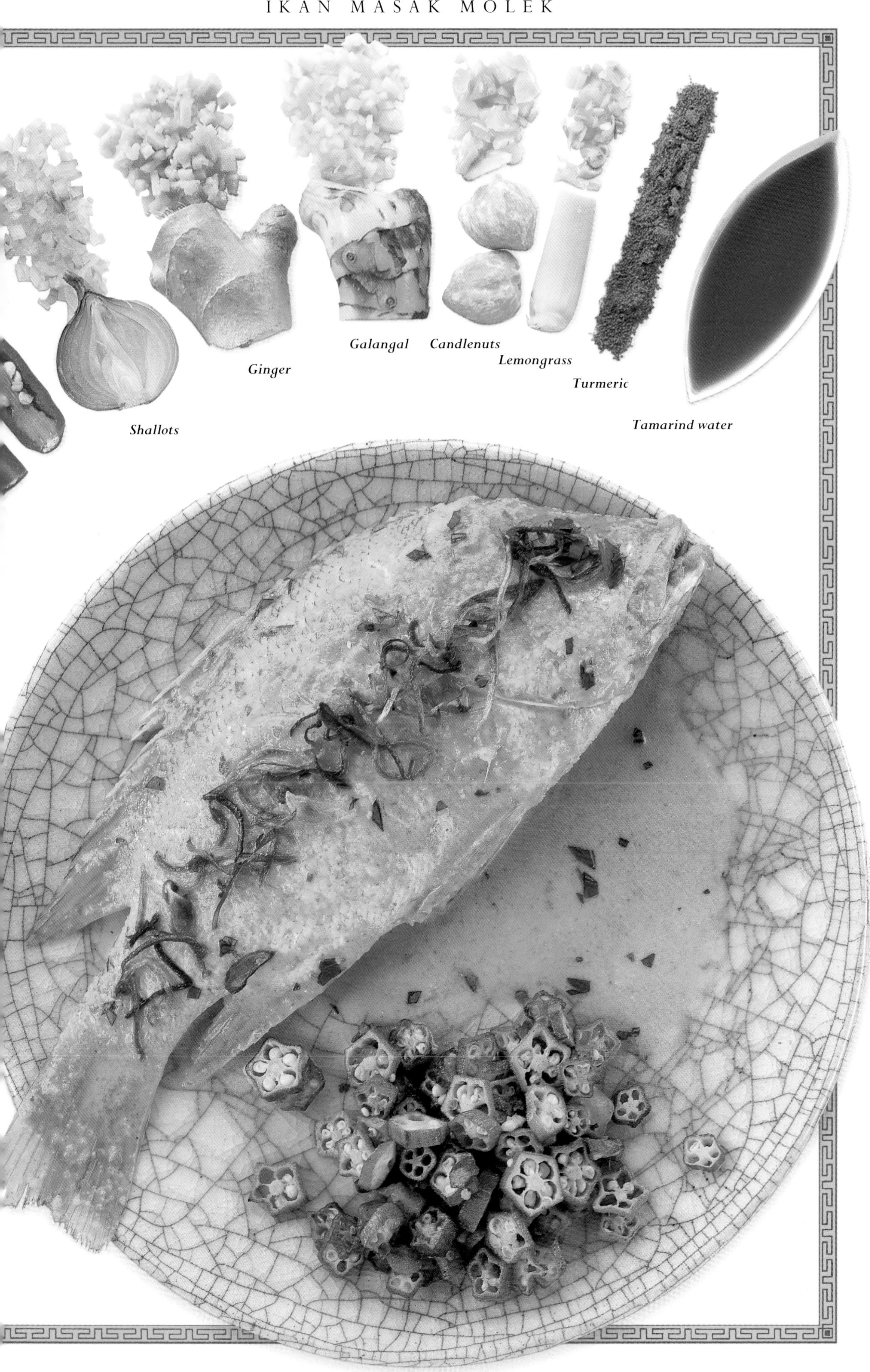
Galangal
Candlenuts
Lemongrass
Ginger
Turmeric
Shallots
Tamarind water

MUC DON THIT

Stuffed squid (Vietnam)

You will find similar recipes for stuffed squid in other Asian countries, but this particular combination of pork, shiitake mushrooms, and golden needles (dried lily buds) is the most successful; the texture and the flavor are just right. Serves 8 as an appetizer, or 4 as a main course with rice and salad.

INGREDIENTS

8 small squid, about 3in (7cm) long, cleaned (see page 150), tentacles reserved and chopped
peanut oil for frying
For the stuffing
2oz (60g) cellophane vermicelli (see page 24), soaked in hot water for 5 minutes, drained
8–10 dried shiitake mushrooms, rehydrated (see page 155), stems removed and caps finely chopped
½oz (15g) golden needles (see page 27), soaked in hot water for 10 minutes, drained and finely chopped, optional
½lb (250g) lean ground pork
2 garlic cloves, finely chopped
4 scallions, cut into thin rounds
3 tsp fish sauce (nuoc mam) (see page 28)
¼ tsp salt
1 small egg, lightly beaten

Golden needles

Shiitake mushrooms

Cellophane vermicelli

Peanut oil

PREPARATION

1 For the stuffing, snip the vermicelli several times in different directions with scissors, to cut them into short lengths. Pat the vermicelli dry with paper towels and place them in a large bowl.
2 Add all the remaining stuffing ingredients, plus the chopped squid tentacles, adding the egg last of all. Mix well, until thoroughly combined.
3 To fill the squid, spoon some of the stuffing into each one, pressing it down, until the squid is about three-quarters full. Close the opening of each pouch with a toothpick.
4 Heat some oil for shallow frying in a wok or skillet. Add the squid and fry, turning them frequently, for 5 minutes. While the squid are cooking, pierce each one in several places with a needle or a fine skewer. Fry the squid for 6–8 minutes longer, or until they are golden brown.
5 Remove the squid from the wok with a slotted spoon and transfer to a plate lined with paper towels, to drain. Discard the toothpicks and slice each squid diagonally into two or three pieces. Serve hot or warm.

KCal 307 P 38g C 19g S 0.6g TF 9g SF 2g UF 5g (4)

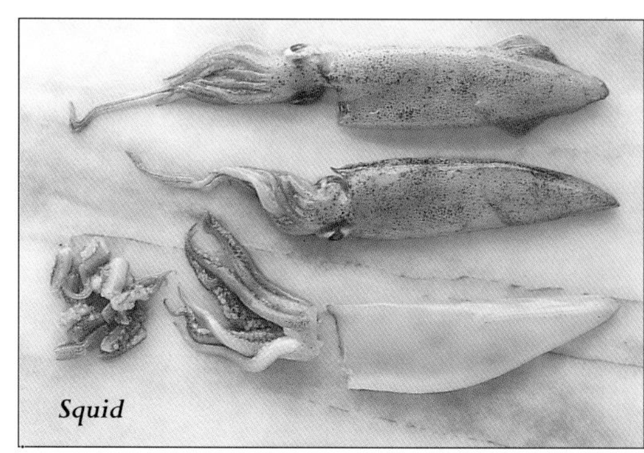

Squid

Ground pork
Garlic
Scallions
Fish sauce
Salt
Egg

OSON

Steamed stuffed fish (Korea)

This method of stuffing fish with different colored vegetables that have been sautéed and seasoned with soy sauce and sesame oil, is typically Korean. Serves 8 as an appetizer or 4 as a main course with a dipping sauce and green salad.

INGREDIENTS

4 fillets of lemon sole, skinned, each 5–6oz (150–175g), each sliced into 4 on the diagonal (see page 150)
¼ tsp salt, plus extra to taste
¼ tsp freshly ground black pepper, plus extra to taste
2 tbsp peanut oil
1 bunch watercress, trimmed
3 medium carrots, cut into julienne strips (see page 154)
6 dried shiitake mushrooms, rehydrated (see page 155), stems removed and caps thinly sliced
¼lb (125g) chestnut mushrooms, thinly sliced
½lb (250g) thin green beans, halved on the diagonal
1 tsp sesame oil
2 tsp light soy sauce
2 tsp cornstarch
2 eggs, separated and beaten, made into 1 thin white omelet and 1 thin yellow omelet, cut into fine strips

For the dipping sauce
1 tsp sesame oil
2 tbsp light soy sauce
2 tbsp rice vinegar (see page 29)
2 tbsp pine nuts, roasted (see page 155), finely chopped
1–2 small dried red chilies, finely chopped

PREPARATION

1 Rub the slices of fish with the salt and pepper and set aside. Coat a nonstick skillet with a little of the oil, add the watercress, and sauté for 2 minutes. Remove from the pan, then sauté the remaining vegetables, each kind separately, in a little more oil, for 2 minutes. Transfer to a plate and sprinkle with the sesame oil and soy sauce.

2 Season the cornstarch with salt and pepper, then rub it over one side of each slice of fish. Arrange a few strips of each vegetable and omelet across the coated side of each slice. Roll up, lengthwise, with the vegetables inside.

3 Line a bamboo steamer (see page 149) with a piece of cheesecloth. Arrange the fish rolls side by side on it, the seams underneath. Cover and steam over boiling water for 5 minutes.

4 Remove the rolls from the steamer and transfer to a warm serving platter. Stand them upright, trimming the ends a little, if necessary.

5 Mix all the sauce ingredients in a very small bowl. Serve the fish hot or warm with the sauce.

KCal 369 P 39g C 12g S 1g TF 19g SF 3g UF 14g (4)

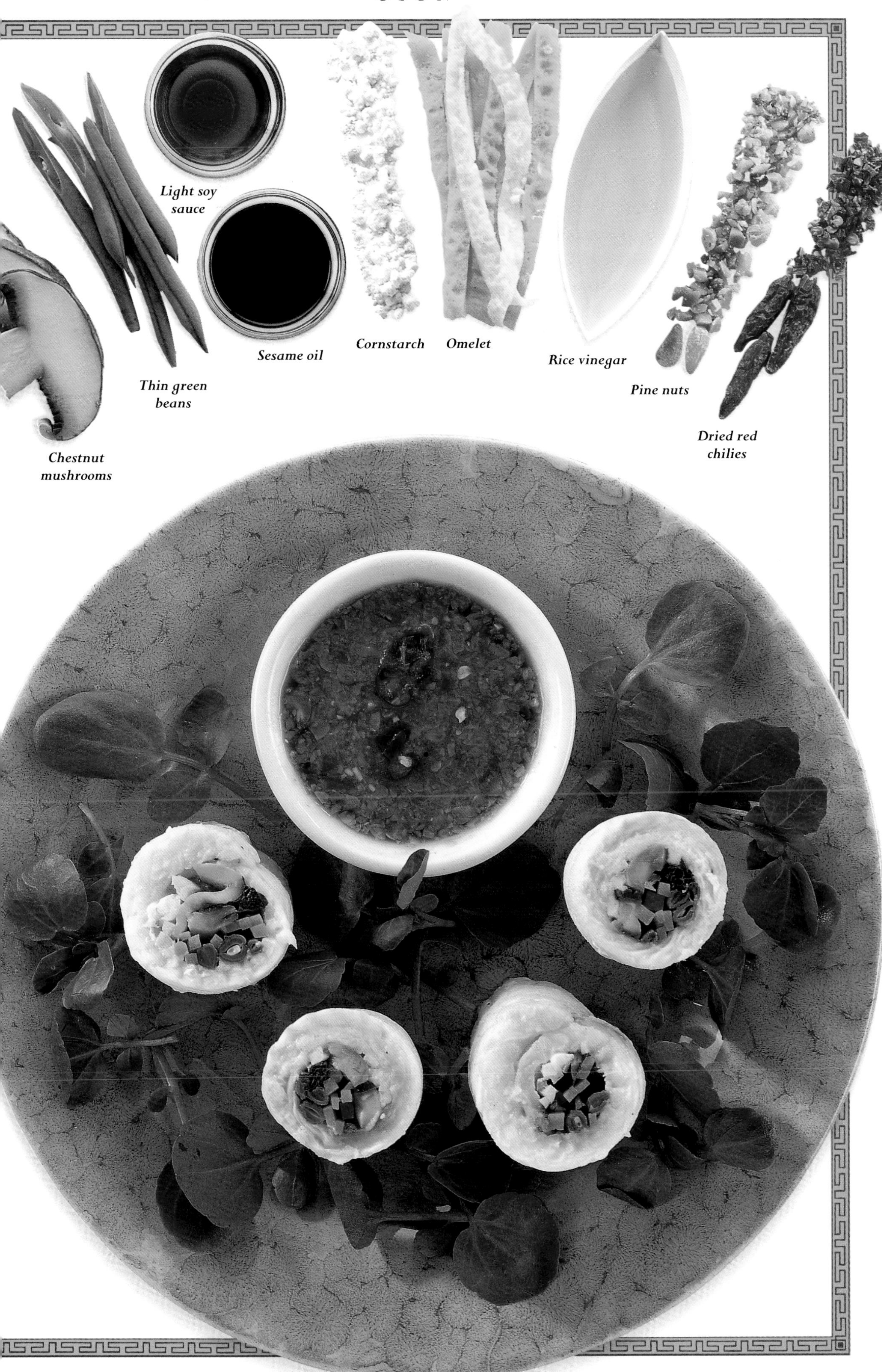
Light soy sauce
Sesame oil
Cornstarch
Omelet
Rice vinegar
Pine nuts
Dried red chilies
Thin green beans
Chestnut mushrooms

GAENG KEO WAN KAI

Green curry of chicken (Thailand)

Thai cooks share their Southeast Asian neighbors' passion for cooking in coconut milk, as well as for sharp- and sour-tasting herbs, pungent garlic, savory shrimp paste, and hot chilies. Here, these ingredients come together in a green curry. Pea eggplants add to the unique flavor, but you can use baby new potatoes, which are also popular in Thailand. Serve with plain boiled rice, and garnish with sliced green chilies.

INGREDIENTS

2 tbsp vegetable oil
1½ lb (750g) boned and skinned chicken thighs and breasts, cut into ¾ in (2cm) cubes
5 cups (1.25 liters) coconut milk (see page 141)
½ lb (250g) pea eggplants (see page 20) or baby new potatoes
1 tbsp chopped fresh cilantro leaves, to garnish

For the paste

2 tbsp chopped fresh cilantro leaves
1 tbsp chopped fresh cilantro roots or stems
3 garlic cloves, finely chopped
2 shallots, finely chopped
2in (5cm) piece of fresh lemongrass, outer leaves removed, center chopped
¾ in (2cm) piece of fresh galangal (see page 27), finely chopped
1 tsp grated kaffir lime zest (see page 22)
1 tsp ground black pepper
1 tbsp each of coriander seed and cumin seed, roasted (see page 155), roughly crushed
½ tsp each of ground nutmeg and mace
5 fresh green chilies, seeded and chopped
1 green pepper, seeded and chopped, optional
2 tsp salt
½ tsp dried shrimp paste (see page 31)
4 tbsp water

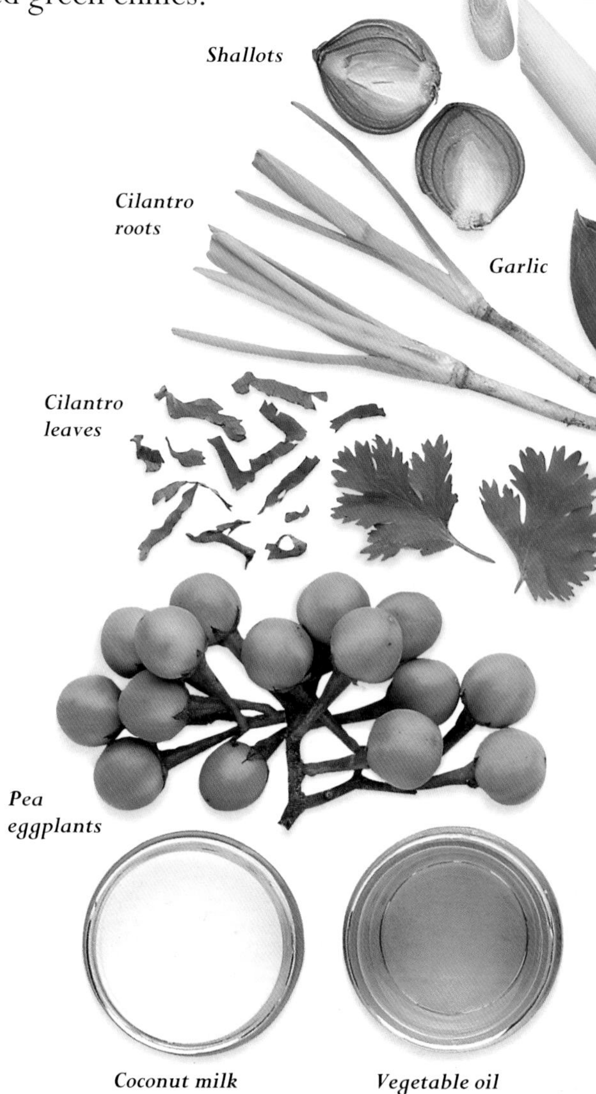

PREPARATION

1 Put all the paste ingredients in a blender and blend until as smooth as possible.
2 Heat the oil in a pan over medium heat. Add the paste mixture and fry for 4 minutes, stirring continuously. Add the chicken to the pan and stir until the pieces are thoroughly coated.
3 Lower the heat, then cover and simmer for 4 minutes. Stir in the coconut milk and simmer, stirring frequently, for 30 minutes.
4 Add the pea eggplants or potatoes and cook for 10–15 minutes, stirring frequently, until tender. Sprinkle with the cilantro, to garnish, then serve.

KCal 381 P 46g C 27g S 1.5g TF 12g SF 3g UF 8g (4)

Cumin seed
Mace
Black pepper
Coriander seed
Nutmeg
Green chili
Green pepper
Kaffir lime zest
Salt
Galangal
Dried shrimp paste
emongrass

SATAY

Satay, in one form or another, has spread in popularity across Asia. It is the perfect fast food, offering an infinite variety of flavors thanks to the accompanying marinades and sauces. It is equally at home served at a wedding reception or barbecue, and the skewers range from elegant metal designer pieces to disposable bamboo.

SATAY DAGING

Skewered beef (Malaysia)

These succulent chunks of meat marinated in soy sauce and spices are usually served with the classic peanut sauce.

See page 67 for recipe.

YAKITORI

Skewered chicken (Japan)

Traditionally, each part of the chicken would be prepared and cooked separately, though here only breast and thigh meat are used.

See page 67 for recipe.

Yakitori Sauce
See page 67 for recipe.

Peanut Sauce
See page 130 for recipe.

Chao Tom

Skewered shrimp balls and shrimp (Vietnam)

These are usually made from shrimp paste shaped around slivers of sugarcane. Here, I use shrimp paste balls and whole shrimp on decorative metal skewers.

See page 66 for recipe.

Lemongrass brush

Cut the end off a stem of fresh lemongrass and beat it until it frays – you have the ideal disposable tool to brush marinade or sauce onto your satay as it cooks.

Pork Satay

Skewered pork (Singapore)

This street-food satay is built up from thin slices of pork interlaced with pieces of pork fat, which are not meant to be eaten but make the meat wonderfully moist and savory.

See page 67 for recipe.

Sate Pusut

Minced fish on skewers (Indonesia)

As usual, the Balinese have taken a new idea and adapted it to be their own. A paste of minced, spiced fish is formed around a flat bamboo blade or the thin upper stem of fresh lemongrass.

See page 66 for recipe.

Nuoc Cham

See page 128 for recipe.

BAAK GING AP

Peking duck with pancakes and hoisin sauce (China)

This is not a difficult dish to make, as was proven to me by my friend Simon Yung, chef at the Oriental Restaurant at the Dorchester Hotel, London. However, you can buy a fully prepared frozen Peking duck (from a Chinese supermarket), then simply roast it and serve with the accompaniments below. Serves 4–6 as a main course.

INGREDIENTS

1 duck, 3½–4lb (1½–2kg)
3 tbsp honey
2 tbsp Chinese red vinegar (see page 29)
3 tbsp Shaohsing wine (see page 29) (optional)
1 cup (250ml) hot water
salt
2in (5cm) piece of fresh ginger, peeled and chopped
10 scallions, the white and green parts separated
To serve
1 cucumber, cut into thin sticks
hoisin sauce or yellow bean sauce (see page 28)
2–3 packages Chinese pancakes (see page 25)

PREPARATION

1 Scald the duck with boiling water (see page 152), then place it on a large baking tray.
2 Mix together the honey, vinegar, Shaohsing wine, if using, and hot water. Pour the mixture all over the top of the duck, turning it to coat the underneath and then brushing the excess from the tray onto the less accessible parts, such as under the wings.
3 Secure the duck on a duck hook (see page 152), placing the hooks under the wings. Hang the duck, undisturbed, in a cool, airy place for 12–24 hours, until the skin is dry.
4 Sprinkle a little salt into the body cavity of the duck, then add the ginger and the green part of the scallions.
5 Place the duck, breast up, on a rack set over a roasting pan. Cook in an oven preheated to 325°F (160°C) for 20–25 minutes, then turn the duck over and roast for 30 minutes, until golden. Turn the duck over again, raise the temperature to 350°F (180°C), and roast for 15 minutes more. Transfer the duck to a carving board and let rest for 5–10 minutes.
6 Cut the white part of the scallions into thin strips and arrange with the cucumber on a plate. Put the hoisin sauce in a bowl. Place the pancakes in a steamer and steam for 10 minutes. Separate each one carefully, then fold in half and arrange on a warm serving dish.

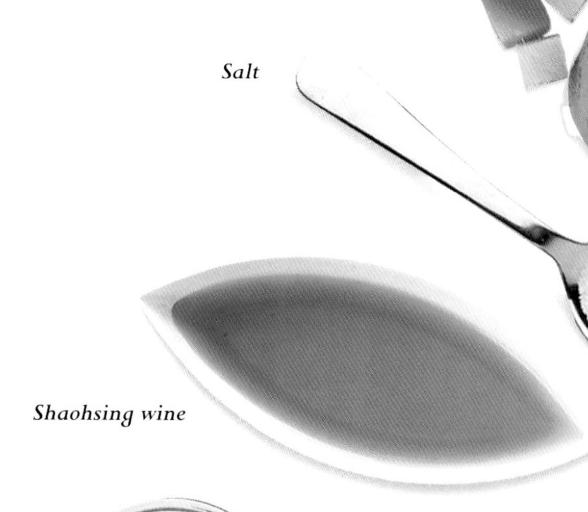

Salt

Shaohsing wine

Chinese red vinegar ***Honey***

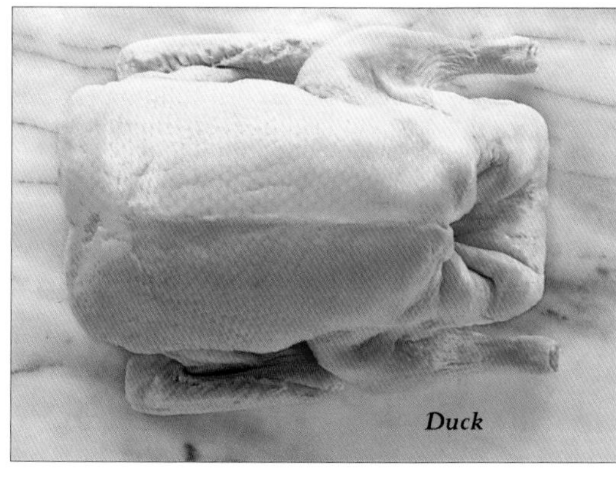

Duck

7 Cut off the crisp duck skin, slice into small pieces, and arrange on a warm platter. Slice the meat into similar size pieces and add to the platter.
8 To eat, place a pancake on a plate, spoon a little hoisin sauce onto the middle of it, and spread with the spoon. Top with some duck skin and meat. Add a few slices of scallion and cucumber and roll up.

KCal 555 P 36g C 68g S 1g TF 14g SF 3g UF 6g (4)

Ginger

Scallions

Cucumber

Hoisin sauce

Chinese pancakes

ROGAN JOSH

Lamb in rich chili sauce with yogurt (India)

This is one of the greatest of all stews – you can make it with lamb, goat, or beef. Traditionally, the fat is left on the meat to give the dish succulence, and the rich flavor is enhanced by cooking in ghee (clarified butter). My version uses lean meat and peanut oil, but by all means use ghee if you prefer. Serves 8 with basmati rice.

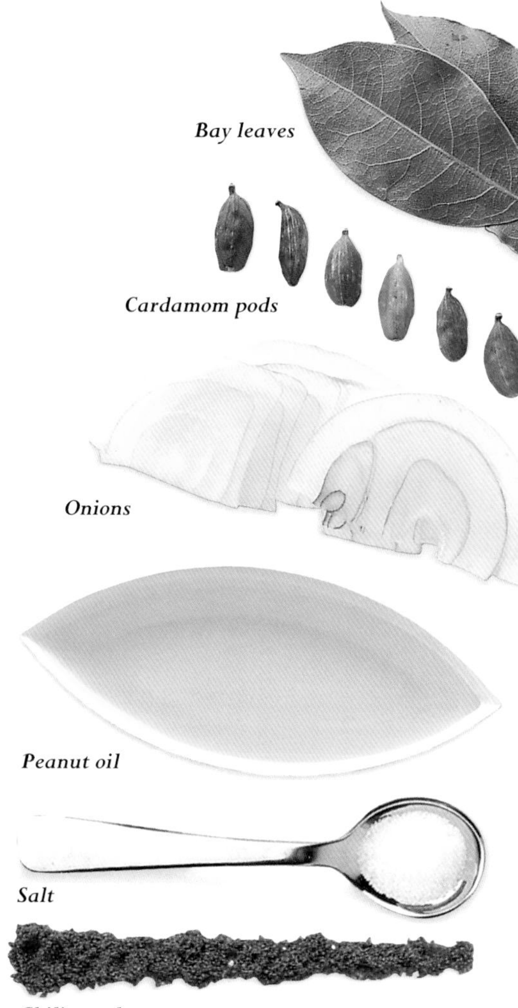

Bay leaves

Cardamom pods

Onions

Peanut oil

Salt

Chili powder

Lean lamb

INGREDIENTS

4lb (2kg) lean lamb from the leg or shoulder, cut into ¾in (2cm) cubes
½ tsp chili powder or cayenne pepper
1 tsp salt, plus extra to taste
¼ cup peanut or vegetable oil
1lb (500g) onions, finely sliced
6 green cardamom pods
2 bay leaves
½ cup (120ml) plain yogurt or 5 tbsp (75ml) yogurt mixed with 3 tbsp tamarind water (see page 101)
5 cups (1.25 liters) hot water
freshly ground black pepper, to taste
½ tsp garam masala (see page 156)

For the paste

4 garlic cloves, chopped
1in (2.5cm) piece of fresh ginger, peeled and chopped
3–6 large fresh red chilies, seeded and chopped
10 black peppercorns, roughly crushed
½in (1cm) piece of cinnamon stick, roughly crushed
2 tsp coriander seed, roughly crushed
2 tsp cumin seed, roughly crushed
3 tsp paprika
3 cloves, roughly crushed
1 tsp salt
½ cup (125ml) water

PREPARATION

1 Put the cubed meat in a bowl, rub all over with the chili powder and salt, and set aside. Put all the ingredients for the curry paste in a blender and blend until smooth.

2 Heat the oil in a large pan, add the onions, and sauté until lightly golden. Add the cardamom pods and bay leaves, and stir once or twice.

3 Add the meat, increase the heat and cook, stirring continuously, for 2 minutes. Cover the pan, lower the heat, and simmer for 3–4 minutes.

4 Uncover the pan, increase the heat, and stir in the paste. Cover and cook for 5 minutes. Add the yogurt, stir, and add the hot water. Cover the pan again and simmer for about 1 hour.

5 Uncover the pan and cook until the sauce is reduced and thick and creamy. Stir and season to taste. Just before serving, add the garam masala and discard the cardamom pods and bay leaves.

KCal 489 P 53g C 9g S 0.7g TF 27g SF 11g UF 14g (8)

Plain yogurt
Black pepper
Garam masala
Garlic
Ginger
Red chilies
Black peppercorns
Cinnamon
Coriander seed
Cumin seed
Paprika
Cloves

BARA-ZUSHI

Sushi rice with julienne of omelet (Japan)

This recipe is very easy to make, and in Japan it is regarded as an everyday dish. Here, I use a stock made by cooking all the mushroom stems for 10 minutes in the soaking water from the dried mushrooms. Alternatively, you can use a homemade fish stock or bonito stock (see page 30).

INGREDIENTS

3 cups (750ml) water
1lb (500g) short-grain Japanese rice (see page 24), washed in several changes of water, drained for 30 minutes
1 cup (250ml) mushroom stock (see introduction, above) or fish stock or bonito stock (see page 30)
1 tbsp mirin (see page 29)
1 tbsp light soy sauce
¼lb (125g) fried tofu (see page 24), quartered
1oz (30g) dried shrimp (see page 31)
8 raw jumbo shrimp, peeled and deveined (see page 82), halved crosswise
2oz (60g) dried shiitake mushrooms, rehydrated (see page 155), stems removed and caps sliced
¼lb (125g) fresh shiitake mushrooms, stems removed and caps sliced
¼lb (125g) button mushrooms, stems removed
¼lb (125g) snow peas or sugar snap peas, halved
2 tsp peanut or vegetable oil
1 egg and 2 egg yolks, beaten, made into 2 thin omelets, cut into fine strips

For the dressing

2 tbsp sugar
⅓ cup (90ml) rice vinegar (see page 29)
1 tsp salt
2 tbsp hot water

PREPARATION

1 Boil the water in a pan. Add the rice and cook, uncovered, for about 10 minutes, until all the water is absorbed. Stir once, then cover, reduce the heat to minimum, and cook for 10–12 minutes.

2 Remove the pan from the heat and set it, still covered, on a very wet dish towel. Let stand for 5 minutes, then transfer the rice to a glass bowl.

3 Mix all the dressing ingredients together in a bowl and pour, a little at a time, into the rice. Mix well, but lightly, then set aside in a cool place.

4 Heat the stock in a pan for 2 minutes. Add the mirin and soy sauce and bring to a boil. Add the fried tofu and dried shrimp and simmer for 3 minutes. Strain the liquid into a skillet, reserving the tofu and shrimp. Reduce the heat, add the jumbo shrimp, and stir for 1 minute.

5 Add the mushrooms and snow peas and cook for 2 minutes, shaking the pan as the liquid evaporates. Stir in the oil and remove from the heat.

6 Spoon the rice onto a serving platter. Mix in the tofu and dried shrimp, and most of the mushrooms, snow peas, and jumbo shrimp, keeping aside a few of each. Arrange the omelet strips over the rice and garnish with the reserved ingredients.

KCal 744 P 33g C 116g S 1.5g TF 14g SF 2g UF 5g (4)

Dried shiitake mushrooms
Fresh shiitake mushrooms
Button mushrooms
Snow peas
Peanut oil
Omelet
Sugar
Rice vinegar
Salt

GADO-GADO

Cooked vegetable salad with peanut sauce (Indonesia)

Indonesians consider this their national dish, but recently the Malaysians have been claiming it as theirs also. For me, it is simply classic Javanese vegetarian food, which I have known all my life and have eaten hundreds of times since I was a little girl. For this dish, the vegetables are usually thoroughly cooked but not overcooked. However, a good Gado-Gado should also have something crunchy and crisp. Here, the crispness comes from the cucumber, while the garnish of shrimp crackers and fried onions provides the crunch. Serves 4–6.

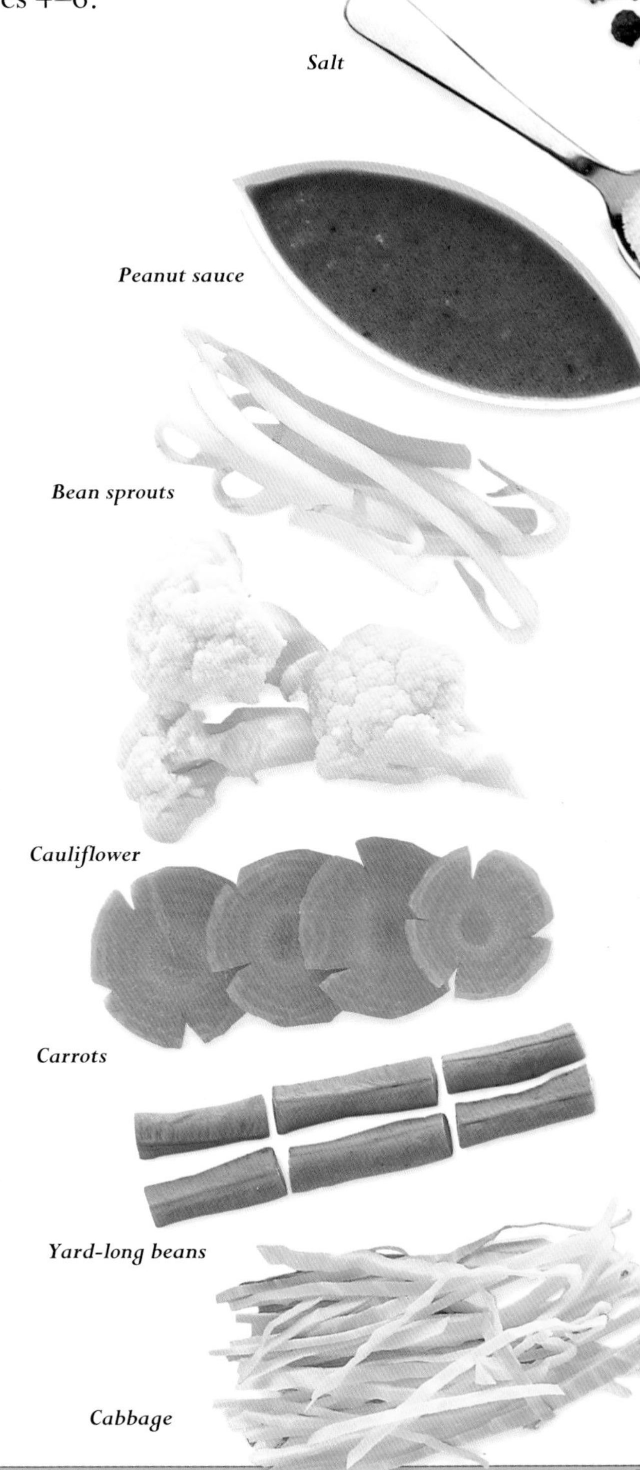

INGREDIENTS

¼ lb (125g) cabbage or scallions, shredded
½ lb (250g) yard-long beans (see page 21) or green beans, cut into ½ in (1cm) lengths
¼ lb (125g) carrots, cut into flower shapes (see page 154)
¼ lb (125g) cauliflower, cut into florets
¼ lb (125g) fresh bean sprouts, rinsed and trimmed
1¼ cups (300ml) Peanut Sauce (see page 130 for recipe)
salt and freshly ground black pepper, to taste

For the garnish

few sprigs of watercress
1–2 eggs, hard-cooked, peeled, and quartered
1 medium potato, boiled in its skin, then peeled and sliced
¼ cucumber, thinly sliced into half moons
6–8 shrimp crackers (see page 31), fried
1–2 tbsp Crisp-Fried Onions (see page 132 for recipe)

PREPARATION

1 For the salad, boil the cabbage, beans, carrots, and cauliflower separately in lightly salted water for 4–5 minutes each. Drain the vegetables in a colander and keep warm. Boil the bean sprouts for 2 minutes, drain, and keep warm with the other vegetables.
2 Heat the Peanut Sauce in a small pan until hot, stirring in a little hot water if it is too thick. Season to taste, then pour the sauce into a small bowl.
3 Arrange the garnish of watercress around the edge of a large serving dish and pile the cooked vegetables in the center of the dish. Arrange the hard-cooked eggs, potatoes, and cucumber on top.
4 Accompany with the shrimp crackers to crumble over the vegetables and sprinkle with the Crisp-Fried Onions. Serve immediately, while still warm, with the sauce, or let the salad stand until cold and sprinkle with the onions just before serving.
5 Alternatively, the salad can be served with the sauce poured over it, and the garnishes arranged separately, allowing everyone to help themselves.

KCal 699 P 21g S 0.6g TF 54g SF 9g UF 41g (4)

Watercress
Eggs
Potato
Cucumber
Shrimp crackers
Crisp-fried onions

RECIPES

The 14 countries covered in this book fall into two distinct groups. India, Sri Lanka, Myanmar, Laos, Thailand, Malaysia, the Philippines, and Indonesia all cook with spices and chilies, and enrich their dishes with yogurt or coconut milk and pungent fish sauces or shrimp pastes. The others – China, Japan, Korea, Vietnam, Cambodia, and Singapore – base the flavor of their cooking on soy sauce and other fermented soybean products, and use much less chili.

Soups

Some of these soups are almost unofficial national dishes in their countries of origin, probably because they are warm, nourishing, and very comforting if you have grown up with them since childhood. For people in the West, they also have the attraction of being exotic. Soup is an essential part of almost every Asian meal, and often becomes a meal in itself. But whatever may be put into it in the way of fish, meat, and vegetables, the basis is always a good clear stock.

Mohinga

Fish soup with rice noodles (Myanmar)

This is the national dish of Myanmar (Burma), and is usually served with lentil fritters as part of a large party dinner or as a family meal. Serves 6–8.

INGREDIENTS

For the stock

1½lb (750g) whole sole or flounder, cleaned
5 cups (1.25 liters) water
3 fresh or dried red chilies, halved
¼ tsp ground turmeric
2 stems of fresh lemongrass
1 tbsp fish sauce (nam pla) (see page 28)

For the accompaniments

1 banana flower (see page 20), optional
8oz (250g) can sliced bamboo shoots, drained and rinsed
1lb (500g) rice noodles (see page 25) or fine egg noodles
2 tbsp Crisp-Fried Onions (see page 132 for recipe)
4 duck or hens' eggs, hard-cooked, peeled, and quartered, or 12 quail eggs, hard-cooked and peeled
2–3 tbsp chopped fresh flat-leaf parsley
8 slices of lemon or lime
chili sauce (see page 28), to serve

To finish the soup

2 tbsp peanut or vegetable oil
1 tsp sesame oil
3 shallots, finely sliced
3 garlic cloves, finely sliced
1 large fresh red chili, seeded and finely sliced
1 tsp finely chopped fresh ginger
2in (5cm) piece of fresh lemongrass, outer leaves removed, center finely chopped
3¾ cups (900ml) coconut milk (see page 141)
1lb (500g) monkfish, filleted and cut into bite-sized pieces, bones reserved for the stock
salt and freshly ground black pepper, to taste

PREPARATION

1 Put all the ingredients for the stock, along with the monkfish bones, in a large pan. Bring to a boil, then reduce the heat and simmer for 5 minutes. Remove the sole or flounder from the pan, transfer to a plate, and let cool.

2 Peel the skin off the sole or flounder, then separate the flesh from the bones and set aside. Return the skin and bones to the stock and simmer for 30 minutes more. Strain the stock through a fine sieve into a bowl and discard the solids.

3 For the accompaniments, discard the two outer layers of the banana flower, if using. Cook the flower in lightly salted boiling water for 6–8 minutes. Drain and quarter the flower, then cut it into fairly thick slices.

4 Cook the bamboo shoots in lightly salted boiling water for 3 minutes, then drain. Arrange them with the banana flower on one side of a large serving dish.

5 Put the rice noodles or egg noodles in a large bowl and pour over plenty of boiling water. Cover and let stand for 3–4 minutes.

6 Drain the noodles in a colander and arrange on the serving dish. Arrange the remaining accompaniments on the dish, placing the chili sauce in a small bowl in the center.

7 To finish the soup, heat the peanut oil and sesame oil in a large pan. Add the shallots, garlic, chili, ginger, and lemongrass and stir-fry for 2 minutes.

8 Stir in the coconut milk and bring to a boil. Add the cooked sole or flounder and raw monkfish, then simmer for 2 minutes. Add the reserved fish stock, season to taste, and heat for another 2–3 minutes.

9 Transfer some of the noodles and the other accompaniments to each serving bowl, ladle over the hot soup, and serve immediately.

KCal 560 P 35g C 79g S 0.6g TF 10g SF 3g UF 6g (6)

Satsumajiru

Miso soup with mixed vegetables (Japan)

Traditionally a fish-based stock (dashi) is added to this soup. This recipe, however, is completely vegetarian and extremely quick to make.

INGREDIENTS

4½ cups (1 liter) cold water
6 tbsp (90g) unsweetened white miso or 4 tbsp red miso (see page 30)
2oz (60g) canned sliced bamboo shoots (drained weight), rinsed and sliced into julienne strips (see page 154)
1 small carrot, sliced into julienne strips (see page 154)
8 fresh shiitake mushrooms or chestnut mushrooms, stems removed and caps thinly sliced
4 asparagus spears or 10 snow peas, very thinly sliced on the diagonal
3 scallions, very thinly sliced on the diagonal
large pinch of seven-spice powder (see page 27), or freshly ground black pepper
salt, to taste

PREPARATION

1 Bring the water to a boil in a pan, then pour ½ cup (125ml) of it over the miso in a bowl, stirring until the miso is dissolved. Return the liquid to the boiling water and reduce the heat to a simmer.

2 Add the bamboo shoots to the pan and simmer for 2 minutes. Add the carrot strips, mushrooms, and asparagus spears or snow peas and simmer for 2 minutes longer.

3 Bring the soup to a boil and add the scallions and the seven-spice or black pepper. Add salt to taste and serve immediately.

KCal 55 P 4g C 8g S 0.9g TF 1g SF 0.1g UF 0.2g (4)

Bun Bo Hue

Noodle soup with beef and lemongrass (Vietnam)

Like most Asian noodle- or rice-based soups, this dish is very substantial and makes a delicious one-dish lunch. It is equally good with or without chili sauce. Serves 6–8.

INGREDIENTS

2 tbsp vegetable oil
1 tbsp tomato paste
1 tsp dried shrimp paste (see page 31)
1 tsp chili sauce (see page 28), optional
2 shallots, finely sliced
½lb (250g) narrow ribbon rice noodles (see page 25)
2 tbsp fish sauce (nuoc mam) (see page 28)
salt and freshly ground black pepper, to taste
2 tbsp chopped fresh cilantro leaves
2 tbsp finely sliced scallions
½ cucumber, peeled, halved lengthwise, seeded, and sliced into half moons, to garnish
3 romaine lettuce leaves, shredded, to garnish

For the stock

1lb (500g) chuck steak or brisket, cut into 2 pieces, some of the fat removed
2 large pork chops, some of the fat removed
2 stems of fresh lemongrass, cut into thirds
1 tsp salt
1 tbsp fish sauce (nuoc mam) (see page 28)
8 cups (2 liters) cold water

PREPARATION

1 Put all the ingredients for the stock in a large pan. Bring to a boil, then simmer for 1–1¼ hours, skimming the froth frequently. Remove the meat and let cool. Strain the stock into a large bowl.
2 Slice the beef and pork thin, discarding the bones of the chops. Set the meat aside.
3 Blend the oil, tomato paste, shrimp paste, and chili sauce, if using, in a bowl. Transfer to a large pan and cook over medium heat for 2 minutes. Add the shallots and stir for a few seconds, then add a ladleful of the stock and simmer for 3 minutes. Add the remaining stock and simmer for 20 minutes.
4 Put the rice noodles in a large pan of boiling water. Remove from the heat, cover, and let stand for 3–4 minutes. Transfer to a colander, rinse under cold running water until cold, then let drain.
5 To serve, add the fish sauce to the stock, season to taste, and reheat. Divide the noodles among the soup bowls, then add the beef and pork. Sprinkle the cilantro and scallions over the meat and ladle some stock into each bowl. Put the cucumber and lettuce on top and serve immediately.

KCal 447 P 33g C 36g S 1g TF 15g SF 5g UF 9g (6)

Salt
Black pepper
Cilantro leaves
Scallions
Cucumber
Romaine lettuce
Lemongrass

Daan Far Tong

Daan Far Tong

Egg drop soup (China)

This is a classic Chinese dish that is popular throughout Southeast Asia. It is a basic soup that depends on the quality of the broth and the freshness of the eggs. If you have heard that adding egg to soup is tricky, do not worry; the eggs will curdle naturally in the hot broth, whichever way you combine them. For serving the soup, bowls with lids are useful, but not essential.

INGREDIENTS

5 cups (1.25 liters) good clear meat or vegetable stock
1 tbsp soy sauce
salt and freshly ground black pepper, to taste
4 small eggs
2 scallions, cut into thin rounds
4 drops of sesame oil, optional

PREPARATION

1 Heat the stock in a pan. Season it well with the soy sauce, and salt and pepper to taste, then simmer for 5 minutes.
2 To serve, break one egg into each of four soup bowls and beat lightly with a fork or chopsticks. Bring the stock to a boil, then pour it onto the egg in each bowl, dividing it equally.
3 Divide the scallions among the bowls. By this time the egg will have floated to the surface of the soup. Add 1 drop of sesame oil to each serving, if using. If the soup bowls have lids, cover them and let stand for 1–2 minutes, before serving.

KCal 76 P 7g C 0.5g S 0.8g TF 6g SF 2g UF 3g (4)

Rasam

Vegetarian soup (India)

In southern India, Rasam is served with some cooked rice added at the end of cooking. However, it also makes a one-dish vegetarian meal, with the rice served separately. Everyone can help themselves to as much rice as they want, and then ladle the soup over it. Serves 4–6.

INGREDIENTS

½ lb (250g) carrots, cut into thin rounds
½ lb (250g) daikon (see page 20), peeled, thinly sliced across
¼ lb (125g) water spinach (see page 21) or watercress
salt and freshly ground black pepper, to taste
¾ cup (125g) cooked long-grain rice (see page 156)

For the broth

10 cups (2.5 liters) water
1 oz (30g) tamarind pulp (see page 30)
¾ cup (90g) red lentils, rinsed and drained
1 large tomato, quartered
1–2 large fresh green chilies, chopped
¼ tsp asafetida (see page 30), optional
1 tsp salt

PREPARATION

1 Put all the ingredients for the broth in a large pan. Bring to a boil, then simmer for 1 hour. Remove from the heat and let cool a little. Strain the broth through a sieve into another pan. Discard the solids.
2 Return the broth to a boil. Add the vegetables, season to taste, and simmer for 5 minutes. Add the rice, simmer for 2 minutes, and serve immediately.

KCal 182 P 9g C 35g S 0.6g TF 1g SF 0.3g UF 0.8g (4)

Laksa Lemak

Hot noodle soup with coconut milk (Malaysia)

The original Laksa Lemak is made with rice noodles or rice sticks, but in Europe, Australia, and North America, many Asian restaurants make it with Chinese-style egg noodles. Serves 8 as a soup or 4 as a one-dish meal. *See page 72 for illustration.*

INGREDIENTS

1 chicken, 3–3½lb (1.5–1.75kg), quartered
5 cups (1.25 liters) water
1lb (500g) raw large shrimp, peeled and deveined (see page 82), shells rinsed and reserved
1 tsp salt, plus extra to taste
½lb (250g) rice noodles or small rice sticks (see page 25) or egg noodles
2½ cups (600ml) very thick coconut milk (see page 141)
freshly ground black pepper, to taste

For the paste

2–4 large fresh red chilies, seeded and chopped
3 candlenuts (see page 22) or 5 blanched almonds, chopped
½in (1cm) piece of fresh ginger, peeled and chopped
½in (1cm) piece of fresh galangal (see page 27), peeled and chopped
3 shallots, chopped
2 garlic cloves, chopped
1 tbsp coriander seed, roughly crushed
2 tbsp tamarind water (see page 101)
2 tbsp peanut or vegetable oil

For the garnish

¼lb (125g) fresh bean sprouts, rinsed and trimmed
3 tbsp finely sliced scallions
4–6oz (125–175g) fried tofu (see page 24), thinly sliced, optional
Crisp-Fried Onions (see page 132 for recipe), optional
1 red chili, seeded and finely chopped, optional

PREPARATION

1 Put all the paste ingredients in a blender and blend until very finely chopped. Put the chicken and water in a pan, bring to a boil, and boil gently for 20 minutes. Sprinkle the peeled shrimp with half the salt, then cover and refrigerate.
2 Remove the chicken from the pan and let cool. Take the meat off the bones, then return the bones and skin to the stock and simmer for 20 minutes more. Add the remaining salt. Cut the meat into bite-sized pieces and refrigerate.
3 Add the shrimp shells to the stock and simmer for 10 minutes. Put the paste in a large pan and cook, stirring frequently, for 4 minutes. Strain in the stock and simmer for 10 minutes.
4 Add the rice noodles to a large pan of boiling water. Cover and let stand for 3–4 minutes. If using egg noodles, cook in boiling water for 3 minutes.
5 Transfer the noodles to a colander to drain, then rinse well under cold running water and drain again.
6 Bring the stock to a boil. Add the coconut milk and simmer for 8 minutes. Add the chicken, return to a boil, and boil for 3 minutes. Add the shrimp, simmer for 3 minutes, then season to taste.
7 Divide the noodles and the first three garnishes among the serving bowls and ladle in the soup. Top with the Crisp-Fried Onions and chili, to serve.

KCal 607 P 45g C 33g S 1g TF 33g SF 13g UF 15g (8)

Kai Tom Ka

Chicken and galangal soup (Thailand)

In Thailand most soups are hot and sour. This one, however, is different in that it is quite sweet and contains coconut milk. Serves 4–6.

INGREDIENTS

½lb (250g) small mushrooms, halved or whole
3 tbsp lime juice
1 tbsp fish sauce (nam pla) (see page 28)
1 tsp chili oil, optional
salt and freshly ground black pepper, to taste
½ cup (125ml) very thick coconut milk (see page 141)
handful of fresh Thai basil leaves (see page 26)

For the stock

2–3 large chicken breasts, on the bone
8 cups (2 liters) cold water
2 stems of fresh lemongrass, cut into thirds
2in (5cm) piece of fresh galangal (see page 27), halved
3 fresh kaffir lime leaves (see page 26)
1 medium onion, sliced
1–2 large fresh red chilies, halved
1 tsp salt

PREPARATION

1 Put all the ingredients for the stock in a large pan and bring to a boil. Boil gently for 15 minutes, skimming off the froth as necessary.
2 Remove the chicken from the pan and transfer to a plate to cool. Take the meat off the bones, then return the skin and bones to the stock and simmer for 35–40 minutes more. Cut the meat into small bite-sized pieces and set aside.
3 Strain the stock through a sieve into another pan. Discard the solids. Return the stock to a boil. Add the mushrooms, lime juice, fish sauce, and chili oil, if using, and simmer for 3 minutes. Add the chicken.
4 Season the soup to taste, then stir in the coconut milk. Simmer for 3 minutes, stirring several times. Add the fresh basil leaves and serve immediately.

KCal 202 P 30g C 7g S 0.9g TF 6g SF 4g UF 2g (4)

SNACKS & APPETIZERS

Throughout Asia there is almost no distinction between snacks, appetizers, starters, and regular meals. Asians developed the art of "grazing" long ago, and they practice it at every culinary level from the simplest snack to the most elaborate and refined delicacy. Spring rolls and dim sum, for example, are some of the most exquisite mouthfuls ever invented. However, I have noticed that the Japanese differ from the rest of us in one respect – they never eat in the street.

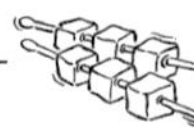

PATTIES

Small filled pies (Sri Lanka)

These patties can be frozen successfully. Makes 25–30 patties. *See illustration on page 35.*

INGREDIENTS

about 2 cups (450ml) peanut oil for deep-frying
For the pastry
¾ lb (375g) shortcrust pastry
or
3 cups (375g) all-purpose flour, plus extra for rolling out
large pinch of salt
1 egg yolk, lightly beaten
4 tbsp butter, melted
6 tbsp (90ml) thick coconut milk (see page 141)
For the filling
1 boned and skinned chicken breast
¼ lb (125g) lamb fillet, in one piece
¼ lb (125g) pork fillet, in one piece
½ tsp salt, plus extra to taste
1 tbsp vegetable oil
1 medium red onion, finely sliced
4 bacon slices, finely diced
1 tsp ground coriander
½ tsp ground cumin
½ tsp ground turmeric
¼ tsp chili powder
large pinch each of ground cloves and cinnamon
seeds of 1 green cardamom pod
1½ in (3cm) piece of fresh lemongrass, bruised
3 fresh or dried curry leaves (see page 26), optional
½ cup (125ml) thick coconut milk (see page 141)
3 eggs, hard-cooked, peeled, and roughly chopped
freshly ground black pepper, to taste

PREPARATION

1 If making the pastry, put the flour, salt, egg, butter, and coconut milk in a food processor and process until well combined into a soft dough. Wrap the dough in plastic wrap and refrigerate for 30 minutes while preparing the filling.

2 For the filling, put the chicken, lamb, and pork in a pan. Cover with water and add the salt. Bring to a boil and boil gently for 30 minutes. Remove the meat from the pan and let cool. (The stock can be used for another dish.)

3 When the meat is cold, put it through the fine disk of a meat grinder, or chop it fine by hand with a chef's knife. Set aside in a cool place.

4 Heat the vegetable oil in a wok or pan. Add the onion and cook for 2 minutes, stirring continuously. Add the bacon and cook, stirring, for 1 minute. Add the ground meat, all the ground spices, the cardamom seed, lemongrass, and curry leaves, if using. Cook, stirring, for 1 minute.

5 Add the coconut milk. Cook for 10 minutes, or until all the milk is absorbed. Season to taste, then transfer the filling to a bowl to cool. Discard the lemongrass and curry leaves, and add the eggs.

6 Remove the pastry from the refrigerator and let stand for few minutes, to soften slightly. Roll out the pastry on a floured board until it is very thin. Cut the pastry into about 20 rounds using a 3½ in (8cm) pastry cutter. Reroll the trimmings and cut out another 5–10 rounds. Discard the leftovers.

7 To fill the patties, take one round of pastry and put a heaping teaspoonful of filling in the center. Fold the pastry over into a half-moon shape, to enclose the filling, and seal the edges with your fingers, and then with a dampened fork. Fill the remaining patties in the same way.

8 Heat the peanut oil in a deep-fat fryer or wok to 350°F (180°C). Add 4 or 5 of the patties to the hot oil and fry for 4–5 minutes, rocking them frequently with a slotted spoon, until golden brown.

9 Remove the patties from the pan and drain on paper towels. Cook the remaining patties in batches, then serve hot, warm, or cold.

KCal 134 P 6g C 8g S 0.2g TF 9g SF 3g UF 5g (per pattie)

Kung Thord

Marinated and fried shrimp (Thailand)

Serve these shrimp the moment you finish frying them. They are equally good served as an appetizer or with drinks, but they must be piping hot.

INGREDIENTS

16 raw jumbo shrimp, peeled and deveined (see page 82)
about 2 cups (450ml) peanut oil for deep-frying

For the marinade

2oz (60g) creamed coconut, chopped
¾ cup (175ml) hot water
1in (2.5cm) piece of fresh galangal (see page 27), peeled and chopped
2in (5cm) piece of fresh lemongrass, outer leaves removed, center chopped
4 fresh cilantro roots or stems, chopped
2 shallots, chopped
3 cloves garlic, chopped
2–4 small dried chilies, chopped
1 tbsp lime juice
1 tsp salt or 1 tbsp fish sauce (nam pla) (see page 28)
2 tsp rice powder (see page 31) or all-purpose flour

PREPARATION

1 Put all the ingredients for the marinade, except the rice powder or all-purpose flour, in a blender and blend until as smooth as possible. Transfer the mixture to a glass bowl and let cool. Stir in the rice powder or all-purpose flour.

2 Add the jumbo shrimp to the marinade and stir until they are thoroughly coated. Cover and refrigerate for 1–2 hours, to marinate.

3 Heat the oil in a deep-fat fryer or a wok to 350°F (180°C). Drain the marinated shrimp in a colander, discarding the marinade. Add half the shrimp to the hot oil and fry for 2–3 minutes.

4 Remove the shrimp from the pan with a slotted spoon and drain on paper towels. Keep the shrimp hot in a warm oven while the second batch is fried, then serve immediately.

KCal 217 P 7g C 5g S 0.6g TF 19g SF 11g UF 7g (4)

SHUEN GUEN

Spring rolls (China)

The spring roll has been a popular Chinese snack for centuries. Today, almost every Asian country has its own version. This recipe uses a vegetarian filling. Makes 20 rolls. See page 34 for illustration.

INGREDIENTS

20 medium frozen spring roll wrappers (see page 25), 9in (23cm) square, defrosted
1 egg white, lightly beaten
about 2 cups (450ml) vegetable oil for deep-frying

For the filling

3 tbsp peanut or vegetable oil
1lb (500g) carrots, cut into thin strips
¼lb (125g) cabbage, finely shredded
7oz (200g) canned sliced bamboo shoots (drained weight), rinsed and cut into thin strips
¾lb (375g) snow peas or thin green beans, thinly sliced on the diagonal
8–10 dried shiitake mushrooms, rehydrated (see page 155), stems removed and caps thinly sliced
½lb (250g) button mushrooms, thinly sliced
2 tsp finely chopped fresh ginger
3 tbsp light soy sauce
6oz (175g) cellophane noodles (see page 25), soaked in hot water for 5 minutes, drained, and cut into short lengths with scissors
6–8 scallions, cut into thin rounds
salt and freshly ground black pepper, to taste

PREPARATION

1 For the filling, heat the oil in a wok. Add the carrots, cabbage, and bamboo shoots and stir-fry for 2 minutes. Add the snow peas or green beans, both types of mushroom, the ginger, and soy sauce and stir-fry for 3 minutes.

2 Add the noodles and scallions and stir-fry rapidly for 2 minutes, until the liquid evaporates but the vegetables are still moist. Season to taste, then remove from the wok and let cool.

3 Place one spring roll wrapper on a flat surface. Put about 2 tablespoons of the cold filling on the corner nearest to you. Flatten the filling a little, then roll the corner of the wrapper over it, toward the center. Fold in the two side flaps. Brush the far corner of the wrapper with a little of the egg white and continue rolling to make a well-sealed bundle. Repeat with the remaining filling and wrappers.

4 Heat the oil in a deep-fat fryer or wok to 350°F (180°C). Add 4 spring rolls, lower the heat a little, and deep-fry for 6–8 minutes, turning the rolls several times, until golden. Remove from the wok with a slotted spoon and drain on paper towels.

5 Keep the spring rolls hot in a warm oven until the remaining batches are fried, then serve immediately. Alternatively, leave the cooked rolls until cold, then briefly refry just before serving.

6 The cooked spring rolls can be frozen for up to 4 weeks. To serve, heat the oil to 300°F (150°C) and deep-fry the frozen rolls for 6–8 minutes, until the filling is heated through and the wrapper is crisp. If the oil is too hot, the outside will blister.

KCal 166 P 3g C 17g S 0.2g TF 4g SF 1g UF 3g (per roll)

PERGEDEL JAGUNG

Corn fritters (Indonesia)

These fritters can be refrigerated for 2 days or frozen for up to 4 weeks. Defrost them completely, then reheat gently in a nonstick skillet for 1–2 minutes. Makes 20–25 fritters. See page 34 for illustration.

INGREDIENTS

4 ears corn or 15oz (475g) canned corn (drained weight)
4 tbsp peanut oil
5 shallots, finely sliced
2 tbsp chopped scallions
1 tsp ground coriander
½ tsp chili powder
1 tsp baking powder
3 tbsp rice powder (see page 31) or all-purpose flour
1 tsp salt, plus extra to taste
1 large egg, lightly beaten
about ⅔ cup (150ml) vegetable oil for frying

PREPARATION

1 To prepare the ears corn, use a sharp knife to slice away the kernels close to the woody cob. Crush the fresh corn kernels or canned corn with a mortar and pestle.

2 Heat half the peanut oil in a pan, add the shallots, and cook for 4 minutes, stirring frequently, until softened but not browned. Remove from the heat and let cool.

3 Transfer the corn to a bowl. Stir in the shallots and all the remaining ingredients, except the oil for frying, and mix well. Add extra salt, if necessary.

4 Heat 5–6 tablespoons (75–90ml) of the vegetable oil in a skillet. Drop a tablespoonful of the fritter mixture into the hot oil and flatten it with a fork. Continue until there are 5 or 6 fritters in the pan. Cook for about 3 minutes on each side, turning them only once.

5 Repeat the process until all the mixture is used, adding more oil to the pan after 2 or 3 batches. Serve the fritters hot or cold.

KCal 100 P 1g C 8g S 0.2g TF 8g SF 2g UF 6g (per fritter)

Samosa

Pastries with vegetable filling (India)

This classic Indian snack is now familiar almost everywhere. Samosa are very easy to make, especially when, as in this recipe, ready-made spring roll wrappers are used. The filling can be made of meat, either lamb or beef, or vegetables. Makes about 30 samosa.

INGREDIENTS

10 large frozen spring roll wrappers (see page 25), 11–12in (28–30cm) square, defrosted
1 egg, beaten
about 2 cups (450ml) vegetable oil for deep-frying

For the filling

2 tbsp ghee (see page 29) or vegetable oil
6 shallots or 1 large onion, finely chopped
2 garlic cloves, finely chopped, optional
½in (1cm) piece of fresh ginger, peeled and chopped
1 tbsp ground coriander
1 tsp ground cumin
½ tsp ground turmeric
¼ tsp chili powder or freshly ground black pepper
pinch of grated nutmeg
pinch of ground cloves
4 medium potatoes, cut into medium dice
8 medium carrots, cut into medium dice
¼–⅓ cup (60–90ml) water
1 tsp salt, plus extra to taste
freshly ground black pepper, to taste
3 tbsp chopped scallions
2 tbsp chopped fresh mint leaves

PREPARATION

1 Cut each spring roll wrapper into 3 equal strips with a pair of scissors. Pile the strips on top of each other, then wrap in a damp dish towel to prevent them from drying out. Refrigerate the wrappers while preparing the filling.

2 For the filling, heat the ghee or vegetable oil in a wok or large pan. Add the shallots or onion, garlic, and ginger and cook, stirring continuously, for 2 minutes. Add the spices and cook, stirring, for a few seconds. Add the diced potatoes and carrots and cook, stirring frequently, for 2 minutes.

3 Add the water and salt to the pan, cover, and simmer, stirring occasionally, for 8–10 minutes. Season to taste, add the scallions and mint, and cook, stirring, for 1 minute. The filling should still be moist. Transfer the mixture to a bowl and let cool.

4 Using one strip of wrapper at a time, make up the samosa, stuffing each one with a dessertspoon of filling (see steps below). It is important to seal the edges of the parcels well so that when the samosa are fried oil cannot seep into the filling.

5 When all the samosa are made, heat the oil in a deep-fat fryer or a wok to 350°F (180°C). Add 3 or 4 of the samosa at a time and fry for 5–6 minutes, rocking them frequently with a slotted spoon, until they are golden brown.

6 Remove the samosa from the pan with the slotted spoon. Drain well on paper towels and keep hot in a warm oven while the remaining batches are fried. Serve hot or warm.

KCal 88 P 1g C 9g S 0.08g TF 3g SF 1g UF 1g (per samosa)

Folding & Filling a Samosa

1 Take one strip of spring roll wrapper at a time and wrap the rest in a damp dish towel. Fold over one corner of the wrapper at a 30° angle and brush it with a little beaten egg.

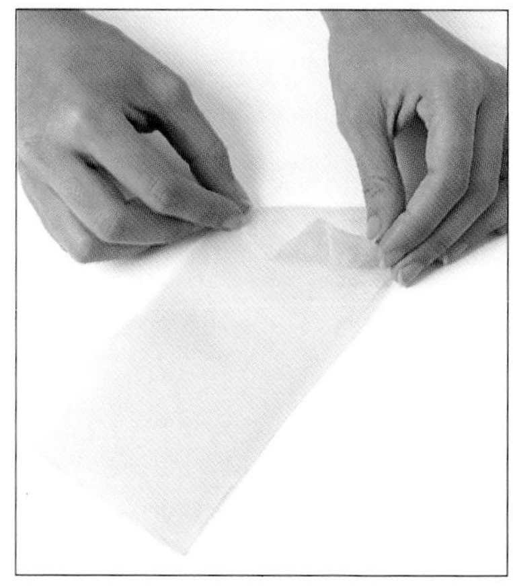

2 Turn the folded corner over again to line up with one side of the strip. Press the edge that has been brushed with egg to seal the wrapper so that it forms a pocket.

3 Put a dessertspoon of filling into the pocket. Place the wrapper on the work surface and fold the pocket over the remaining pastry, brushing the edge with egg to seal.

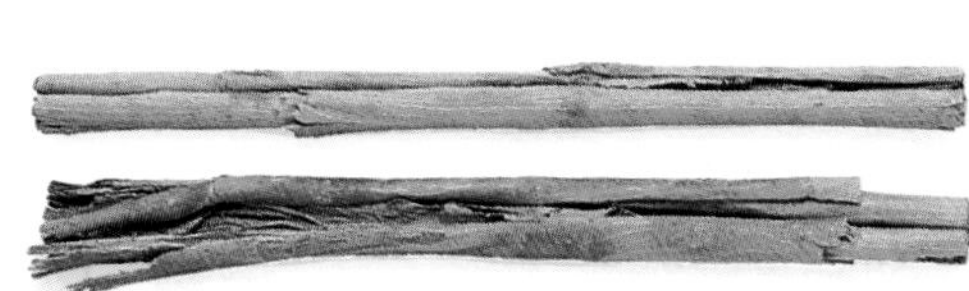

SATE PUSUT

Skewered minced fish (Indonesia)

These satays need no extra sauce – they are spicy enough already. Makes 16 satays. See page 44 for illustration.

INGREDIENTS

salt and freshly ground black pepper, to taste
1½ lb (750g) cod fillet or filleted monkfish tail
3 tbsp chopped scallions or chives
1 egg white, lightly beaten

For the marinade

4 shallots, chopped
2 garlic cloves, chopped
2 candlenuts (see page 22) or
4 blanched almonds, roughly chopped
2 cloves
½ in (1cm) piece of cinnamon stick
¼ tsp grated nutmeg
1 tsp dried shrimp paste (see page 31)
1 tsp sugar
¼ tsp ground turmeric
2in (5cm) piece of fresh lemongrass, outer leaves removed, center chopped
1 fresh kaffir lime leaf (see page 26), shredded
2 tbsp water
2 tbsp lemon or lime juice
2 tbsp peanut or vegetable oil

PREPARATION

1 Put all the marinade ingredients in a blender and blend until as smooth as possible. Transfer the mixture to a pan and simmer, stirring frequently, for 4–5 minutes. Season to taste, then remove from the heat and let cool.

2 Finely chop the cod or monkfish with a sharp knife. Transfer to a glass bowl and add the scallions or chives, the egg white, and the cold marinade mixture. Mix well, then refrigerate for at least 2 hours or, if possible, overnight.

3 Shape the fish mixture into balls, each the size of a walnut. To thread onto skewers, hold a fish ball in the palm of your hand, then push 2 bamboo skewers or a lemongrass stalk through the middle of it. Form the fish ball into a sausage shape around the skewers. Repeat with the remaining fish balls.

4 Grill the satays over charcoal, or under a preheated hot broiler, for 2 minutes on each side, then serve immediately.

KCal 59 P 9g C 1g S 0.05g TF 2g SF 0.4g UF 1.5g (per skewer)

CHAO TOM

Skewered shrimp balls and shrimp (Vietnam)

This recipe is an adaptation of the traditional version where shrimp paste is skewered onto sugarcane sticks. Serve with Nuoc Cham or Peanut Sauce (see pages 128 and 130 for recipes). Makes 8 satays. See page 45 for illustration.

INGREDIENTS

32 raw medium shrimp, peeled and deveined (see page 82), tails left whole
salt and freshly ground black pepper, to taste
2 tbsp sesame seeds
2 tbsp bread crumbs
½ tsp each of chili oil and sesame oil
1 tbsp peanut oil

For the shrimp paste

1lb (500g) raw small shrimp, peeled and deveined (see page 82)
1 egg white
½ tsp salt
½ tsp sugar
¼ tsp ground black pepper
2oz (60g) pork fat, chopped, optional
2 tsp rice powder (see page 31) or potato starch
2 garlic cloves, finely chopped
1 tsp finely chopped fresh ginger
1 tsp fish sauce (nuoc mam) (see page 28)

PREPARATION

1 Rub the medium shrimp with salt and pepper and set aside. For the paste, process the small shrimp, egg white, salt, sugar, and pepper in a food processor until smooth. Add the remaining paste ingredients and process until well mixed. Transfer the mixture to a bowl, cover, and refrigerate for 1 hour.

2 Combine the sesame seeds and bread crumbs on a flat plate. Divide the shrimp paste into 24 portions. Roll each portion in the sesame and bread-crumb mixture, shaping it into a ball.

3 Thread the whole shrimp and the shrimp balls alternately onto 8 skewers, allowing 4 shrimp and 3 shrimp balls per skewer. Arrange the skewers on a well-oiled baking sheet and cook in an oven preheated to 400°F (200°C) for 10 minutes.

4 Mix the chili oil and sesame oil with the peanut oil. Transfer the skewers to a broiler pan and broil for 2 minutes on each side, brushing them with the oil mixture. Serve the Chao Tom immediately.

KCal 152 P 17g C 3g S 0.4g TF 8g SF 2g UF 6g (per skewer)

Satay Daging

Skewered beef (Malaysia)

Serve Satay Daging with Peanut Sauce or Nuoc Cham (see pages 130 and 128 for recipes). Makes 18 satays. *See page 44 for illustration.*

INGREDIENTS

2lb (1kg) rump steak or topside, cut into 1in (2.5cm) cubes

For the marinade

3 shallots, finely sliced
2 garlic cloves, crushed
2in (5cm) piece of fresh ginger, peeled and finely chopped
1 tbsp coriander seed, roasted (see page 155) and roughly crushed
1 tsp ground cumin
½ tsp chili powder
½ tsp coarsely ground black pepper
2 tbsp light soy sauce
1 tbsp peanut oil
1 tbsp distilled white vinegar or lemon juice
½ tsp salt
1 tsp grated jaggery or light brown sugar

PREPARATION

1 Mix all the ingredients for the marinade in a glass bowl. Add the cubes of beef and stir well to coat. Cover and refrigerate for at least 2 hours or, if possible, overnight.

2 Thread the meat onto 18 skewers, allowing 3 or 4 pieces per skewer. Cook the satay over charcoal, or under a preheated hot broiler, for 8 minutes, turning them several times. Serve immediately.

KCal 78 P 13g C 0.6g S 0.2g TF 3g SF 1g UF 2g (per skewer)

Pork Satay

Skewered pork (Singapore)

Here, a piece of pork fat is put between the meat cubes on each skewer to give additional flavor. Serve with Peanut Sauce (see page 130 for recipe). Makes 18 satays. *See page 45 for illustration.*

INGREDIENTS

2lb (1kg) pork tenderloin or leg meat, cut into pieces not more than ½in (1cm) long and 1in (2.5cm) wide
¼lb (125g) thick pork fat, cut the same as the pork

For the marinade

4 garlic cloves, crushed
1 tsp ground black pepper
1 tsp ground Szechwan pepper
2 tsp five-spice powder (see page 27)
2 tbsp each of light soy sauce and clear honey
¼ tsp salt

PREPARATION

1 Mix all the ingredients for the marinade in a glass bowl. Add the pieces of meat and stir well to coat. Cover and refrigerate overnight.

2 Thread the meat and fat onto 18 bamboo or metal skewers, allowing about 5 pieces of meat and 1 or 2 pieces of fat per skewer. Place the fat between the meat cubes and pack tightly together.

3 Arrange the satays on a rack set over a roasting pan. Cook in an oven preheated to 350°F (180°C) for 30 minutes, then turn the satays over and cook for 20 minutes. Brown under a hot broiler for 3–4 minutes, if necessary, then serve immediately.

KCal 116 P 13g C 2g S 0.2g TF 6g SF 2g UF 3g (per skewer)

Yakitori

Skewered chicken (Japan)

The glaze for the chicken doubles as a dipping sauce. Makes 8 skewers. *See page 44 for illustration.*

INGREDIENTS

2 boned and skinned chicken breasts and 4 boned and skinned chicken thighs, cut into ¾in (2cm) cubes
4 scallions, stems only, cut into ¾in (2cm) pieces

For the glaze/sauce

4 tbsp dark soy sauce
2 tbsp mirin (see page 29)
2 tbsp sake (see page 29)
1 tbsp sugar
1 tbsp tamari soy sauce (see page 28)
¼ tsp salt
1¾ cups (400ml) water

PREPARATION

1 For the glaze, mix half of all the ingredients, except the water, in a glass bowl. Blend in ½ cup (120ml) of the water and set aside.

2 Thread the pieces of chicken and pieces of scallion onto 8 short bamboo or wooden skewers, allowing 3 or 4 pieces of meat and 2 pieces of scallion per skewer.

3 For the sauce, mix the remaining dark soy sauce, mirin, sake, sugar, tamari soy sauce, salt, and water in a pan. Simmer for 10 minutes, then remove from the heat and transfer the sauce to a serving bowl.

4 Pour the glaze onto a flat plate and turn the skewered chicken in it, to coat well. Cook the yakitori over charcoal, or under a preheated broiler, for 5–6 minutes, turning them several times. Serve immediately with the sauce.

KCal 81 P 14g C 4g S 0.8g TF 0.9g SF 0.3g UF 0.6g (per skewer)

Tempura

Mixed seafood and vegetables deep-fried in batter (Japan)

Deep-frying in batter is a traditional method of cooking in many countries. Although this recipe is Japanese, some Japanese cooking experts would tell you that it originally came from the West.

INGREDIENTS

1 small purple eggplant, halved across, each half cut into 8 segments, lengthwise
1 medium red onion, cut into 8 rings
1 red or yellow pepper, seeded and cut into 10 pieces
8 raw large shrimp, peeled and deveined (see page 82)
2 medium squid, cleaned and each cut into 8 rings (see page 150), tentacles discarded
¼lb (125g) small skinned sole fillet, cut into 8 pieces
about 2 cups (450ml) sunflower oil for deep-frying

For the batter

2 egg yolks
2 cups (475ml) ice-cold water
4 cups (500g) all-purpose flour
pinch of salt

For the dipping sauce

4 tbsp light soy sauce
4 tbsp mirin (see page 29)
½ cup (125ml) bonito stock (see page 30)
2 tsp finely chopped fresh ginger

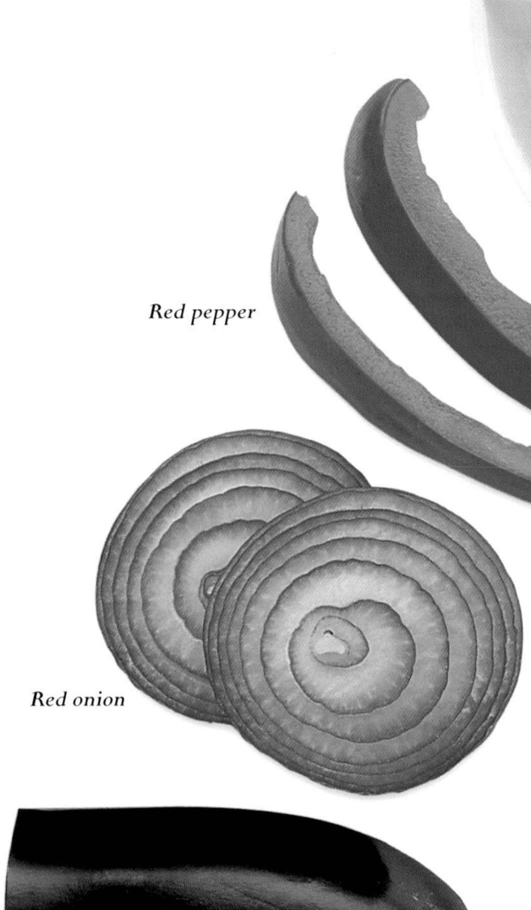

PREPARATION

1 Dry the pieces of vegetables and seafood thoroughly with paper towels.

2 Prepare the batter a half quantity at a time. Put one egg yolk in a bowl and beat it lightly with a fork. Pour in half the ice-cold water and whisk lightly. Sift in half the flour and salt and stir lightly with a fork or a pair of chopsticks. Do not beat the batter, it is supposed to be lumpy.

3 Heat the oil in a deep-fat fryer or wok to 350°F (180°C). Dip the vegetables, one piece at a time, into the batter, then plunge into the hot oil until 4 or 5 pieces are frying together. Cook for 2–3 minutes, then remove with a slotted spoon and drain on paper towels. Keep warm while the remaining vegetables are battered and cooked.

4 In a clean bowl, make the second batch of batter with the remaining ingredients. Dip half of the shrimp into the batter and fry for 2–3 minutes, turning them with a slotted spoon as they cook.

5 Drain the shrimp on paper towels and keep warm with the vegetables. Repeat with the remaining shrimp. Coat and fry the squid and fish in two batches each, then drain and keep warm.

6 Put all the sauce ingredients, except the ginger, in a pan. Bring to a boil, then simmer for 2 minutes. Add the ginger, stir once, then transfer to a bowl. Serve with the tempura.

KCal 655 P 32g C 106g S 1.4g TF 15g SF 2g UF 10g (4)

Mirin
Salt
Light soy sauce
All-purpose flour
Bonito stock
Fresh ginger
Egg yolks
Sunflower oil

Siu Mai

Steamed wonton with shrimp and pork (Singapore)

When making these dim sum it is essential to buy wonton wrappers that are made for steaming – they are slightly thicker than those for deep-frying. Serve as an appetizer or as part of a dim sum lunch. Makes 20–24.

INGREDIENTS

6–8oz (175–250g) wonton wrappers for steaming (see page 25), defrosted if frozen

For the filling

¾lb (375g) raw shrimp, peeled and deveined (see page 82), chopped

½lb (250g) ground pork

1 tsp salt

3oz (90g) fresh shiitake mushrooms or cultivated mushrooms, chopped

6 canned water chestnuts, chopped

2 tsp light soy sauce

1 tsp sugar

2 tbsp finely chopped scallions

¼ tsp freshly ground black or white pepper

1 egg white, lightly beaten

PREPARATION

1 For the filling, put the chopped shrimp, ground pork, and salt in a bowl and knead them together with your hands until well mixed.

2 Add all the remaining filling ingredients and mix well with a wooden spoon. Cover and refrigerate for 30 minutes, or longer, if possible.

3 To fill the wonton wrappers, using scissors, snip off a little from the corners of each wrapper.

4 Put 1 tablespoon of the filling in the center of each wrapper and gather up the edges to make a bag. Lift it onto your hand, then squeeze gently in the middle as if to form the neck of a bag.

5 Open the bag at the top and press the filling down with a dampened teaspoon, to flatten the top. Continue until all the wrappers are filled.

6 To cook the Siu Mai, steam them in batches in a bamboo steamer (see page 149), or in an ordinary steamer, for 8–10 minutes per batch.

7 Alternatively, if you do not have a steamer, arrange some Siu Mai on an oiled plate. Set a trivet or a soup plate upside down in the bottom of a large pot and add enough hot water to come to the top of it. Stand the plate on top. Bring the water to a boil, cover the pot, and cook for 12–15 minutes.

8 Serve the Siu Mai hot or warm, accompanied by a hot-flavored dipping sauce such as chili sauce (see page 28), if desired.

KCal 264 P 20g C 12g S 0.8g TF 4g SF 2g UF 2g (6)

Rempah-Rempah

Shrimp and bean sprout fritters (Malaysia)

Serve these fritters as a snack with drinks. Makes about 20 fritters. See illustration on page 34.

INGREDIENTS

about 2 cups (450ml) vegetable oil for deep-frying

20 small raw shrimp, peeled and deveined (see page 82)

For the fritters

½lb (250g) raw shrimp, peeled and deveined (see page 82), chopped

½lb (250g) fresh bean sprouts, rinsed and trimmed

¼lb (125g) rice powder (see page 31) or all-purpose flour

2 tsp baking powder

1 tsp ground coriander

pinch of ground turmeric

2 fresh red chilies, seeded and finely chopped

4 scallions, finely sliced

1 tsp light soy sauce

1 tsp salt

2 eggs, beaten

PREPARATION

1 Put all the ingredients for the fritters in a glass bowl and mix together well with a spoon.

2 Heat the oil in a deep-fat fryer or wok to 350°F (180°C). Take a tablespoonful of the fritter mixture, place a whole shrimp on top, then flatten it so that the whole shrimp is set into the top of the fritter. Repeat with the remaining mixture and shrimp.

3 Put 4 or 5 of the fritters into the hot oil and deep-fry for 3 minutes. Remove from the pan with a slotted spoon and drain on paper towels. Keep warm while the remaining batches are fried. Serve the fritters warm or cold.

KCal 63 P 4g C 6g S 0.2g TF 3g SF 0.5g UF 2g (per fritter)

SUSHI

Rice rolls (Japan)

The Japanese use a bamboo rolling mat (see page 149) to make rolled sushi, but a double thickness of foil will work equally well. Make the sushi as close to serving as possible, they keep fresh for only 1–2 hours. Makes 24 sushi and serves 6. See page 35 for illustration.

INGREDIENTS

For the rice

2 cups (500g) short-grain Japanese rice (see page 24), washed in several changes of water and left to drain for 30 minutes
2 cups (500ml) cold water
10–12oz (300–375g) sliced smoked salmon
1 thin cucumber, cut in half lengthwise and seeded, each half sliced lengthwise into 4 strips

For the dressing

4 tbsp rice vinegar (see page 29)
2 tbsp sugar
1 tbsp hot water
½–1 tsp salt

PREPARATION

1 Put the rice and cold water in a heavy-based pan. Bring to a boil and boil, uncovered, for about 10 minutes, until all the water is absorbed. Stir once with a spoon, then reduce the heat to very low.

2 Cover the pan and let the rice cook undisturbed for 10–12 minutes. Remove the pan from the heat and let stand, still covered, on a wet dish towel for 5 minutes. Transfer the rice to a wooden, ceramic, or glass bowl and let cool for a few minutes.

3 Mix all the dressing ingredients together in a small glass bowl, then pour over the rice, a little at a time, and mix in gently. Do not stir the rice vigorously; the action should be like gently tossing a salad. Taste the rice as you add the dressing, you may not need all of it. Cover the bowl with a damp dish towel and set aside in a cool place.

4 Line a bamboo rolling mat, or a double thickness of foil, about 10in (24cm) square, with plastic wrap. Divide the rice and smoked salmon slices into 4 portions.

5 Arrange a quarter of the smoked salmon on the rolling mat or foil, top with a quarter of the rice, then arrange 2 strips of cucumber on top and roll up (see steps below).

6 Remove the rolled sushi from the mat or foil and keep rolled in the plastic wrap. Repeat the rolling process with the remaining rice portions and smoked salmon. Refrigerate the rolls for 10 minutes before serving.

7 To serve, remove the plastic wrap from the sushi and cut each roll across into 6 slices. Arrange the rolls on a serving platter and serve immediately.

KCal 106 P 5g C 20g S 0.3g TF 1.1g SF 0.3g UF 0.8g (per sushi)

ROLLING SUSHI

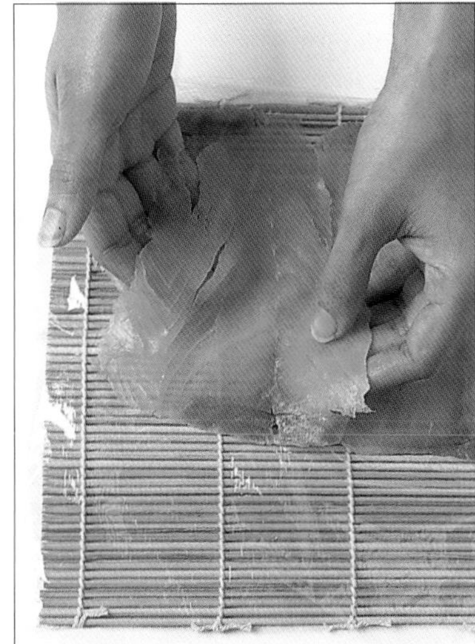

1 Arrange a quarter of the smoked salmon slices, with the long sides running top-to-bottom, to cover only about half the length of the mat, but almost its full width. Leave about a ½in (1cm) margin on either side.

2 Spread one portion of the seasoned rice over the smoked salmon to cover all but a narrow strip along the furthest edge. Level the rice by pressing it lightly with the back of a fork to give an even layer.

3 Place 2 strips of cucumber across the rice. Using the mat or foil as a guide, roll up the sushi away from you into a compact sausage, making sure the plastic wrap and the mat or foil are not rolled into the rice.

INDONESIA & MALAYSIA

Strong flavors, delicately balanced and blended; textures that range from crunchy to chewy, crisp to soft; the subtle use of sourness and the tang of hot chilies – all these bring to life the cooking of Indonesia and Malaysia.

LAKSA LEMAK
Malaysian hot noodle soup with coconut milk. (See page 61 for recipe.)

RUJAK
Indonesian hot, spicy fruit salad. (See page 137 for recipe.)

OSENG OSENG AYAM DENGAN SAYURAN
Indonesian stir-fried chicken with vegetables. (See page 86 for recipe.)

NASI KUNING
Malaysian savory yellow rice. (See page 126 for recipe.)

FISH & SEAFOOD

Fish is a staple food of almost all Asian countries, whether from the deep ocean or the village pond. To the cook it offers opportunities and a challenge. Luckily most fish recipes can be made with a variety of different species; the important thing is to buy the freshest fish available, particularly if the dish is to be eaten raw or lightly cooked. Short cooking times are typical of these recipes – shrimp and scallops, for example, become very tough if overdone. The flavors of Asian fish cuisine are clear and emphatic, and the balance of herbs, spices, and seasoning is vital.

PEPES IKAN

Marinated fish baked with coconut (Indonesia)

This classic Javanese dish, now an acknowledged Indonesian specialty, is cooked everywhere with regional variations. Needless to say, in Indonesia we prefer to cook it wrapped in banana leaves. A good alternative is to use a circle of baking parchment as the wrapper and cook "en papillote."

INGREDIENTS

4 tbsp tamarind water (see page 101)
½ tsp salt, plus extra to taste
2 garlic cloves, finely chopped
¼ tsp chili powder
4 double fillets of trout, 6–7oz (175–200g) each, or 4 boned and skinned fish steaks
3 tbsp peanut oil
4 shallots, finely sliced
2–4 large fresh red chilies, seeded and finely sliced
1 tsp ground coriander
2 tsp chopped fresh ginger
½ stem of fresh lemongrass, outer leaves removed, center chopped
handful of fresh mint leaves
1–1½ cups (125–175g) grated fresh coconut (see page 133) or 1½ cups (125g) dried coconut soaked in ½ cup (125ml) warm water for 5 minutes
freshly ground black pepper, to taste
fresh banana leaves (see page 20) or baking parchment

PREPARATION

1 Combine the tamarind water, salt, garlic, and chili powder in a bowl. Add the fish and turn until well coated. Cover and marinate for 1 hour.
2 Remove the fish from the marinade and transfer to a plate. Reserve the marinade.
3 Heat the oil in a large shallow pan. Add the shallots and chilies and stir-fry for 2–3 minutes. Stir in the coriander, ginger, lemongrass, and mint leaves. Simmer for 1 minute.
4 Add the fresh or dried coconut, and simmer, stirring frequently, for 6–8 minutes. Add the marinade and cook, stirring frequently, for 1 minute. Season to taste, then add the fish. Stir, cover the pan, and remove from the heat.
5 Cut the banana leaf into four 12in (30cm) squares, or cut baking parchment into four 12in (30cm) circles. Place one piece of fish in the center of each square or circle and divide the coconut mixture among them, spreading it over the fish.
6 Fold the banana leaf over to make a bundle and secure in place with bamboo skewers. Alternatively, fold the paper circle in half and tightly fold the edges together, to seal.
7 Place the bundles on a baking sheet and bake in an oven preheated to 350°F (180°C) for 15–20 minutes, or until the fish is cooked through. Serve the bundles sealed, allowing the diners to open their own.

KCal 469 P 37g C 6g S 0.3g TF 33g SF 17g UF 14g (4)

Patrani Machchi

Baked fish wrapped in banana leaves (India)

This is the Indian version of what the people of Java call Pepes Ikan (see opposite). I would not be surprised if this is another of the many dishes that have traveled from Persia via India to Indonesia. Serve with vegetables of your choice and rice. See page 134 for illustration.

INGREDIENTS

4 fillets of flounder or turbot, 5–6oz (150–175g) each
½ tsp salt
juice of 1 small lemon
4 tbsp grated fresh coconut (see page 133)
or 3 tbsp dried coconut
3 tbsp finely chopped fresh cilantro leaves
fresh banana leaves (see page 20) or foil

For the paste

1 tbsp coriander seed, roasted (see page 155), roughly crushed
1 tsp cumin seed, roasted (see page 155), roughly crushed
2 garlic cloves, chopped
2 tsp white poppy seeds (see page 23), roughly crushed
2 tbsp tamarind water (see page 101)
or distilled white vinegar
1 tsp sugar
1 fresh green and 1 red chili, seeded and chopped
2 tbsp peanut oil
½ tsp salt, plus extra to taste

PREPARATION

1 Rub the fish all over with the salt and lemon juice and let stand in a cool place for 30 minutes.

2 Put all the paste ingredients in a blender and blend until as smooth as possible. Transfer the paste mixture to a bowl and stir in the grated fresh or dried coconut and the cilantro leaves. Add more salt, if necessary.

3 If using banana leaves, cut them to cover a large piece of foil about 16in (40cm) square. Alternatively, just use a double layer of foil. Arrange the fish fillets in a single layer on top of the leaves or foil and rub each piece well, on both sides, with the paste mixture.

4 Fold the banana leaves and foil over the fillets to enclose them, securing the banana leaves with bamboo skewers and turning the edges of the foil over to seal and make a loose bundle. Put the bundle directly on the shelf of an oven preheated to 375°F (190°C) and bake for 15–20 minutes.

5 Unwrap the bundle and transfer the fish and the cooking juices to a large ovenproof dish. Place under a preheated hot broiler for 2–3 minutes, to lightly brown the tops, then serve immediately.

KCal 239 P 27g C 5g S 0.7g TF 15g SF 6g UF 7g (4)

Lachap Longlei Guin

Deep-fried sole with chili bean sauce and asparagus (China)

I watched chef Simon Yung of the Dorchester Hotel, London, prepare this classic Cantonese dish. Naturally, as a professional chef, his presentation is impressive, with the fish skeleton formed into a boat shape and deep-fried until crisp. Making it at home, I use only the fish fillet. Serves 2 as a main course or 4 as an appetizer.

INGREDIENTS

2 skinned Dover sole fillets, each 8–10oz (250–300g), each cut into 4 thin slices on the diagonal (see page 150)
1 tsp light soy sauce
few drops of sesame oil
4 large fresh shiitake mushrooms or chestnut mushrooms, stems removed and caps sliced
1oz (30g) canned sliced bamboo shoots, cut into fine julienne strips (see page 154)
1 small carrot, cut into fine julienne strips (see page 154)
3 scallions, cut into ¾in (2cm) lengths
2 tsp cornstarch
salt and freshly ground black pepper, to taste
about 1¼ cups (300ml) vegetable oil for deep-frying
6 asparagus spears, about 3in (7cm) long
2 tbsp chopped fresh cilantro leaves, to garnish

For the sauce

2 tbsp chili bean sauce (see page 28)
¼ green pepper, seeded and finely diced
1 garlic clove, crushed and finely chopped
1–2 tsp rice vinegar (see page 29)
3 tbsp hot water

PREPARATION

1 Sprinkle the fish slices with the soy sauce and sesame oil. Divide the mushrooms, bamboo shoots, carrot, and scallions into 8 equal portions and arrange each portion on a slice of fish. Roll up each slice with the vegetables inside.

2 Sprinkle some of the cornstarch and a little salt and pepper over each roll and rub it in gently.

3 Mix all the sauce ingredients in a small pan. Heat the oil in a wok until very hot. Add the fish rolls and cook for 2 minutes only. Remove the rolls from the wok with a slotted spoon. Transfer to a heated serving platter and keep warm.

4 Heat the sauce in the pan and, at the same time, cook the asparagus in the wok for 10 seconds. Remove the asparagus from the wok and drain on paper towels. Pour the hot sauce over the fish rolls and arrange the asparagus around it. Sprinkle with the cilantro, to garnish, then serve immediately.

KCal 501 P 50g C 11g S 0.8g TF 29g SF 3g UF 20g (2)

Plea Tray

Fish salad (Cambodia)

Every Asian community seems to have its own favorite fish salad, and if life were longer it would be fascinating to travel around and collect all of them. Luckily, all the ones I have found so far, including this one by Rosine Ek of Chez Rosine Cuisine du Cambodge, Paris, can be made with fish that are readily available in the West without losing the flavor of Asia.

INGREDIENTS

4 tbsp fresh lime juice
2 tsp finely chopped fresh lemongrass, center only
1 tsp finely chopped fresh galangal (see page 27)
1–3 fresh red bird's-eye chilies, finely chopped
1 tsp sugar
2 tsp fish sauce (nuoc mam) (see page 28)
¼ tsp salt, plus extra to taste
¾ lb (375g) salmon fillet, cut into thin strips (see page 150)
½ medium cucumber or 1 small cucumber, peeled
2 shallots, very finely sliced
1 red pepper, seeded and cut into very fine strips
handful each of 2 types of fresh mint leaves
2–3 iceberg lettuce leaves, finely shredded

PREPARATION

1 Mix the lime juice, lemongrass, galangal, chilies, sugar, fish sauce, and salt together in a bowl. Add the strips of fish, turning them until well coated, then let marinate in a cool place for 2–3 hours.

2 Cut the cucumber in half lengthwise, and scoop out and discard the seeds, using a teaspoon. Slice the cucumber into very thin half-moon shapes.

3 Put the cucumber slices in a glass serving bowl. Add the shallots, red pepper, both types of mint, and the lettuce, and mix together well.

4 Remove the strips of fish from the marinade and transfer to the salad. Season the marinade with more salt, if desired, and pour it over the salad. Toss all the ingredients together until thoroughly mixed, then serve immediately.

KCal 205 P 21g C 6g S 0.4g TF 11g SF 2g UF 7g (4)

TERIYAKI

Glazed grilled fish (Japan)

Teriyaki is a grilled (yaki) dish with a sauce that forms a glaze (teri) during cooking. Traditionally, it is arranged on a platter lined with chrysanthemum leaves, decorated with a flower carved from daikon (mooli), and served with a small pile of shredded pink pickled ginger. As I have never managed to carve the flower successfully, I simply pile up fine matchsticks of daikon and ginger next to the fish. Serve the fish hot, followed by plain boiled Japanese rice with some vegetables or a salad, if desired.

INGREDIENTS

4 halibut steaks, 5–6oz (150–175g) each, cut about 2in (5cm) thick
1 tsp coarse sea salt
4 tbsp peanut oil
2 tbsp finely shredded pink pickled ginger (see page 31), to garnish
¼lb (125g) daikon (see page 20), cut into tiny julienne strips (see page 154), soaked in ice water, to garnish

For the marinade/glaze

2 tbsp sake (see page 29)
2 tbsp mirin (see page 29)
5 tbsp (75ml) dark soy sauce
1 tbsp sugar

PREPARATION

1 Rub the fish steaks all over with the salt and let stand for 30 minutes. Rinse well under cold running water, then dry on paper towels.

2 Combine the ingredients for the marinade in a glass bowl. Add the fish steaks and marinate for 1–2 hours, turning them several times.

3 Remove the fish steaks from the marinade and arrange side by side, on a broiler pan. Cook under a preheated hot broiler for 5–8 minutes, turning once, until golden brown all over.

4 Pour the marinade into a small pan. Heat for 2–3 minutes, or until it has thickened and caramelized. Using the back of a spoon, glaze the fish steaks all over. Return the fish to the broiler and cook for 2–3 minutes more.

5 Arrange the teriyaki on a serving platter and garnish with a small pile of shredded pink pickled ginger and another of daikon.

KCal 297 P 33g C 8g S 1.9g TF 14g SF 3g UF 10g (4)

IKAN MASAK TAUCO

Fish in black bean sauce (Malaysia)

Here I recommend flounder and black bean sauce, but you could use yellow bean sauce and the freshest fillets of any white fish. Serve with rice or noodles, or simply with some salad for a light lunch.

INGREDIENTS

4 skinned fillets of flounder, 6–7oz (175–200g) each, or cod or monkfish
½ tsp salt
1 tsp freshly ground black pepper
1 tbsp light brown sugar
2 tbsp all-purpose flour
4 tbsp peanut or soy oil
6 shallots or 1 large onion, very finely sliced
2–5 fresh green chilies, seeded and thinly sliced
½lb (250g) small mushrooms, thinly sliced
1 tsp light soy sauce
3 scallions, cut into thin rounds

For the paste

2 tbsp black bean or yellow bean sauce (see page 28)
2 garlic cloves, chopped
2in (5cm) piece of fresh ginger, chopped
¼ tsp chili powder
1 tbsp tamarind water (see page 101) or lemon juice
2 tbsp peanut or soy oil

PREPARATION

1 Rub the fish fillets all over with the salt and pepper. Mix the sugar and flour together in a small bowl and rub over one side of the fillets. Roll up the fillets, floured side out, then secure with a wooden toothpick, and set aside.

2 Put all the paste ingredients in a blender and blend until as smooth as possible. Transfer the paste mixture to a small bowl.

3 Heat the oil in a large nonstick skillet. Add the fish rolls and cook, turning them frequently, for 2–3 minutes. Remove from the pan with a slotted spoon and transfer to a plate, then carefully remove the toothpicks.

4 Reheat the skillet. Add the shallots or onion and cook, stirring almost continuously, for about 2 minutes. Add the paste mixture, green chilies, and mushrooms and cook, stirring frequently, for 2–3 minutes. Increase the heat and stir in the soy sauce and scallions.

5 Return the rolls to the pan and stir carefully until they are coated with the black bean sauce. Lower the heat, then cover the pan and cook for 1 minute only. Remove the pan from the heat and let stand, still covered, for 2 minutes before serving.

KCal 360 P 33g C 14g S 0.7g TF 20g SF 4g UF 14g (4)

IKAN MASAK LADA

Pan-fried fillet of cod coated in chilies (Malaysia)

Chili lovers will appreciate this popular Malaysian dish. It does not need to be blisteringly hot, because if you choose the right chilies – large red ones – they are not very hot. Serve with rice, or noodles, and salad.

INGREDIENTS

4 pieces of cod fillet, 5–6oz (150–175g) each
½ tsp salt, plus extra to taste
½ tsp freshly ground white pepper, plus extra to taste
5 tbsp (75ml) peanut or vegetable oil
10 large fresh red chilies or 2 red peppers, seeded and finely chopped
4 shallots, very finely chopped
2 garlic cloves, finely chopped
2 tsp finely chopped fresh ginger
2 tsp ground coriander
1 tbsp tamarind water (see page 101)

PREPARATION

1 Rub the fish all over with the salt and pepper, and let stand for 10–15 minutes.
2 Heat the oil in a skillet. Add the fish fillets in a single layer and cook over medium heat for 2 minutes. Turn the fillets over with a spatula and cook for 2 minutes more.
3 Remove the fish from the pan and transfer to a plate. Add the chilies or red peppers, shallots, and garlic to the pan and cook, stirring almost continuously, for 6 minutes. Add the ginger and ground coriander. Season to taste and cook, stirring continuously, for 2 minutes.
4 Add the tamarind water to the pan, then increase the heat and cook, stirring continuously, for 2 minutes. Add 2 tablespoons of hot water to the mixture if it looks too dry.
5 Arrange the fish fillets on top of the chili mixture, cook for 1 minute, then turn them over and cook for 1 minute more. Remove the pan from the heat, cover, and let stand for 2 minutes before serving.

KCal 276 P 29g C 6g S 0.3g TF 15g SF 3g UF 11g (4)

SUZUKI SASHIMI

Raw sea bass with vegetables and dipping sauce (Japan)

I admit I have made this dish only once, but it was a great success. My fish was caught at four o'clock in the morning off the coast of Cornwall, delivered to my house in London at eleven, and eaten that evening. I would not attempt to prepare sashimi with anything less fresh. Good sashimi is unbeatable, so I have included this recipe for those who are lucky enough to live by the sea where truly fresh fish is easily available. Make the dipping sauce well in advance; it will keep refrigerated in an airtight jar for 2–3 days.

INGREDIENTS

½ medium cucumber, halved lengthwise
1lb (500g) very fresh sea bass fillet, cut into very thin slices (see page 150)
1 lemon, cut into wedges
handful of fresh mint leaves, to garnish
wasabi paste (see page 31), to serve
For the dipping sauce
½ cup (125ml) dark soy sauce
1 tbsp sake (see page 29)
1 tbsp mirin (see page 29)
2 tbsp tamari soy sauce (see page 28)
1oz (30g) bonito flakes (see page 30)

PREPARATION

1 For the dipping sauce, combine the dark soy sauce, sake, and mirin in a small pan. Bring to a boil, then simmer for 5 minutes. Remove the pan from the heat and add the tamari soy sauce and bonito flakes. Let stand for about 5 hours.
2 Scoop out and discard the seeds of the cucumber using a teaspoon, then cut the cucumber into julienne strips (see page 150).
3 To serve, arrange the fish slices on 4 plates, put the cucumber julienne and lemon wedges on top, and garnish with the mint. Put the wasabi and the dipping sauce in separate small bowls, so each guest has his or her own.
4 To eat, the lemon is squeezed over the fish. A slice of fish is picked up with chopsticks and dipped into the wasabi, then into the dipping sauce. The fish is eaten alternately with a little cucumber.
5 Alternatively, the fish can be eaten like a salad, with a knife and fork, and mixed with some salad greens, if desired, with the wasabi and the dipping sauce mixed together and poured over.

KCal 164 P 28g C 4g S 3.4g TF 3g SF 0.5g UF 1.5g (4)

NGA WEHIN

Basic fish curry (Myanmar)

Some Burmese curries are similar to Thai curries, others are more closely related to Indian curries. It is hard to tell which side of the family this one favors, for it is a basic curry that contains neither coconut milk nor yogurt. It is worth using the whole fish, with bones and head, as this gives a tasty sauce.

INGREDIENTS

½ grouper or ocean perch or 2 butterfish, 2–2½ lb (1–1.25kg) in total
3¾ cups (900ml) water
2in (5cm) piece of fresh ginger, thinly sliced
1 tsp ground turmeric
½ tsp salt, plus extra to taste
1 tbsp fish sauce (nam pla) (see page 28)
1 stem of fresh lemongrass, cut into 3 pieces
freshly ground black pepper, to taste
3 tbsp chopped fresh cilantro leaves, to garnish

For the paste

5 shallots, chopped
3 garlic cloves, chopped
2–6 small dried red chilies
1 tsp finely chopped fresh lemongrass, center only
2 tbsp tamarind water (see page 101)
3 tbsp vegetable oil
1 tbsp fish sauce (nam pla) (see page 28)
2 red tomatoes, peeled and chopped

PREPARATION

1 Put the fish in a pan with the water, ginger, turmeric, salt, fish sauce, and lemongrass. Bring to a boil, then simmer for 8–10 minutes.
2 Remove the fish from the pan and let cool. Take the fish off the bones in large pieces and set aside. Return the skin and bones to the stock and simmer for 20 minutes more. Strain the stock into a bowl and discard the solids.
3 Put all the paste ingredients in a blender and blend until as smooth as possible. Transfer the paste to a pan and bring to a boil. Cook, stirring frequently, for 3 minutes. Add the strained stock and cook for another 15–20 minutes, until the sauce is reduced.
4 Season to taste, and add the fish. Heat through for 3–4 minutes, then sprinkle with the cilantro leaves to garnish, and serve immediately.

KCal 356 P 50g C 5g S 1g TF 15g SF 2g UF 10g (4)

HOJAN HSIN TAIJI

Stir-fried scallops in oyster sauce (China)

When prepared in a Chinese restaurant kitchen, this classic Cantonese dish is stir-fried only for a few seconds over a fierce heat. At home, the flame under my wok is much less powerful, so this takes me about 5 minutes to cook. It is important to have every ingredient prepared in advance and right on hand. See page 96 for illustration.

INGREDIENTS

12 raw scallops, cut horizontally in half
1 tsp cornstarch
1 tbsp light soy sauce
¼ tsp freshly ground white pepper, plus extra to taste
1 tbsp Shaohsing wine (see page 29) or dry sherry
4 tbsp peanut oil
1 small celery heart with the leaves, roughly chopped
6 fresh shiitake mushrooms, stems removed, caps quartered
3 scallions, cut into ½in (1cm) lengths on the diagonal
2 ripe tomatoes, peeled, seeded, and quartered, optional
salt, to taste

For the sauce

2 tbsp oyster sauce
1 tbsp Shaohsing wine (see page 29) or dry sherry
2 tsp very finely chopped fresh ginger
1 tsp very finely chopped garlic
½ tsp cornstarch
1 tbsp light soy sauce
½ tsp sesame oil

PREPARATION

1 Place the scallops in a bowl and rub with the cornstarch, soy sauce, white pepper, and Shaohsing wine. Let stand in a cool place.
2 Put all the ingredients for the sauce, except the sesame oil, in a bowl. Mix together until well blended, then set aside.
3 Heat a wok until hot and add the peanut oil. When the oil starts to smoke, add the scallops and stir-fry for 1 minute. Remove the scallops from the wok with a slotted spoon and transfer to a bowl.
4 Add the celery and mushrooms to the wok and stir-fry for 1–2 minutes. Remove from the wok with the slotted spoon and transfer to a plate. Discard the oil remaining in the wok.
5 Reheat the wok, pour in the sauce mixture, and cook, stirring continuously, for 1–2 minutes. Raise the heat and add the scallions and tomatoes, if using, and stir-fry for 30 seconds.
6 Add the scallops along with any cooking juices, the celery, and mushrooms. Stir-fry for another 30 seconds, then stir in the sesame oil. Season to taste and serve immediately.

KCal 191 P 12g C 6g S 0.9g TF 12g SF 2g UF 9g (4)

Homok Talay

Mixed seafood in coconut milk (Thailand)

Asia offers dozens, if not hundreds, of variations on the hot pot, but the main ingredients are usually fish and shellfish or meat and vegetables. Serve with rice.

INGREDIENTS

2 squid, ½ lb (250g) each, cleaned (see page 150) and cut into bite-sized pieces, tentacles discarded
8–12 live mussels, scrubbed and washed
8 raw scallops, cut across, in half
8 raw jumbo shrimp, legs removed
4 cooked crab claws
handful each of fresh mint leaves and basil leaves
salt and freshly ground black pepper, to taste
8 small fresh red chilies, to garnish

For the sauce

3 tbsp vegetable oil
4 shallots or 1 medium onion, chopped
3 garlic cloves, chopped
1–3 large fresh red chilies, seeded and finely chopped
2 tsp finely chopped fresh ginger
½ tsp ground turmeric
seeds of 3 green cardamom pods
2 tbsp tamarind water (see page 101)
2 fresh kaffir lime leaves (see page 26)
1 stem of fresh lemongrass, cut into 3 pieces
1 tsp salt
1 tsp sugar
3¾ cups (900ml) very thick coconut milk (see page 141)
1 tsp fish sauce (nam pla) (see page 28), optional

PREPARATION

1 Add the squid pieces to a pan of lightly salted boiling water and cook for 4–5 minutes. Drain in a colander and set aside.

2 Pick over the mussels and discard any with broken shells or those that feel much too heavy for their size. Put the mussels in a pan of boiling water and cook for 1 minute.

3 Remove the pan from the heat and let the mussels stand for a few minutes, until the shells open. Discard any mussels that remain closed, and rinse the open ones to rid them of any sand.

4 For the sauce, heat the oil in a large heavy-based pan. Add the shallots, garlic, chilies, and ginger and cook, stirring continuously, for 2 minutes.

5 Add the turmeric, cardamom seeds, tamarind water, lime leaves, lemongrass, salt, and sugar. Stir once and add the coconut milk. Bring to a boil, then lower the heat a little and cook, stirring frequently, for 30–40 minutes, or until the sauce is reduced by half its volume.

6 Add all the seafood, the mint, and basil leaves and cook for 4–5 minutes. Season to taste, then remove the lime leaves and lemongrass and garnish with the chilies.

KCal 568 P 34g C 21g S 1g TF 39g SF 24g UF 11g (4)

Shallots
Garlic
Large red chili
Fresh ginger
Ground turmeric
Cardamom pods
Tamarind water
Kaffir lime leaves
Lemongrass
Sugar
Fish sauce
Coconut milk

Peeling & Deveining Shrimp

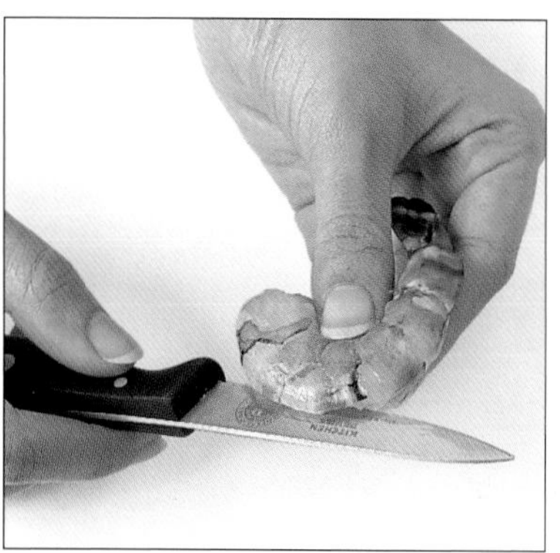

1 Remove and discard the head and shell of the shrimp. Make a short cut along the back of the shrimp to reveal the black vein or intestine.

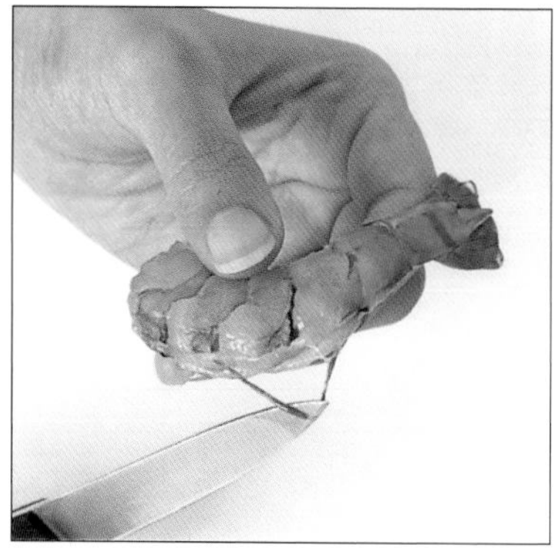

2 Using the tip of a knife, pull out and discard the intestine. By keeping the cut along the back short, the shrimp will remain straight when cooked.

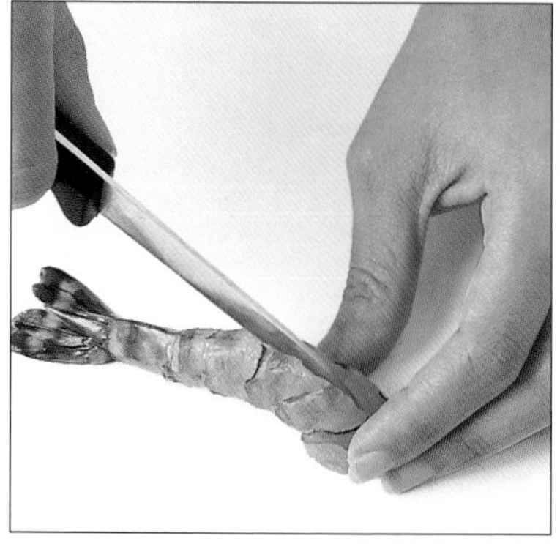

3 To make the shrimp curl or "butterfly" during cooking, make a longer cut down the back of the shrimp when removing the intestine.

Sambal Goreng Udang

Sambal Goreng Udang

Shrimp in rich coconut sauce (Indonesia)

For centuries, this has been a classic and very popular dish throughout Java. It has now become one of the better-known dishes in Indonesian cuisine. Serve with rice and stir-fried vegetables or a salad.

INGREDIENTS

2 cups (450ml) hot water
2 fresh kaffir lime leaves (see page 26) or bay leaves
2in (5cm) piece of fresh lemongrass
4oz (125g) creamed coconut, broken into pieces
16–20 raw jumbo shrimp, peeled and deveined (see steps opposite)
2 ripe tomatoes, peeled, seeded, and chopped
¼lb (125g) snow peas or sugar snap peas

For the paste

3 shallots or 1 small onion, chopped
2 garlic cloves, chopped
2in (5cm) piece of fresh ginger, peeled and sliced
3 large fresh red chilies, seeded and chopped
1 tsp dried shrimp paste (see page 31), optional
2 candlenuts (see page 22) or macadamia nuts or blanched almonds, chopped
1 tsp ground coriander
1 tsp paprika
½ tsp salt, plus extra to taste
1 tbsp tamarind water (see page 101) or lemon juice
2 tbsp peanut or vegetable oil
3 tbsp cold water

PREPARATION

1 Put all the paste ingredients in a blender and blend until as smooth as possible. Transfer the mixture to a pan, bring to a boil.

2 Cook for 4 minutes, stirring frequently. Add the hot water, lime leaves or bay leaves, and lemongrass. Return to a boil, then simmer for 20 minutes.

3 Add the creamed coconut and stir until dissolved. Simmer, stirring continuously, for 3–4 minutes more. Season with more salt, if desired.

4 Bring the sauce to a rolling boil. Add the shrimp and cook, stirring continuously, for 2 minutes.

5 Add the tomatoes and snow peas or sugar snap peas and simmer for another 2 minutes only. Do not cook the mixture for any longer or the shrimp will become tough and tasteless. Discard the lime leaves or bay leaves and lemongrass before serving.

KCal 331 P 12g C 7g S 0.4g TF 29g SF 20g UF 7g (4)

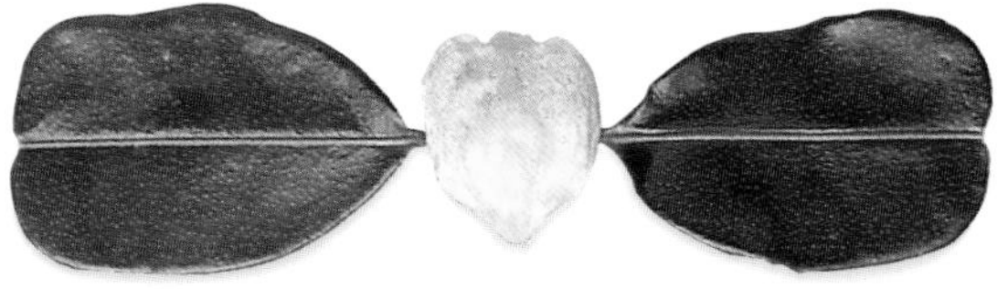

Jingha Kari

Shrimp curry (India)

This curry is very similar to one cooked for me by a Burmese friend long ago in central Java – it was quite delicious. The difference is that my friend used finely chopped young coconut flesh, which is, I suppose, the alternative to the yogurt used here. Serve with a rice pilaf, such as Navratan Pullao (see page 126 for recipe).

INGREDIENTS

4 tbsp peanut or vegetable oil
2 medium onions, finely sliced
2 fresh green chilies, seeded and finely sliced
2in (5cm) piece of cinnamon stick
8–10 cloves
4 tbsp hot water
4 tbsp low-fat plain yogurt, lightly whisked
salt and freshly ground black pepper, to taste
16–20 raw jumbo shrimp, peeled and deveined (see steps opposite)
3 tbsp chopped fresh flat-leaf parsley or cilantro, to garnish

For the paste

6 garlic cloves, chopped
2 tsp finely chopped fresh ginger
½ tsp chili powder
½ tsp ground turmeric
1 tsp ground coriander
1 tbsp tamarind water (see page 101) or lemon juice
4 tbsp cold water

PREPARATION

1 Put all the paste ingredients in a blender and blend until as smooth as possible. Transfer the paste mixture to a bowl and set aside.

2 Heat the oil in a pan. Add the onions and cook, stirring frequently, for 8 minutes. Remove from the pan with a slotted spoon and transfer to a bowl.

3 Pour off the oil from the pan, leaving about 1 tablespoon. Return the pan to the heat, add the chilies, cinnamon, and cloves, and stir-fry for 1 minute. Return the onions to the pan, add the paste mixture, and stir-fry for 1 minute.

4 Stir in the hot water and simmer for 5 minutes. Add the yogurt and seasoning and cook, stirring, for 1–2 minutes. Increase the heat and add the shrimp. Stir until they are coated, then cover the pan and cook over medium heat for 3 minutes.

5 Remove the pan from the heat and let stand, tightly covered, for 2 minutes. Discard the cinnamon stick and cloves. Transfer the curry to a heated serving dish and sprinkle with the chopped parsley or cilantro, to garnish.

KCal 174 P 10g C 8g S 0.09g TF 12g SF 2g UF 9g (4)

JUI JIN JEUN HO HAI

Deep-fried soft-shell crab (China)

Soft-shell crabs (small blue crabs that have just molted) are a delicacy, especially on the East Coast, where they are extremely popular. Serves 2 on its own or 4 as part of a main course with 2 other dishes.

INGREDIENTS

4 fresh soft-shell crabs, cleaned and rinsed
1 egg yolk, lightly beaten
1 tbsp cornstarch blended with 2 tbsp cold water
about 1¼ cups (300ml) oil for deep-frying
2 tsp finely chopped garlic
1 fresh large red chili, seeded and chopped or ½ tsp crushed red pepper flakes
1 tsp light soy sauce

For the marinade

½ tsp each salt and freshly ground white pepper
1 tsp sugar
2 tbsp Shaohsing wine (see page 29) or dry sherry

PREPARATION

1 Combine all the marinade ingredients in a bowl, add the crabs, and turn to coat. Let marinate for 10 minutes. Transfer the crabs to a plate and reserve the marinade.

2 Brush the crabs with the egg yolk, then coat with the cornstarch mixture and set aside for a few minutes.

3 Heat a wok until hot, then add the oil and heat to 325°F (160°C). Add the crabs and cook for 1 minute. Remove from the heat for 1 minute. Return the wok to the heat and cook the crabs for 3–4 minutes, or until golden.

4 Remove the crabs from the wok with a slotted spoon and transfer to a plate, to drain. Carefully pour off the oil from the wok.

5 Place the wok over medium heat. Add the garlic and chili and stir-fry for a few seconds. Add the soy sauce and the reserved marinade and stir-fry for a few seconds more. Return the crabs to the wok and stir until they are coated with the sauce.

KCal 415 P 23g C 8g S 1.1g TF 31g SF 4g UF 23g (2)

ALIMANGO TAUSI

Stuffed crab with yellow bean sauce (Philippines)

To give substance to the stuffing, the Filipinos like to use fruit, typically guava. But other fruits, such as apple or quince, are also delicious. This dish is usually deep-fried or steamed. Here, however, it is baked in the oven. Serve with rice or noodles, or just a mixed green salad.

INGREDIENTS

4 small whole cooked crabs, about ¾ lb (375g) each
1 medium guava or apple or quince, peeled and quartered, then seeded or cored
3 tbsp peanut oil
2 shallots, finely sliced
2 garlic cloves, finely sliced
1 tbsp yellow bean sauce (see page 28)
2 small dried red chilies
2 tsp finely chopped fresh ginger
1 tbsp light soy sauce
3 eggs, lightly beaten
2 tbsp chopped scallions
salt and freshly ground black pepper, to taste

PREPARATION

1 Plunge the crabs into a large pan of boiling water and simmer for 5 minutes. Remove from the pan and let cool.

2 When cold, prepare and clean the crabs (see page 151). Clean and reserve the shells. Thinly slice the quartered guava or apple or quince, crosswise, into a bowl of lightly salted water.

3 Heat the oil in a wok. Add the shallots, garlic, yellow bean sauce, chilies, and ginger and stir-fry for 2 minutes. Add the drained fruit and stir-fry for another 2 minutes. Add the soy sauce, then cover the wok and cook over low heat for 2 minutes. Stir in the beaten egg and scallions and season to taste. Cook, stirring continuously, for 1–2 minutes.

4 Divide the crab meat among the crab shells and spoon the fruit and egg mixture equally over the crab. Arrange the shells on a baking sheet and bake in an oven preheated to 350°F (180°C) for 10–15 minutes, until the egg starts to brown. Place the crabs under a preheated hot broiler to brown more, if desired.

KCal 334 P 32g C 6g S 0.9g TF 20g SF 4g UF 13g (4)

Hoy Lai Phad Nam Prik Phao

Braised clams with basil (Thailand)

In Thailand there are at least three different kinds of basil. For this dish you can use any of them, though it is perhaps easier to find anise basil or Thai basil. Alternatively, ordinary sweet basil will do very well. *See page 111 for illustration.*

INGREDIENTS

2lb (1kg) clams, soaked in cold water
3 tbsp peanut or vegetable oil
3 shallots, finely sliced
3 garlic cloves, finely chopped
2 large fresh green chilies, seeded and cut on the diagonal into 3 slices
1 tsp chili sauce (see page 28), optional
1 tbsp fish sauce (nam pla) (see page 28)
handful of fresh Thai basil leaves (see page 26)
2 fresh red chilies, seeded and diced, to garnish

PREPARATION

1 Scrub the clams in their soaking water, then rinse under cold running water. Set the clams aside in a colander, discarding any with broken shells, or those that do not close when lightly tapped.
2 Heat the oil in a pan, add the shallots, garlic, and green chilies and stir-fry for 1 minute. Add the chili sauce, if using, and stir in the clams. Increase the heat and stir-fry for 4 minutes, or until the clams open. Discard any clams that remain closed.
3 Stir in the fish sauce and most of the basil leaves. Scatter over the remaining basil leaves and red chilies, to garnish, and serve immediately.

KCal 154 P 16g C 2g S 0.9g TF 9g SF 2g UF 7g (4)

Dhallo Badun

Fried squid curry (Sri Lanka)

Long cooking seems to be preferred in Asia, especially for curry. This is because the curry sauce needs to reduce slowly, which improves the flavor and also makes it look more appetizing. In this recipe, however, instead of cooking the squid for an hour in the curry sauce, I cook the raw squid for just a few minutes and add it to the long-cooked sauce just before serving. Serves 6–8 as a main course with plain boiled rice or a rice pilaf, plus 2 other dishes.

INGREDIENTS

2lb (1kg) small squid, cleaned (see page 150) and cut into thin rings, tentacles cut into 2in (5cm) lengths
¾ cup (175ml) peanut or vegetable oil for frying
6 shallots or 1 large onion, finely sliced
4 garlic cloves, finely chopped
2 tsp finely chopped fresh ginger
1 stem of fresh lemongrass, cut into 3 pieces
5 fresh or dried curry leaves (see page 26), optional
½–1 tsp chili powder
1 small cinnamon stick
1 tsp ground coriander
½ tsp ground cumin
½ tsp fenugreek seed
½ tsp fennel seed
2 cloves
2 green cardamom pods
¼ cup (60ml) hot water
2 tbsp distilled white vinegar
salt and freshly ground black pepper, to taste
2½ cups (600ml) coconut milk (see page 141)

PREPARATION

1 Rinse the squid pieces under cold running water, then transfer to a colander and let drain completely.
2 Heat 3 tablespoons of the oil in a pan. Add the shallots or onion and cook, stirring frequently, until they begin to brown. Add the garlic, ginger, lemongrass, curry leaves, and all the dried spices and cook, stirring frequently, for 2 minutes.
3 Add the hot water and vinegar, then season to taste. Bring to a boil, then simmer for 5 minutes. Stir in the coconut milk and bring almost to a boil. Reduce the heat and simmer, uncovered, for about 1 hour. Adjust the seasoning, if necessary.
4 Heat the remaining oil in a wok. Add the drained squid in 2 or 3 batches and cook for 3 minutes per batch. Remove the squid from the wok with a slotted spoon and transfer to the simmering sauce. Simmer, stirring once or twice, for 2 minutes more, then serve immediately.

KCal 276 P 27g C 11g S 0.3g TF 14g SF 3g UF 10g (6)

POULTRY

The domestic hen is descended from the jungle fowl of Southeast Asia, and anyone who has driven along country roads in Indonesia will know that they have retained many of their wild, unpredictable ways. Ducks are migrants, domesticated in China and Europe; they are, strictly, exotics in places like Bali, where you may see a flock marching to the rice fields behind a boy with a white flag.

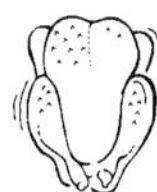

TSOI PE TSA JI GAI

Deep-fried crispy-skin chicken (China)

The preparation of this Cantonese dish is very much like that for Peking Duck (see page 46 for recipe). However, the crispness of the skin here is the result of deep-frying twice.

INGREDIENTS

1 tbsp five-spice powder (see page 27)
1 tsp salt
1 tsp sugar
1 chicken, 3–3½ lb (1.5–1.75kg), scalded with boiling water (see page 152)
2 tbsp rice vinegar (see page 29)
3 tbsp clear honey
about 5 cups (1.25 liters) vegetable oil for deep-frying
3 scallions, each cut into 3 pieces
3 thick slices of peeled fresh ginger

PREPARATION

1 Mix the five-spice powder, salt, and sugar together and rub over the scalded chicken, and inside the body cavity. Mix the vinegar with the honey and rub all over the chicken skin.
2 Secure the chicken on a duck hook (see page 152) and hang in a cool, airy place for 2–3 hours.
3 Heat a large wok, and when hot pour in the vegetable oil. Heat the oil until it reaches about 325°F (160°C). Put the scallions and ginger into the cavity of the chicken.
4 Add the chicken to the wok and fry until the skin is golden, about 8 minutes. Remove the chicken from the wok, transfer to a colander, and drain well.
5 Just before serving, reheat the oil. Prick the chicken skin all over with a fork and return the chicken to the oil. Deep-fry for about 10 minutes, until the chicken is well cooked and the skin is just a little browner and crisper than before. Remove from the wok and drain well on paper towels. Cut the chicken into quarters and serve.

KCal 649 P 47g C 15g S 0.7g TF 45g SF 11g UF 31g (4)

OSENG OSENG AYAM DENGAN SAYURAN

Stir-fried chicken with vegetables (Indonesia)

This kind of stir-fry – a little meat with plenty of vegetables – is typical of many Southeast Asian countries, where meat is expensive and vegetables are cheap and abundant. Beef, pork, or lamb can be used instead of chicken. Serves 4–6 with rice. See page 73 for illustration.

INGREDIENTS

3 tbsp peanut oil
3 shallots, finely sliced
1 tsp finely sliced fresh ginger
1 large fresh red chili, seeded and sliced
1 tsp grated jaggery (see page 30) or light brown sugar
1 tsp dried shrimp paste (see page 31), optional
1 skinless chicken breast, cut into thick slices
1 tbsp light soy sauce
6 tbsp (90ml) hot water
⅓lb (175g) fine asparagus, tips separated from stems and stems cut in half on the diagonal
⅓lb (175g) button mushrooms
⅓lb (175g) baby corn, halved lengthwise
1 large yellow pepper, seeded and cut into 8–10 strips
¼lb (125g) snow peas, halved on the diagonal if large
salt and freshly ground black pepper, to taste

PREPARATION

1 Heat the oil in a wok. Add the shallots, ginger, and chili and stir-fry for 1–2 minutes. Add the jaggery and shrimp paste, if using, and stir briefly.
2 Add the chicken and stir-fry for 3–4 minutes. Stir in the soy sauce and hot water and simmer for 3 minutes. Add the asparagus stems, mushrooms, and baby corn and stir again. Lower the heat, then cover and simmer for 3 minutes.
3 Add the asparagus tips, yellow pepper, and snow peas. Stir-fry for 2 minutes and season to taste. Stir-fry for 2 minutes longer, then serve.

KCal 171 P 14g C 8g S 0.8g TF 9g SF 2g UF 7g (4)

Kyet Thar Hin

Chicken curry with limes (Myanmar)

The use of lime in this dish indicates that it is more closely related to the curries of Thailand than India. Serve with rice and a green salad.

INGREDIENTS

3 tbsp vegetable oil
1 tsp sesame oil
3 medium onions, finely chopped
2 garlic cloves, chopped
1 tsp ground turmeric
1 tbsp ground coriander
2 cinnamon sticks
4 cloves
3 fresh kaffir lime leaves (see page 26)
4 skinned and boned chicken breasts and 4 thighs
3 tbsp Balachaung (see page 132 for recipe)
1 stem fresh lemongrass, cut into 3 pieces
6oz (175g) canned chopped tomatoes
1 tsp freshly ground black pepper
1 tbsp fish sauce (see page 28)
juice of 2 limes
salt, to taste
1 lime, cut into wedges, to garnish

PREPARATION

1 Mix the vegetable oil and sesame oil together in a bowl, then transfer to a large ovenproof casserole dish and place over medium heat. Add the onions and cook, stirring frequently, for 5 minutes.
2 Stir in the garlic, ground turmeric and coriander, cinnamon sticks, cloves, and lime leaves. Add the chicken pieces and stir until they are coated.
3 Add the Balachaung and stir-fry for 2 minutes. Add the lemongrass and tomatoes, then cover and simmer for 30 minutes.
4 Uncover the dish and increase the heat a little. Add the black pepper, fish sauce, and lime juice. If the mixture is too thick, add a little hot water.
5 Cook the chicken for 10 minutes more, adding salt, if necessary. Serve the curry immediately or cook it more, until the chicken is very tender and almost falling off the bones.
6 To cook the curry longer, cover the dish and place in an oven preheated to 325°F (160°C). Cook for 20 minutes, then reduce the temperature to 225°F (110°C) and cook for up to 1 hour longer, if desired.
7 Remove the cinnamon sticks, cloves, lime leaves, and lemongrass. Skim off some of the oil from the sauce and garnish with the lime wedges, to serve.

KCal 363 P 44g C 13g S 1.3g TF 13g SF 2g UF 10g (4)

Gaeng Ped Kai

Red curry of chicken (Thailand)

There are three main types of curry in Thailand: green, red, and massaman. The green and red curries are "city" curries as opposed to "jungle" curry, which is much stronger and spicier. Serve with plain boiled rice.

INGREDIENTS

1½ lb (750g) boned chicken breasts and thighs, cut into ¾ in (2cm) cubes
5 cups (1.25 liters) coconut milk (see page 141)
½ lb (250g) baby new potatoes
For the paste
4 shallots, finely chopped
3 garlic cloves, finely chopped
2in (5cm) piece of fresh lemongrass, outer leaves removed, center chopped
¾ in (2cm) piece of fresh galangal (see page 27), finely chopped
1 tsp grated kaffir lime rind (see page 22)
1 tsp ground black pepper
1 tbsp coriander seed, roasted (see page 155), roughly crushed
1 tsp cumin seed, roasted (see page 155), roughly crushed
½ tsp each of ground mace and nutmeg
5 fresh red chilies, seeded and chopped
1 red pepper, seeded and chopped, optional
1 tsp salt, plus extra to taste
½ tsp dried shrimp paste (see page 31)
2 tbsp each of water and vegetable oil
2 tbsp tamarind water (see page 101)
For the garnish
1 tbsp chopped fresh red chilies
1 tbsp chopped fresh cilantro leaves
2 tbsp roasted peanuts, roughly chopped

PREPARATION

1 Put all the paste ingredients in a blender and blend until as smooth as possible. Transfer the paste mixture to a large pan and simmer, stirring frequently, for 4 minutes. Add the chicken and stir until coated. Cover and simmer for 4 minutes.
2 Add the coconut milk to the pan and simmer, stirring frequently, for 30 minutes. Season to taste. Add the potatoes and cook, stirring frequently, for 10–15 minutes, or until tender. Garnish with the chilies, cilantro leaves, and peanuts.

KCal 444 P 48g C 34g S 1g TF 15g SF 3g UF 11g (4)

Pipian

Chicken and pork in peanut sauce (Philippines)

Normally served as a very thick rice-flour porridge with meat and peanut butter, this lighter version of Pipian includes sliced boiled chicken, pork, and ham, and a peanut sauce. Serves 8–10 with rice.

INGREDIENTS

1 chicken, 3lb (1.5kg), halved lengthwise
2lb (1kg) pork leg meat, in one piece, skin removed
1lb (500g) uncooked ham, in one piece, skin and fat removed
1 large onion, halved
4 garlic cloves
10 cups (2.5 liters) water
For the peanut sauce
3 tbsp vegetable oil
4 shallots, finely sliced
3 garlic cloves, finely sliced
2 tsp paprika
½ tsp ground turmeric
½ tsp freshly ground white pepper, plus extra to taste
¼ lb (125g) shelled peanuts, fried and ground to a powder
2 tbsp tamarind water (see page 101) or lemon juice
salt, to taste

PREPARATION

1 Put the chicken, pork, and ham in a large pan with the onion, garlic, and water. Bring to a boil, then let it simmer for 1–1¼ hours.
2 Remove the meat from the stock and let cool. Strain 2½ cups (600ml) of the stock into a bowl and skim. Remove the chicken from the bones in large pieces, discard the fat from the pork, and trim the ham. Slice all the meat thinly and set aside.
3 For the sauce, heat the oil in a pan or wok. Add the shallots and garlic and cook, stirring continuously, for 2 minutes. Add the paprika, ground turmeric, and pepper and stir again.
4 Add the measured stock, bring to a boil, then simmer for 2 minutes. Add the ground peanuts, stir once, and simmer for 5 minutes. Add the tamarind water or lemon juice and season to taste.
5 Stir the meat into the sauce and simmer for 3 minutes, until heated through, then serve immediately. Alternatively, arrange the cold meat on a platter and serve the sauce separately.

KCal 435 P 61g C 6g S 0.8g TF 19g SF 4g UF 13g (8)

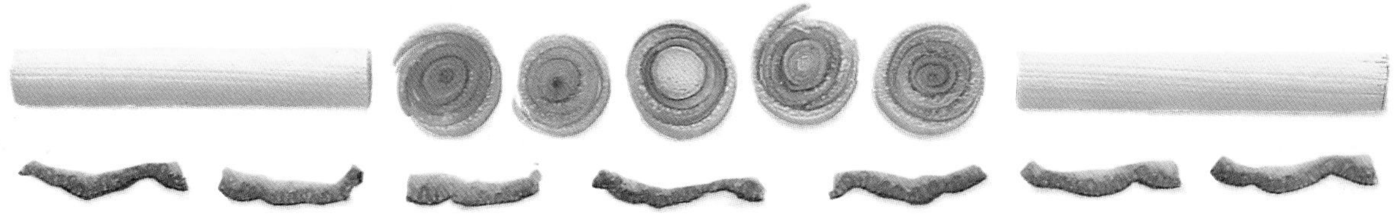

Dui Ga Nhoi Thit

Stuffed boned chicken legs (Vietnam)

Traditionally, this dish is made with a whole chicken, boned from the neck so the skin remains intact. The result is quite impressive, but it takes time and skill. This short-cut version uses only chicken legs. Serve hot as a main course, or cold, thinly sliced, as an appetizer with Nuoc Cham (see page 128 for recipe) as a dipping sauce.

INGREDIENTS

4 large chicken legs (drumstick and thigh in one piece), boned in one piece (see page 152)
juice of half a lemon
salt and freshly ground black pepper, to taste
2 tbsp vegetable oil or clarified butter
For the stuffing
2 boned and skinned chicken thighs, chopped
⅓ lb (175g) pork tenderloin, chopped
2 large fresh red chilies, seeded and chopped
3 shallots, chopped
2 garlic cloves, chopped
2 stems of fresh lemongrass, outer leaves removed, center chopped
1 tsp sugar
2 tbsp fish sauce (nuoc mam) (see page 28)
2 tbsp vegetable oil
1oz (30g) wood ears, rehydrated (see page 155)
2oz (60g) cellophane noodles (see page 25), soaked in hot water for 5 minutes, then drained

PREPARATION

1 Put the boned legs in a bowl and rub with the lemon juice and salt and pepper. Cover and refrigerate while preparing the stuffing.
2 For the stuffing, put the chopped chicken and pork in a food processor and process for a few seconds. Transfer to a bowl.
3 Put all the remaining stuffing ingredients, except the wood ears and noodles, into the food processor and process to a paste. Add to the ground meat and mix well.
4 Slice the wood ears into thin strips and cut the noodles into short lengths with a pair of scissors, then mix into the stuffing mixture.
5 Heat a little of the oil in a skillet, add a teaspoon of the stuffing mixture, and fry until cooked through. Taste, then add some salt and pepper to the remaining stuffing mixture, if required, mixing well.
6 Using a spoon, press some of the stuffing into the center of each drumstick and then the thigh, working carefully so that the meat and skin can be folded over neatly to hold the stuffing in place.
7 Arrange the legs in an ovenproof dish, then brush all over with the remaining oil. Place in an oven preheated to 325°F (160°C) and roast for 45–50 minutes. Serve the chicken, hot or cold, cut into thick slices.

KCal 371 P 38g C 20g S 0.7g TF 15g SF 2g UF 12g (4)

Dhansak

Chicken cooked with lentils and vegetables (India)

This is an adaptation, somewhat simplified, of a grand Parsee dish. It is usually served with rice only, as vegetables are already included.

INGREDIENTS

2 tbsp vegetable oil
1 tsp cumin seed
1 medium onion, finely sliced
8 boned and skinned chicken thighs
1 tsp finely chopped fresh ginger
6 garlic cloves
1 medium eggplant, cut across into 4, each piece quartered
2 tbsp chopped fenugreek leaves (see page 26), optional
1½ tsp salt, plus extra to taste
¼ tsp ground black pepper
1 tsp garam masala (see page 156)
For the lentils
2 tsp ground coriander
½ tsp ground cumin
½ tsp chili powder
½ tsp dry mustard
¼ tsp fenugreek seed, ground
½ tsp ground turmeric
1 cup (125g) green lentils, rinsed
2½ cups (600ml) cold water
1 medium potato, cut into 8 pieces

PREPARATION

1 Put all the ingredients for the lentils in a large pan. Bring to a boil, then cover and simmer for 20 minutes. Remove the pan from the heat and mash the lentils and potatoes a little with a spoon or potato masher.
2 Heat the oil in another pan. Add the cumin seed and onion and cook, stirring frequently, for 2–3 minutes. Add the chicken and ginger and cook, stirring, for 2 minutes longer.
3 Add the garlic, eggplant, fenugreek leaves, salt, and pepper to the chicken. Cover and cook for 20 minutes. Stir in the lentil mixture, cover, and simmer for 5 minutes. Stir in the garam masala and more salt, if necessary. Transfer the Dhansak to a platter and serve immediately.

KCal 304 P 31g C 28g S 0.8g TF 9g SF 1g UF 7g (4)

Sze Chuan Jar Gai

Fried chicken Szechwan style (China)

For this Szechwan dish the dark meat from the drumstick and thigh is preferred. Red and green chilies are normally used, but here I have substituted red chilies and green pepper to make it less fiery. Serve with rice.

INGREDIENTS

4 boned chicken drumsticks and 4 boned thighs, cut into ¾in (2cm) cubes, the skin left on
1 small egg white
1 tbsp cornstarch
1 tbsp dark soy sauce
½ cup (125ml) vegetable oil
3 large fresh red chilies, seeded and cut into ½in (1cm) pieces
1–2 tbsp crushed garlic
1 large green pepper, seeded and cut into ½in (1cm) pieces
handful of fresh flat-leaf parsley
2 tbsp rice wine (see page 29) or medium-dry sherry
1 tsp sesame oil

For the sauce

2 tbsp light soy sauce
½ tsp salt
1 tsp sugar
¼ tsp chili powder or ground black pepper
2 tsp rice vinegar (see page 29)
1 tsp cornstarch
2 tbsp cold water

PREPARATION

1 Put the chicken pieces in a glass bowl and add the egg white, cornstarch, and dark soy sauce. Stir well to mix thoroughly. Let stand in a cool place for 20 minutes.

2 Mix all the sauce ingredients together in another bowl. Heat a wok over high heat. Add the oil and heat until very hot.

3 Add the chicken pieces in 2 batches and cook, stirring quickly, for 2 minutes per batch. Remove the chicken with a slotted spoon.

4 Add the chilies to the wok and stir-fry for 2 minutes. Remove with the slotted spoon and scatter over the chicken. Carefully pour off most of the oil, leaving about 3 tablespoons in the wok.

5 Reheat the oil in the wok, add the garlic, and cook for a few seconds, stirring vigorously. Add the green pepper and stir-fry for 1 minute, then add the parsley, and the chicken with the chilies.

6 Stir in the wine or sherry over high heat. Pour in the sauce mixture, stir-fry for 1 minute, then add the sesame oil and serve immediately.

KCal 373 P 19g C 9g S 1.1g TF 30g SF 5g UF 23g (4)

Green pepper

Garlic

Red chili

Vegetable oil

Dark soy sauce

Cornstarch

Egg white

Chicken drumsticks

Chicken thighs

Sesame oil
Rice wine
Light soy sauce
Salt
Sugar
Chili powder
Rice vinegar
Flat-leaf parsley

MURGH SALAR JUNG

Chicken in cashew and coconut sauce (India)

This is an adaptation of a recipe by my friend Joyce Westrip. Serve with rice.

INGREDIENTS

4 skinless chicken breasts
½ cup (120ml) vegetable oil
3 large onions, finely sliced
1¾ cups (400ml) coconut milk (see page 141)
2 tbsp Serundeng (see page 133 for recipe), to garnish

For the marinade

1¼ cups (300ml) plain yogurt, lightly whisked
¼ tsp ground cloves and cinnamon
½ tsp salt
½ tsp crumbled saffron strands, soaked in 3 tbsp warm milk for 15 minutes

For the paste

2 tsp white poppy seeds (see page 23), roughly crushed
10 cashew nuts, chopped
2 shallots, chopped
3 tsp finely chopped fresh ginger
1 tsp finely chopped garlic
2–3 dried red chilies, chopped
1 tsp coriander seed, roasted (see page 155), roughly crushed
½ tsp cumin seed, roasted (see page 155), roughly crushed
2 green cardamom pods, roughly crushed
1 tsp fennel seeds, roughly crushed
6 black peppercorns, roughly crushed
½ tsp salt, plus extra to taste
3 tbsp vegetable oil
½ cup (125ml) hot water

PREPARATION

1 Mix all the marinade ingredients together in a bowl. Add the chicken and marinate for 4 hours in a cool place, or overnight in a refrigerator.
2 Put all the paste ingredients in a blender and blend until as smooth as possible.
3 Heat the vegetable oil in a wok, add the onions, and cook until well browned. Remove half the onions with a slotted spoon and transfer to a large pan. Drain the remaining onions on paper towels.
4 Reheat the onions in the pan. Stir in the paste mixture and bring to a boil. Reduce the heat and simmer for 6–8 minutes, stirring frequently.
5 Add the chicken and marinade to the pan, turning the meat until it is coated. Simmer for 10 minutes. Add the coconut milk, bring to a boil, then cook over medium heat for 25–30 minutes. Season to taste. Transfer to a warm platter, sprinkle with the reserved fried onions and the Serundeng, then serve.

KCal 518 P 41g C 28g S 0.9g TF 30g SF 6g UF 21g (4)

AYAM GORENG JAWA

Javanese fried chicken (Indonesia)

If you prefer not to deep-fry the chicken, simply serve it at the end of the cooking time in step 3 – it tastes just as good. Serve with rice and a vegetable dish such as Orak-Arik (see page 113 for recipe).

INGREDIENTS

2½ cups (600ml) coconut milk (see page 141)
1 chicken, 3½ lb (1.75kg), cut into 8–10 pieces (see page 153)
about 2½ cups (600ml) vegetable oil for deep-frying

For the paste

6 shallots, chopped
1 tsp ground coriander
3 candlenuts (see page 22) or 5 blanched almonds, chopped
1 large fresh red chili, seeded and chopped
¼ tsp ground turmeric
½ in (1cm) piece of fresh galangal (see page 27), peeled and chopped
2in (5cm) piece of fresh lemongrass, outer leaves removed, center chopped
1 tsp salt, plus extra to taste
1 tsp grated jaggery (see page 30) or light brown sugar

PREPARATION

1 Put all the paste ingredients, plus ⅓ cup (90ml) of the coconut milk, in a blender and blend until as smooth as possible.
2 Transfer the mixture to a large pan and simmer, stirring frequently, for 6 minutes. Add the chicken and stir until coated with the paste mixture.
3 Add the remaining coconut milk and bring to a boil. Lower the heat and simmer, uncovered, for 1 hour, or until all the liquid is absorbed. Season with salt, if required. Remove from the heat and serve, if desired, or leave until cold.
4 Heat the oil in a large wok. Add half the chicken pieces and fry, moving them around occasionally, for 10–12 minutes, until the skin is golden and crisp. Remove from the pan and drain on paper towels. Fry the remaining chicken, then serve hot or warm.

KCal 734 P 56g C 10g S 0.8g TF 53g SF 13g UF 36g (4)

BEBEK BETUTU

Traditional long-cooked Balinese duck (Indonesia)

Here, I use kale or spinach as an alternative to the usual stuffing of cassava leaves, but the recipe still includes the traditional mix of Balinese spices. Serves 4–6 with rice.

INGREDIENTS

⅓–½lb (175–250g) curly kale or spinach, blanched in boiling water for 2 minutes, squeezed dry, and shredded
1 duck, 3½–4lb (1.75–2kg)
For the paste
5 shallots or 2 medium onions, chopped
4 garlic cloves, chopped
5 fresh red chilies, seeded and chopped
2 candlenuts (see page 22) or macadamia nuts, chopped (optional)
2 tsp coriander seed, roughly crushed
1 tsp cumin seed, roughly crushed
2 cloves, roughly crushed
2 green cardamom pods, roughly crushed
1in (2.5cm) piece of cinnamon stick, roughly crushed
¼ tsp ground or grated nutmeg
½ tsp ground turmeric
¼ tsp ground white pepper, plus extra to taste
½in (1cm) piece of fresh galangal (see page 27), peeled and chopped
2in (5cm) piece of fresh lemongrass, outer leaves removed, center chopped
1 tsp dried shrimp paste (see page 31)
3 tbsp tamarind water (see page 101) or lime juice
2 tbsp each of peanut oil and water
1 tsp salt, plus extra to taste

PREPARATION

1 Put all the paste ingredients in a blender and blend until as smooth as possible. Transfer the paste mixture to a pan and simmer for 6–8 minutes, stirring frequently. Season to taste, then transfer the paste to a glass bowl and let cool.
2 Mix half the cold paste with the shredded kale or spinach. Rub the remaining paste over the duck, inside and out. Stuff the shredded greens into the duck. Loosely wrap the duck in 2 or 3 layers of foil, folding the foil over at the top to seal.
3 Put the duck in a roasting pan and place in the center of an oven preheated to 325°F (160°C). Cook for 2 hours, then reduce the temperature to 250°F (120°C) and cook for 3–4 hours longer.
4 Unwrap the duck and transfer it to a large dish. Spoon off and discard the oil from the cooking juices. For the sauce, pour the juices into a pan, add the stuffing from the duck, and heat through.
5 Carve the duck – it will be very tender, so the meat will come off the bones easily – then transfer the meat to a heated serving platter. Serve the duck immediately, with the sauce poured over it or served separately in a bowl.

KCal 316 P 32g C 12g S 0.8g TF 16g SF 4g UF 12g (4)

HAK TJIN TJAN NAH HIU

Stir-fried duck with black pepper (China)

I find that a stir-fry like this tastes much better if the slices of meat are marinated first.

INGREDIENTS

4 duck breasts, each cut into 6 thin slices on the diagonal
½ cup (125ml) vegetable oil
8 scallions, each cut into 3 pieces
2 tbsp Shaohsing wine (see page 29) or dry sherry
1 tbsp dark soy sauce
salt and freshly ground black pepper, to taste
For the marinade
1 tbsp light soy sauce
1 tbsp Shaohsing wine (see page 29) or dry sherry
1 tsp ginger juice (see page 155)
½ tsp chili oil
¼ tsp ground black pepper

PREPARATION

1 Mix all the marinade ingredients together in a large bowl. Add the pieces of duck, turning them until coated, then marinate in a cool place for 2–3 hours.
2 Heat a wok and pour in the oil. When the oil is very hot, add the duck slices and stir-fry for 2 minutes. Remove from the wok with a slotted spoon and transfer to a plate.
3 Carefully pour off most of the oil from the wok, leaving about 1 tablespoon behind. Reheat the oil in the wok and add the scallions. Stir-fry for 30 seconds, then add the duck.
4 Pour the wine or sherry over the meat, then carefully swirl the wok and tip it slightly so that the alcohol catches alight and flames the duck. Alternatively, light it with a match. Once the flames have died down, add the soy sauce and salt and pepper, to taste. Stir-fry the duck for about 30 seconds more, then serve immediately.

KCal 300 P 26g C 1g S 0.7g TF 20g SF 4g UF 15g (4)

Kalio Bebek

Duck pieces in rich coconut sauce (Indonesia)

In other Asian countries Kalio is known as "Indonesian curry." In fact, it is not a true curry, since it does not use all the spices that are usually present in a curry paste.

INGREDIENTS

1 duck, 4lb (2kg), cut into 8–10 pieces (see page 153), most of the fat removed
2 tbsp distilled white vinegar
8 cups (2 liters) boiling water
8 cups (2 liters) coconut milk (see page 141)
5 shallots, finely chopped
4 garlic cloves, finely chopped
2–6 large fresh red chilies, seeded and finely chopped
½–1 tsp chili powder, optional
2 tsp finely chopped fresh ginger
1 tsp ground turmeric
¾in (2cm) piece of fresh galangal (see page 27)
1 stem of fresh lemongrass, cut across into 2 pieces
1 tsp salt, plus extra to taste
freshly ground black pepper, to taste

PREPARATION

1 Wash the duck pieces in cold water and place in a bowl. Rub with the vinegar, then pour over the boiling water and let stand for 5 minutes. (The vinegar reduces the duck odor, while the boiling water melts the fat.) Drain the duck in a colander.

2 Put all the remaining ingredients in a large pan and add the duck. Bring to a boil, then lower the heat until the coconut milk bubbles gently.

3 Cook uncovered for 1½ hours, stirring frequently, until the sauce is quite thick and the meat is tender. Season to taste and discard the galangal and lemongrass before serving.

KCal 318 P 30g C 27g S 1.2g TF 11g SF 4g UF 6g (4)

Batakh Vindaloo

Duck curry (India)

A variation of the classic pork vindaloo from Goa, this curry uses plenty of garlic and chilies, and has little fat.

INGREDIENTS

4–6 duck breasts, skinned, each cut across into 5 pieces
6 tbsp (90ml) vegetable oil
2 large red onions, finely sliced
½ cup (125ml) hot water
salt and freshly ground black pepper, to taste

For the marinade

3 tbsp red wine vinegar
½ tsp chili powder
½ tsp salt

For the paste

3 shallots, chopped
5–8 garlic cloves, chopped
½ in (1cm) piece of fresh ginger, peeled and chopped
4–8 large fresh red chilies, seeded and chopped
1 medium red pepper, seeded and chopped
1 tsp cumin seed, roughly crushed
2 tsp coriander seed, roughly crushed
½ in (1cm) piece of cinnamon stick, roughly crushed
2 cloves, roughly crushed
1 tsp grated jaggery (see page 30) or light brown sugar
2 tbsp vegetable oil
1 tbsp distilled white vinegar
2 tbsp tamarind water (see page 101)

PREPARATION

1 Put the duck pieces in a bowl. Mix the marinade ingredients together, then pour over the duck and rub well into the meat. Let stand for 10 minutes.

2 Put all the paste ingredients in a blender and blend until as smooth as possible.

3 Heat the oil in a wok, add the onions and cook, stirring frequently, for 6–8 minutes, or until they begin to brown. Remove the onions with a slotted spoon and transfer to a large pan.

4 Add half the duck pieces to the wok and cook for 3 minutes, stirring frequently. Remove with the slotted spoon and transfer to a bowl. Cook the remaining duck pieces.

5 Reheat the onions in the pan and stir for a few seconds. Add the paste mixture and simmer, stirring frequently, for 8 minutes.

6 Add the duck, along with any juices that have accumulated in the bowl. Stir once or twice, then add the hot water.

7 Cover the pan, bring to a boil, and simmer for 40 minutes. Season to taste. Cook, uncovered, for 10–15 minutes, then serve hot.

KCal 474 P 32g C 15g S 0.4g TF 33g SF 5g UF 25g (4)

Sech Tea Ang-Krueng

Roasted and grilled duck with spices (Cambodia)

Rosine Ek, the chef-proprietor of Chez Rosine Cuisine du Cambodge, Paris, gave me this recipe. It can be made with pork, lamb, or beef, but my favorite is the recipe that uses duck breasts, as described here. Serve with rice and a green salad or a selection of raw vegetables.

INGREDIENTS

4 duck breasts

For the marinade

2 tsp finely chopped lemongrass, center part only
1 garlic clove, finely chopped
2 shallots, finely chopped
2 tsp dark soy sauce
½ tsp freshly ground black pepper
2 tsp fish sauce (nuoc mam) (see page 28)
2 tbsp coconut milk (see page 141)

For the sauce

½ cup (125ml) water
2 tsp fish sauce (nuoc mam) (see page 28)
1 tbsp distilled white vinegar
½ tsp sugar
2–3 tbsp ground roasted peanuts
4 tbsp coconut milk (see page 141)
salt, to taste

PREPARATION

1 Mix all the ingredients for the marinade in a glass bowl. Add the duck breasts and marinate for 2 hours, or overnight in the refrigerator.

2 For the sauce, mix the water, fish sauce, vinegar, and sugar in a pan. Bring to a boil, then simmer for 5 minutes. Remove from the heat and set aside.

3 Remove the duck breasts from the marinade and arrange on a rack in a roasting pan. Place in an oven preheated to 350°F (180°C) and roast for 20–25 minutes, turning them once. Remove the duck from the oven and place under a preheated hot broiler to brown more.

4 Cut each duck breast diagonally into 4 slices and arrange on a serving platter. Reheat the sauce and bring to a boil. Add the ground peanuts and cook, stirring, for 1 minute. Add the coconut milk and some salt, if necessary, and simmer for 2 minutes. Pour the sauce over the duck and serve immediately.

KCal 260 P 29g C 4g S 0.8g TF 14g SF 4g UF 10g (4)

CHINA

The philosophy of *yin* and *yang* underlies the ancient Chinese classification of foods into "cold" and "hot." These must be balanced if a meal is to be spiritually correct, healthy, and delicious. Even the colors of these classic dishes suggest which ones are vigorous and assertive, and which are cooling and contemplative.

HOJAN HSIN TAIJI
Stir-fried scallops in oyster sauce.
(See page 79 for recipe.)

CHAR SIU PAAIH GWAT
Pork spare ribs in barbecue sauce.
(See page 102 for recipe.)

HAHNG
YAHN DAUH FUH
Almond float. (See page 137 for recipe.)

LO HAN CHAI
Buddha's delight. (See page 115 for recipe.)

MEAT

It is only recently that people in Asia have bred animals just for their meat. Years ago, for most of us, fresh meat was holiday food, and usually pretty tough. For that reason, Asian women became experts at preparing and cooking meat in a variety of ways – cutting it into thin slices, marinating it, adding herbs and spices, or slow-cooking it in coconut milk – to produce tender and aromatic results. I have kept the traditional flavors of these dishes, but have adapted the recipes to suit the good meat we are now used to in the West.

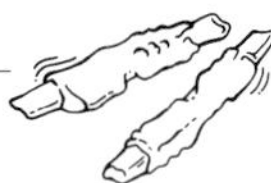

CHAR SIU

Roast strips of pork (China)

This is a classic Cantonese dish. Serve hot, as you would serve traditional roast pork, or mix cold slices with stir-fried vegetables, fried rice, or fried noodles.

INGREDIENTS

2lb (1kg) boneless pork with some fat, from the neck end or leg, cut into 4 strips
2 tbsp clear honey
For the marinade
2 tbsp sugar
1 tbsp light soy sauce
2 tbsp yellow bean sauce (see page 28)
2 tbsp hoisin sauce
1 tbsp oyster sauce, optional
1 tsp five-spice powder (see page 27)
1 tbsp Shaohsing wine (see page 29) or dry sherry
½ tsp salt

PREPARATION

1 Mix all the marinade ingredients together in a glass bowl. Add the meat and rub all over with the mixture. Marinate for 4–5 hours, turning the meat several times and rubbing it with the marinade.
2 Remove the pork from the marinade and arrange on a wire rack in a single layer, without touching. Place over a roasting pan half-filled with cold water.
3 Put the pork in an oven preheated to 375°F (190°C) and roast for 30 minutes. Dip the pork strips back into the marinade, turning them until well coated. Rearrange on the rack and return to the oven. Lower the temperature to 350°F (180°C) and cook for 30–35 minutes.
4 Transfer the pork to a serving plate. Brush with the honey, then cut into thin slices and serve.

KCal 407 P 55g C 25g S 1g TF 10g SF 4g UF 6g (4)

MOO WAN

Sweet pork with marigold (Thailand)

Quite often a dish that is easy to make turns out to be the most popular. Here, the addition of kapi *(Thai dried shrimp paste) gives the pork an authentic flavor. The marigold petal garnish is simple but effective.*

INGREDIENTS

1lb (500g) pork tenderloin, cut into bite-sized pieces
1 tbsp dark soy sauce
¼ tsp salt, plus extra to taste
2 tbsp peanut or vegetable oil
1 onion, finely chopped
2 tbsp grated jaggery (see page 30) or dark brown sugar
2 tbsp fish sauce (nam pla) (see page 28)
1 tbsp light soy sauce
½ tsp ground white pepper
¼ tsp freshly ground black pepper, plus extra to taste
½ cup (120ml) hot water
1 tsp dried shrimp paste (kapi) (see page 31)
2 tbsp chopped fresh cilantro leaves, to garnish
handful of fresh or dried marigold petals (see page 22), to garnish

PREPARATION

1 Place the pork in a glass bowl and rub with the dark soy sauce and salt. Let stand.
2 Heat the oil in a wok. Add the onion and cook until soft. Add the sugar and fish sauce and stir vigorously until the sugar is caramelized.
3 Add the pork, stir-fry for 3 minutes, then add the light soy sauce, white and black pepper, and hot water. Stir-fry over high heat for 3 minutes.
4 Add the shrimp paste and stir-fry for 1–2 minutes more. Season to taste and sprinkle with the chopped cilantro and marigold petals, to garnish.

KCal 263 P 29g C 14g S 1.4g TF 11g SF 3g UF 7g (4)

PAD SOM SIN MOO

Pork in coconut milk with pickled onions (Laos)

Like their Thai neighbors, the Lao use a lot of coconut milk in their cooking. Serve with plain steamed rice.

INGREDIENTS

4 large boneless pork chops, the lean meat cut into ½in (1cm) cubes, the fat reserved and roughly chopped
6 garlic cloves, finely sliced
1 tsp ground white pepper, plus extra to taste
2 tsp salt, plus extra to taste
2½ cups (600ml) thick coconut milk (see page 141)
20 Asian red onions (see page 21) or pickling onions, peeled
juice of 1–2 limes
1 tbsp sugar
4 tbsp water
1 tbsp fish sauce (nam pla) (see page 28)
2 tbsp chopped scallions, the green part only
4 tbsp chopped fresh cilantro leaves

PREPARATION

1 Put the chopped pork fat in a pan and heat it until it becomes oily. Add the cubes of meat and the garlic and cook, stirring frequently, for 3 minutes.
2 Remove and discard the pieces of fat. Add the ground pepper and half the salt to the pan, stir once, and then add the coconut milk.
3 Bring the mixture to a boil, then reduce the heat until the coconut milk bubbles slowly. Cook uncovered for 30–35 minutes longer, or until the coconut milk is quite thick.
4 Put the Asian red onions or pickling onions in a pan with the lime juice, sugar, water, and the remaining salt. Simmer until all the liquid has evaporated and the onions are caramelized.
5 Add the fish sauce to the thickened coconut milk, increase the heat, and stir-fry for 3 minutes. Season to taste, then add the scallions, chopped cilantro leaves, and the caramelized onions, and serve immediately.

KCal 320 P 26g C 20g S 1.5g TF 16g SF 12g UF 3g (4)

Cha Dum

Pork loaf (Vietnam)

This dish requires really good-quality ham. If all you can find is the watery kind, it is better to leave it out. Serve with a green salad and Nuoc Cham (see page 128 for recipe). The loaf can also be added to casseroles or used as a sandwich filling.

INGREDIENTS

½lb (250g) fresh shiitake mushrooms or 10 dried shiitake mushrooms, rehydrated (see page 155), stems removed and caps thinly sliced
1½lb (750g) ground lean pork
4–6oz (125–175g) good-quality cured ham, finely diced
5 scallions, finely chopped
1 tbsp fish sauce (nuoc mam), plus extra to taste
½ tsp salt, plus extra to taste
1 tsp freshly ground black pepper
3 large eggs, lightly beaten

PREPARATION

1 In a large bowl, mix the mushrooms with all the remaining ingredients, kneading them together for a few seconds. Cook a small spoonful of the mixture in a little oil and taste for seasoning. Add more salt or fish sauce to the remaining loaf mixture, if desired.

2 Pack the mixture into an oiled 2lb (1kg) loaf pan, pressing it down with the back of a spoon. Cover the pan with several layers of foil, then place in the top of a steamer. Cover with the lid and steam for 60–80 minutes, or until the center of the loaf is cooked through.

3 Alternatively, put the loaf pan in a roasting pan. Pour enough warm water around the loaf pan to come halfway up the sides. Place in an oven preheated to 350°F (180°C) and cook for 60–80 minutes, or until the center of the loaf is cooked through.

4 Remove the loaf pan from the steamer or roasting pan and let cool slightly. Turn the loaf out of the pan onto a serving platter and let stand until cold. Serve thinly sliced.

KCal 355 P 55g C 1g S 1.1g TF 15g SF 5g UF 8g (4)

Adobong Baboy

Red stew of pork (Philippines)

I am told that Adobo, or "Adobong," has long held an honored place in the cuisine of the Philippines. There, a red stew usually takes its color from annatto seed, but here I use the more widely available paprika and ground turmeric instead. Serves 6–8 with plenty of rice.

INGREDIENTS

3lb (1.5kg) pork leg meat, cut into ¾in (2cm) cubes
6–8 garlic cloves, finely chopped
½ cup (125ml) distilled white vinegar or rice vinegar (see page 29)
5 cups (1.25 liters) water
2 fresh kaffir lime leaves (see page 26) or bay leaves
1 tsp salt, plus extra to taste
3 tbsp vegetable oil
3 shallots, chopped
2 garlic cloves, crushed
1–2 large fresh red chilies, seeded and chopped
1 tsp paprika
1 tsp ground turmeric
¾ cup (175ml) very thick coconut milk (see page 141)
2 tbsp fish sauce (nam pla) (see page 28)
freshly ground black pepper, to taste

PREPARATION

1 Put the pork, garlic, vinegar, and water in a large pan. Bring to a boil, and boil gently for 40 minutes, skimming occasionally. Add the lime leaves or bay leaves and salt and cook for 5 minutes.

2 Remove the meat from the pan with a slotted spoon and transfer to a colander to drain. Boil the stock for 30 minutes longer, skimming the froth. Strain 2½ cups (600ml) of the stock into a bowl.

3 Heat the oil in a large pan. Add the shallots, garlic, and chilies and cook for 2 minutes. Add the paprika and turmeric and stir for a few seconds. Add about 5 tablespoons of the coconut milk and stir once or twice.

4 Add the meat and stir until the pieces are colored with the paprika and turmeric. Add the measured stock and fish sauce and cook for 30 minutes. Add the remaining coconut milk and cook over medium heat for 20 minutes. Season to taste and serve.

KCal 368 P 56g C 3g S 0.9g TF 15g SF 5g UF 8g (6)

Making Tamarind Water

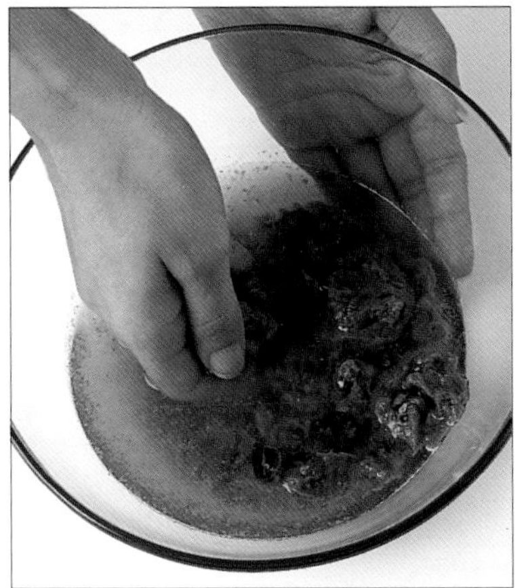

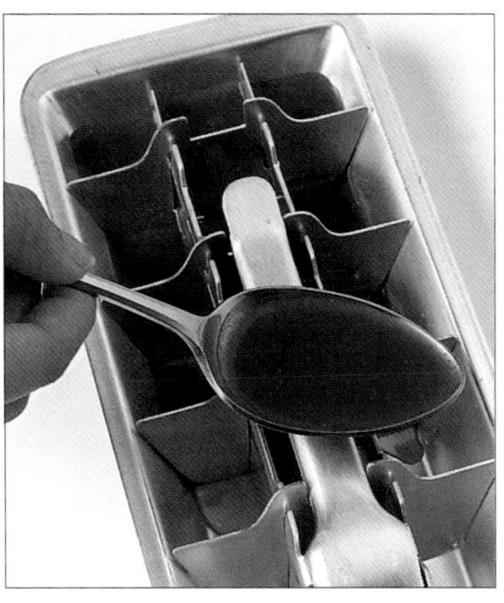

1 Place a block of tamarind pulp in a large bowl. Add enough hand-hot water to cover, then squeeze the pulp between your fingers until it has separated from the seeds and the water is brown.

2 Pour the mixture into a sieve set over a pan. Strain off the liquid, mashing the pulp against the sides of the sieve. Bring the liquid in the pan to a boil, then simmer for 10 minutes. Let cool.

3 Spoon 1 tablespoon of liquid into each section of an ice-cube tray, then freeze. Remove the cubes from the tray and store in freezer bags. Use one cube for each tablespoon of tamarind water.

Vindaloo

Pork cooked in hot and sour sauce (India)

This traditional Goan dish can be short-cooked using pork fillet, or long-cooked using pork leg meat. Serves 6–8 with plenty of rice. *See page 135 for illustration.*

INGREDIENTS

3lb (1.5kg) pork tenderloin or lean leg meat, cut into ½in (1cm) cubes
½ cup (120ml) vegetable oil
3 large red or white onions, finely sliced
6 fresh or dried curry leaves (see page 26), optional
¾ cup (175ml) or 3¾ cups (900ml) hot water
salt and freshly ground black pepper, to taste

For the marinade

3 tbsp red wine vinegar
1 tsp salt
½ tsp chili powder

For the paste

4 shallots, chopped
6–8 garlic cloves, chopped
4–8 large fresh red chilies, seeded and chopped
1 large red pepper, seeded and chopped
¾in (2cm) piece of peeled fresh ginger, chopped
1 tbsp coriander seed, roughly crushed
2 tsp cumin seed, roughly crushed
2 cloves, roughly crushed
½in (1cm) piece of cinnamon stick, roughly crushed
1 tsp grated jaggery (see page 30) or dark brown sugar
2 tbsp vegetable oil
2 tbsp distilled white vinegar
2 tbsp tamarind water (see steps above)

PREPARATION

1 Mix all the marinade ingredients together. Put the pork in a bowl and rub with the marinade. Let marinate for 10 minutes. Put the paste ingredients in a blender and blend until as smooth as possible.

2 Heat the vegetable oil in a wok, add the onions, and cook, stirring frequently, for 8–10 minutes. Remove from the wok with a slotted spoon.

3 Add the meat to the wok in 3 or 4 batches and cook for 3 minutes per batch. Remove the meat from the wok with the slotted spoon.

4 Put the onions in a large pan. Place over medium heat and reheat them, stirring for a few seconds. Add the paste mixture and simmer, stirring frequently, for 8 minutes. Add the meat and the curry leaves and stir until well coated.

5 If using pork tenderloin, add the ¾ cup (175ml) hot water. For leg meat, add the 3¾ cups (900ml) hot water. Bring to a boil, then cover and simmer for 20 minutes for the fillet, or 1 hour and 20 minutes for the leg meat. Season to taste, cook uncovered for 1 minute, then serve immediately.

KCal 499 P 57g C 12g S 0.5g TF 25g SF 5g UF 18g (6)

Twaejigogi Saektchim

Stuffed pork with vegetables (Korea)

At first glance this dish looks complicated to make. In fact, it is quite straightforward, and after cooking it a few times, I find I enjoy it more and more. Serve with rice.

INGREDIENTS

1–1¼ lb (500–625g) pork tenderloin, cut into 4 crosswise
1 tsp each of salt and freshly ground black pepper
4 tbsp vegetable oil
2 tbsp pine nuts, roasted (see page 155), to garnish

For the filling

2–3 tbsp vegetable oil
1 tsp sesame oil
1 large carrot, cut into julienne strips (see page 154)
2 small zucchini, cut into julienne strips (see page 154)
8 button mushrooms, finely sliced
6 dried shiitake mushrooms, rehydrated (see page 155), stems removed and caps finely sliced

For the sauce

2 tbsp dried shrimp (see page 31)
2 tbsp chopped fresh ginger
1 garlic clove, chopped
¼ tsp sugar or 1 tbsp mirin (see page 29)
1 tbsp light soy sauce
pinch of salt
4 tbsp water

PREPARATION

1 Rub the pork with the salt and pepper and let stand for 5 minutes. Heat the oil in a skillet, add the pieces of pork, and cook for 3–4 minutes, turning them frequently. Remove from the pan and set aside. Wipe the pan clean.
2 For the filling, mix the vegetable oil and sesame oil together and heat in the skillet. Add the carrot, stir-fry for 1 minute, then remove from the pan. Cook the remaining vegetables in separate batches for 1 minute each.
3 Put all the sauce ingredients in a blender and blend until as smooth as possible. Transfer the mixture to a small pan and simmer for 4 minutes. Pass the sauce through a sieve into a small bowl.
4 Make 4 parallel cuts across each piece of meat, taking care not to cut right through. Place the pork in a heatproof dish that is deep enough to hold the juices that form during cooking.
5 Stuff some of the carrots into a cut in one portion of meat. Fill the remaining cuts with some of the other vegetables, keeping each type separate.
6 Stuff the other pieces of pork in the same way. Arrange the remaining vegetables on top of the meat, so that the colors match those of the stuffing.
7 Pour the sauce evenly over the vegetables and pork. Place the dish in a steamer, cover, and steam over rapidly boiling water for 10–12 minutes. Remove the dish from the steamer, sprinkle with the pine nuts, to garnish, and serve immediately.

KCal 391 P 34g C 8g S 1.3g TF 25g SF 4g UF 19g (4)

Char Siu Paaih Gwat

Pork spareribs in barbecue sauce (China)

Here is the Chinese original of the Thai steamed and grilled spareribs (see opposite). The ribs can be eaten with rice or noodles, or just by themselves with salad. See page 96 for illustration.

INGREDIENTS

8 cups (2 liters) water
½ tsp salt
2lb (1kg) pork spareribs, cut into 3–3½ in (7–8cm) lengths
3 tbsp vegetable oil
2 tsp finely chopped fresh ginger
6 shallots, finely chopped
2 tbsp dark soy sauce
2 tbsp light soy sauce
2 tbsp hoisin sauce
1 tsp sugar
1 tsp freshly ground black pepper
4 tbsp hot water
2 tbsp Shaohsing wine (see page 29) or dry sherry
⅓ cup (90ml) chicken stock
scallion brushes (see page 155), to garnish

PREPARATION

1 Boil the water in a large pan and add the salt. Add the ribs to the pan and simmer for 4 minutes. Drain the ribs and pat dry with paper towels.
2 Heat the oil in a large, heavy-based casserole dish. Add the ribs and stir-fry for 3 minutes. Add the ginger and shallots and stir-fry for 2 minutes.
3 Add the two types of soy sauce, the hoisin sauce, sugar, and black pepper. Increase the heat, stir-fry for 30 seconds, then add the hot water. Stir again and cover the dish.
4 Place the casserole in an oven preheated to 325°F (160°C) and cook for 1–1¼ hours. Stir in the Shaohsing wine or sherry, then remove the ribs from the sauce and arrange them, side by side, in a large roasting pan.
5 Return the ribs to the oven, increase the temperature to 400°F (200°C), and cook for 10–15 minutes more. Transfer the remaining sauce from the casserole to a small pan. Add the chicken stock and reheat. Arrange the ribs on a plate, garnish with the scallions, and serve with the sauce.

KCal 475 P 38g C 5g S 1.5g TF 33g SF 10g UF 21g (4)

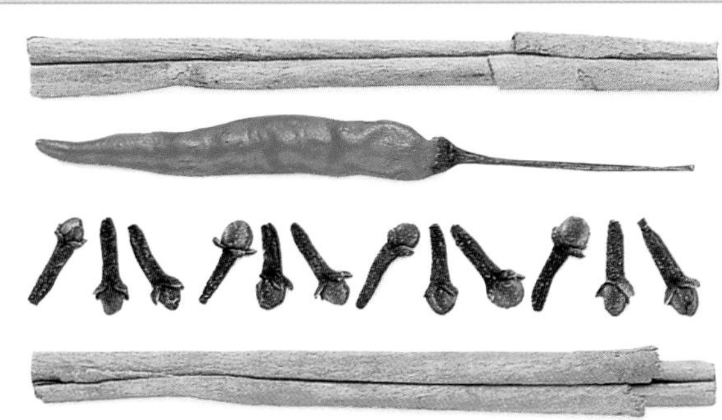

GRADOOK MOO NUENG TAO JEAW

Steamed and grilled spareribs with yellow bean sauce (Thailand)

This is one of the many popular Thai dishes with a strong Chinese influence. The Thai version has bird's-eye chilies and tamarind added to the sauce.

INGREDIENTS

2lb (1kg) pork spareribs, cut into 3in (7.5cm) lengths
½ cup (125ml) hot water
salt and freshly ground black pepper, to taste

For the marinade / sauce

4 tbsp yellow bean sauce (see page 28)
2 garlic cloves, crushed
2–6 fresh red bird's-eye chilies, crushed
¼ tsp ground cloves
¼ tsp ground cinnamon
2 tbsp ginger juice (see page 155)
2 tbsp tamarind water (see page 101)
1 tbsp dark soy sauce
2 tsp fish sauce (nam pla) (see page 28)
1 tsp grated jaggery (see page 30) or dark brown sugar

PREPARATION

1 Mix all the marinade ingredients together in a glass bowl. Put the ribs in another bowl, then coat well with a third of the marinade. Let stand in a cool place for 2 hours, or refrigerate overnight.

2 Transfer the remaining marinade to a pan. Add the hot water and boil, stirring frequently, for 5 minutes. Season to taste, then let cool.

3 Bring the ribs back to room temperature, then place in a steamer and cook for 1 hour. Remove the ribs from the steamer and let stand until cold. (Up to this point everything can be prepared well in advance and refrigerated.)

4 Allow the ribs and sauce to come back to room temperature. Pour half the sauce into a pan and bring to a boil to reheat.

5 Arrange the ribs on a broiler pan and place under a preheated hot broiler. Cook for 4–5 minutes, turning them frequently and brushing with the remaining sauce. Pour the reheated sauce into a bowl and serve as a dipping sauce with the ribs.

KCal 402 P 38g C 7g S 0.8g TF 25g SF 9g UF 14g (4)

MASSAMAN

Beef curry (Thailand)

The original recipe for this dish traveled with Islam from the Middle East to Asia. The Thais have put their signature on this Massaman – that is, Muslim – curry by adding their own favorite ingredients of cilantro root, kaffir lime peel, and fish sauce.

INGREDIENTS

3 tbsp vegetable oil
2 large onions, finely sliced
2lb (1kg) brisket or chuck steak, most of the fat removed, cut into ¾in (2cm) cubes
2 pieces of dried galangal (see page 27)
3–5 pieces of dried kaffir lime peel (see page 22)
3 cloves
2 stems of fresh lemongrass, halved
1½in (3cm) piece of cinnamon stick
1 tsp salt, plus extra to taste
3¾ cups (900ml) hot water
2½ cups (600ml) coconut milk (see page 141)
¾lb (375g) small new potatoes
2 tbsp tamarind water (see page 101)
1–2 tsp grated jaggery (see page 30) or dark brown sugar
2 tbsp roasted peanuts, chopped, to garnish

For the paste

2–6 large fresh red chilies, seeded and chopped
4 garlic cloves, chopped
2 tbsp coriander seed, roasted (see page 155), roughly crushed
1 tbsp cumin seed, roasted (see page 155), roughly crushed
¼ tsp grated nutmeg
3 cilantro roots (see page 26) or stems, chopped
1 tbsp fish sauce (nam pla) (see page 28)

PREPARATION

1 Heat the oil in a pan. Add the onions and cook, stirring, for 6–8 minutes, until they begin to brown. Stir in the meat. Add the galangal, lime peel, cloves, lemongrass, and cinnamon. Stir and add the salt and water. Bring to a boil, cover, and cook over medium heat for 55–60 minutes, stirring frequently.

2 Put all the paste ingredients, plus 4 tablespoons of the coconut milk, in a blender and blend until as smooth as possible. Transfer the paste to a small pan and simmer, stirring frequently, for 8 minutes.

3 Remove the galangal, lime peel, lemongrass, cloves, and cinnamon from the meat. Add the new potatoes and stir in the paste, blending well.

4 Simmer, uncovered, for 5 minutes. Add the rest of the coconut milk, the tamarind water, and sugar. Cook, uncovered, for 30 minutes. Add more salt, to taste, and sprinkle with the peanuts to garnish.

KCal 646 P 60g C 41g S 1.1g TF 29g SF 8g UF 18g (4)

Huhng Siu Ngauh

Red-cooked beef with broccoli (China)

In Chinese cooking, the term "red-cooked" refers to any food that is slow-cooked in soy sauce. Long cooking is a convenient way to cook for large numbers, as the dish can be prepared well in advance and reheated when required without any deterioration of the flavor or texture. Serves 6–8 with steamed or boiled white rice.

INGREDIENTS

4lb (2kg) piece of rolled brisket, cut across in half
8 cups (2 liters) water
1 tsp salt, plus extra to taste
1 large onion, roughly chopped
3 slices of peeled fresh ginger
3 tbsp vegetable oil
2 tsp finely chopped fresh ginger
1 tsp freshly ground black pepper, plus extra to taste
4 tbsp dark soy sauce
½in (1cm) piece of cassia bark (see page 27) or cinnamon stick
1 star anise
3¾ cups (900ml) hot water
4 tbsp Shaohsing wine (see page 29) or dry white wine
1–1½lb (500–750g) broccoli, cut into small florets

PREPARATION

1 Put the beef, water, salt, onion, and sliced ginger in a large pan and bring to a boil. Lower the heat a little, then cover and boil gently for 1 hour.
2 Remove the beef from the stock and transfer to a cutting board. Strain the stock into a bowl and skim well. Measure and reserve 2½ cups (600ml) of the stock. Cut the beef into 1in (2.5cm) cubes and pat dry with paper towels.
3 Heat the oil in a large casserole dish, add the cubed beef, and stir-fry for 2 minutes. Add the chopped ginger, the black pepper, soy sauce, cassia bark or cinnamon stick, and the star anise and stir-fry for a few seconds.
4 Add the hot water and stir once. Cover the casserole, place in an oven preheated to 300°F (150°C) and cook for 1 hour and 20 minutes.
5 Remove the casserole from the oven and add the wine and the reserved stock. Stir once and season to taste. Remove the cassia bark or cinnamon stick and star anise. Cover the casserole and return to the oven. Lower the temperature to 250°F (120°C) and cook for 1 hour.
6 Remove the casserole from the oven and place over medium heat. Add the broccoli florets, simmer uncovered for 8–10 minutes, then serve.

KCal 581 P 77g C 7g S 1.2g TF 27g SF 9g UF 14g (6)

Vegetable oil

Fresh ginger

Onion

Salt

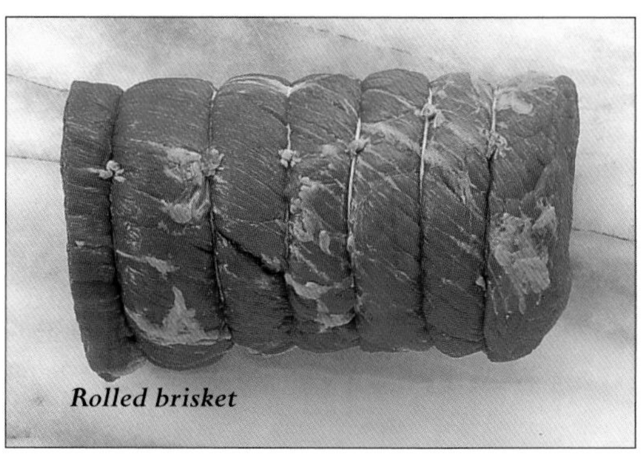

Rolled brisket

Black pepper
Dark soy sauce
Cassia bark
Star anise
Shaohsing wine
Broccoli

SUKIYAKI

Beef and vegetable hot pot (Japan)

This recipe is based on recollections of a magnificent sukiyaki prepared by a visiting Japanese professor at my university in central Java. He cooked it in a true sukiyaki pot (see page 149) at the dining table, while his wife passed around the guests' bowls as they were filled and refilled. Chopsticks are normally used to cook and eat with, but where hot oil is concerned you may feel safer with a spoon and fork or tongs. Serve with Japanese rice.

INGREDIENTS

4 eggs, optional
soy sauce, to serve
7oz (200g) shirataki (see page 24), optional
about 4 tbsp vegetable oil
1½ lb (750g) very thinly sliced beef sirloin (see page 152)
6 scallions, thinly sliced on the diagonal
1 lb (500g) firm tofu (see page 24), cut into 16 cubes
¼–⅓ lb (125–175g) fresh shiitake mushrooms or chestnut mushrooms, thinly sliced
⅓ lb (175g) watercress

For the broth

about 2½ cups (600ml) clear beef or chicken stock
3 tbsp dark soy sauce
1 tbsp mirin (see page 29)
4 tbsp sake (see page 29)
1–2 tsp sugar, optional

PREPARATION

1 Mix all the broth ingredients in a pan. Bring to simmering point and keep hot, so it can be taken to the table in a bowl. Alternatively, pour the broth into a fondue pot, so it can simmer at the table.
2 Arrange a sukiyaki pot (see page 149) or an electric skillet on the dining table, and turn on the heat. Provide each diner with a small bowl of cooked rice, an empty soup bowl, and a pair of chopsticks. Place an unbroken egg on a small plate by the side of each empty bowl. On the table there must also be a small bowl of soy sauce.
3 If using the shirataki, cook them in a large pan of boiling salted water for 3–4 minutes. Drain well in a colander, then rinse under cold running water and drain again.
4 To serve, put 1–2 tablespoons of the oil in the hot sukiyaki pot or skillet. When the oil is hot, add 4–8 slices of the meat and cook, turning them several times. Add a few pieces of scallion, 4 pieces of tofu, a few slices of mushroom, and sprigs of watercress to the pot or pan. Stir for 1–2 minutes, then add a ladle of simmering broth and some of the shirataki, if using, and heat through.
5 Everybody helps themselves from the pot or pan: the egg, if desired, is broken over the food in the soup bowl, then some of the broth is spooned over it. The egg is stirred until it scrambles in the hot stock, then a few drops of soy sauce are added.
6 The cook adds more ingredients and broth to the pot as they become depleted. The rice is eaten between the meat and vegetables or by itself at the end of the meal.
7 The broth remaining in each bowl is drunk like tea from a cup, but if preferred a soup spoon can be used.

KCal 485 P 57g C 6g S 0.9g TF 25g SF 6g UF 17g (4)

BOXAO MANG

Beef with bamboo shoots (Vietnam)

You can find Indonesian, Malaysian, Singaporean, and Filipino variations of the classic Southeast Asian dish on the same theme. Serves 2 with rice or noodles.

INGREDIENTS

4 tbsp peanut or soy oil
¾ lb (375g) rump steak, cut across the grain into ¾ in (2cm) wide strips (see page 152)
7oz (200g) canned bamboo shoots, drained and rinsed, sliced lengthwise into thin strips
4 scallions, thinly sliced on the diagonal
3 tbsp sesame seeds, roasted (see page 155) and crushed with a mortar and pestle

For the Nuoc Cham

2 tbsp fish sauce (nuoc mam) (see page 28)
2 garlic cloves, crushed
1–2 small dried red chilies, finely chopped
juice of half a lime or lemon
large pinch of salt
large pinch of sugar, optional

PREPARATION

1 Put all the ingredients for the Nuoc Cham in a small glass bowl and mix together with a teaspoon. Set aside until required.
2 Heat a wok until very hot, then add half the oil, and heat it until smoking. Add the beef and stir-fry quickly for 1 minute. Remove the beef with a slotted spoon and transfer to a plate.
3 Add the remaining oil to the wok and heat until smoking. Add the bamboo shoots and stir-fry for 1 minute. Add the scallions and stir-fry for 1 minute more.
4 Add the Nuoc Cham and stir-fry over very high heat for 30 seconds. Add the beef and crushed sesame seeds. Stir-fry for 30 seconds longer to heat the beef through, then serve immediately.

KCal 573 P 49g C 4g S 1.7g TF 41g SF 9g UF 29g (2)

Gule Kambing

Aromatic lamb stew (Indonesia)

In central Java Gule Kambing is made with goat meat. I use lamb, usually the neck or leg. Serves 6–8 with plenty of plain white rice.

INGREDIENTS

3–4lb (1.5–2kg) lean lamb, cut into ½in (1cm) cubes
2½ cups (600ml) hot water
2in (5cm) piece of cinnamon stick
1 stem of fresh lemongrass, cut into 3 pieces
2 fresh kaffir lime leaves (see page 26) or bay leaves
1–1½ cups (250–375ml) thick coconut milk (see page 141)
salt and freshly ground black pepper, to taste
2 tbsp Crisp-Fried Onions (see page 132 for recipe), to garnish
handful of fresh flat-leaf parsley, to garnish

For the paste

5 shallots or 1 onion, chopped
4 garlic cloves, chopped
3 candlenuts (see page 22) or macadamia nuts, roughly chopped
2–4 large fresh red chilies, seeded and chopped
¼ tsp ground white pepper
2 tsp chopped fresh ginger
1 tsp chopped fresh galangal (see page 27)
1 tsp ground turmeric
2 tsp ground coriander
2 cloves, roughly crushed
1 tsp salt
4 tbsp tamarind water (see page 101)
3 tbsp vegetable oil

PREPARATION

1 Put all the paste ingredients in a blender and blend until as smooth as possible. Transfer the paste mixture to a large pan and simmer, stirring frequently, for 6–8 minutes.
2 Add the meat and cook, stirring continuously, for 2 minutes. Add the hot water, cinnamon stick, lemongrass, and lime leaves or bay leaves. Cover and simmer for 30 minutes.
3 Add the coconut milk and cook, uncovered, over low heat for 30–40 minutes, stirring frequently. The exact cooking time will depend on the desired consistency of the sauce.
4 Season to taste, then remove the cinnamon stick, lemongrass, and lime leaves or bay leaves.
5 Transfer the stew to a serving bowl and sprinkle with the Crisp-Fried Onions and chopped fresh parsley, to garnish.

KCal 523 P 52g C 8g S 0.5g TF 31g SF 13g UF 15g (6)

Kambing Korma

Lamb curry with coconut milk (Malaysia)

This curry is very similar to the Muslim lamb korma of central India, except that it is not made with yogurt. Often, as in India, it is served with roti (bread), especially at lunchtime. For an evening meal, it is served with rice. Serves 6–8 with roti or rice.

INGREDIENTS

2lb (1kg) mutton or lamb leg meat, cut into ¾in (2cm) cubes
1 tsp salt, plus extra to taste
5 tbsp (75ml) ghee (see page 29) or vegetable oil
5 shallots or 1 large red onion, finely chopped
6 garlic cloves, finely chopped
2 tsp chopped fresh ginger
2 tsp finely chopped fresh lemongrass, center only
2in (5cm) piece of cinnamon stick
2 fresh or dried curry leaves (see page 26) or bay leaves
2½ cups (600ml) hot water
1 cup (250ml) very thick coconut milk (see page 141)
freshly ground black pepper, to taste

For the dry spice mixture

2 tsp coriander seed
1 tsp cumin seed
1 tsp fennel seed
seeds of 3 green cardamom pods
4 cloves
10 black peppercorns

PREPARATION

1 Roast the dry spice mixture (see page 155) for 3 minutes, then let cool. Grind to a fine powder in a spice mill or with a mortar and pestle.
2 Place the meat in a large glass bowl. Sprinkle with the ground spices and the salt, and mix together. Let stand in a cool place for 15–20 minutes.
3 Heat the ghee or oil in a wok or large shallow pan. Add half the meat and cook for 5 minutes, stirring continuously. Remove the meat from the wok with a slotted spoon and transfer to a plate. Cook the remaining meat and remove from the wok.
4 Reheat the wok, add the shallots or onion, and stir-fry for 5 minutes. Add the garlic, ginger, and lemongrass and stir-fry for 2 minutes more.
5 Return the meat to the wok, add the cinnamon stick and curry leaves or bay leaves, and stir once. Add the hot water, then cover and simmer for 40–45 minutes.
6 Stir in the coconut milk and simmer for 20 minutes, stirring frequently. Season to taste, and remove the cinnamon stick and curry leaves or bay leaves before serving.

KCal 447 P 35g C 6g S 0.5g TF 32g SF 19g UF 10g (6)

Aloo Gosht

Meat curry with potatoes (India)

Lamb is the usual meat for this curry, but you will also find this dish made with beef or chicken, depending on where you are in Asia. Serve with roti (bread) or rice.

INGREDIENTS

4 medium potatoes, cut across in half, each half quartered
4 large or 8 small lamb chops
7oz (200g) canned chopped tomatoes
½ cup (120ml) hot water
4 tbsp plain yogurt
salt and freshly ground black pepper, to taste

For the paste

4 shallots, chopped
2 garlic cloves, chopped
8 white peppercorns, roughly crushed
¼ tsp chili powder
1 tbsp coriander seed, roughly crushed
2 tsp cumin seed, roughly crushed
1 tsp ground turmeric
¼ tsp salt
3 tbsp vegetable oil
4 tbsp water

PREPARATION

1 Put the potatoes in a large bowl of lightly salted cold water until ready to use. Put all the paste ingredients in a blender and blend until as smooth as possible. Transfer the paste mixture to a pan and simmer, stirring frequently, for 4–5 minutes.

2 Add the lamb chops to the pan, and cook, turning frequently, until they are brown all over. Drain the potato pieces, add them to the pan and cook, stirring continuously, for 2–3 minutes.

3 Add the chopped tomatoes, cover, and simmer for 15 minutes. Add the hot water, cover, and cook over medium heat for 20 minutes, or until the potatoes are tender.

4 Add the yogurt, a spoonful a time, stirring briskly. Simmer for 5 minutes, season to taste, and serve.

KCal 384 P 26g C 34g S 0.3g TF 18g SF 5g UF 11g (4)

Dalcha

Lamb cooked with lentils (India)

This everyday Indian dish is simple to make and the ingredients are readily available. Any dhal or lentils can be made into Dalcha, but my own favorite is red lentils. Serve with rice.

INGREDIENTS

1lb (500g) lean lamb leg meat, cut into ¾in (2cm) cubes
1 medium onion, finely sliced
1 tsp ground cumin
2 tsp finely chopped fresh ginger
1½ tsp salt, plus extra to taste
3 tbsp tamarind water (see page 101)
2 medium purple eggplants, halved crosswise, each half quartered
¼lb (125g) thin green beans, halved
4 ripe tomatoes, peeled and quartered
½ tsp chili powder
handful of fresh cilantro leaves, to garnish

For the lentils

1 tsp ground coriander
¼ tsp chili powder
½ tsp dry mustard
½ tsp fenugreek seed, ground
½ tsp ground turmeric
8oz (250g) split red lentils, washed and drained
2½ cups (600ml) water

For the fried ingredients

4 tbsp vegetable oil
1 large onion, sliced
2–3 dried chilies, each cut into 3 pieces
1 garlic clove, crushed
½ tsp each of yellow mustard seed and cumin seed
4 fresh or dried curry leaves (see page 26), optional
large pinch of asafetida (see page 30), optional

PREPARATION

1 For the lentils, put the ingredients in a pan. Bring to a boil, then cover and simmer for 15 minutes.
2 Add the cubed lamb and onion. Stir, then add the cumin, ginger, and salt. Cook, stirring continuously, for 1–2 minutes until all the ingredients are mixed. Stir in the tamarind water, then cover and cook over low heat for 20 minutes.
3 Add the eggplants and beans and cook, covered, for 8 minutes. Add the tomatoes and chili powder and simmer for 4 minutes. Taste and season with more salt, if desired.
4 For the fried ingredients, heat half the vegetable oil in a heavy-bottomed skillet. Add the onion and cook until golden brown. Remove the onion with a slotted spoon and drain on paper towels.
5 Pour the rest of the oil into the skillet. Add the chilies, garlic, mustard and cumin seed, curry leaves, and asafetida, if using, and stir-fry for 1 minute.
6 Transfer the Dalcha to a serving platter and spoon the fried ingredients over it, along with half the oil in the skillet. Sprinkle with the fried onions and the fresh cilantro, to garnish.

KCal 583 P 45g C 52g S 0.9g TF 24g SF 6g UF 15g (4)

Khoua Sin Fahn

Venison in rich coconut sauce (Laos)

I am told that in Laos, as in several Asian countries, what we call venison is the meat of a much smaller animal than the Western deer. The meat is cooked in thick coconut milk until the water evaporates, so that by the end of cooking the meat is fried in the oil. Serves 6–8.

INGREDIENTS

8 cups (2 liters) thick coconut milk (see page 141)
3lb (1.5kg) venison, from the saddle or haunch, cut into ¾in (2cm) cubes
1 tsp salt, plus extra to taste
4 tbsp chopped scallions

For the paste

4 garlic cloves, chopped
2–4 large fresh red chilies, seeded and chopped
5 shallots, chopped
3 fresh kaffir lime leaves (see page 26), chopped

PREPARATION

1 Put all the paste ingredients, plus ⅓ cup (90ml) of the coconut milk, in a blender and blend until as smooth as possible. Transfer the paste mixture to a large pan. Add the venison, salt, and the remaining coconut milk and stir well.
2 Bring the mixture to a boil, then reduce the heat a little so that the coconut milk bubbles gently. Cook for 1½ hours, stirring occasionally, until the coconut milk has reduced and thickened.
3 Transfer the mixture to a wok and cook until the sauce becomes oily. Cook, stirring frequently, for 15 minutes, until the sauce is thick. Season to taste and add the scallions. Cook, stirring continuously, for 1 minute, then serve.

KCal 617 P 60g C 19g S 0.70g TF 34g SF 27g UF 5g (6)

THAILAND

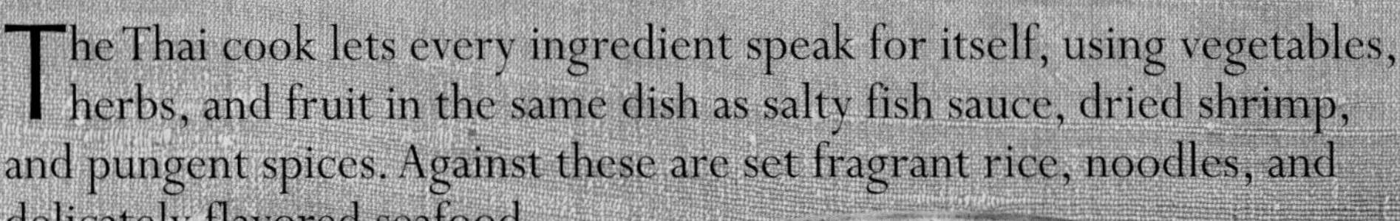

The Thai cook lets every ingredient speak for itself, using vegetables, herbs, and fruit in the same dish as salty fish sauce, dried shrimp, and pungent spices. Against these are set fragrant rice, noodles, and delicately flavored seafood.

YAM WOON SEN
Spicy salad of cellophane noodles, shrimp, and pork.
(See page 119 for recipe.)

YAM PLA
MUEK MAMUANG
Green mango and squid salad.
(See page 119 for recipe.)

HOY LAI PHAD
NAM PRIK PHAO
Braised clams with basil. *(See page 85 for recipe.)*

VEGETABLES & SALADS

In Western cookbooks, recipes for vegetable dishes and salads are often found in separate chapters. But in Asia we have never made much of a distinction between cooked and raw produce. We like to harvest our vegetables when they are young and tender and need little or no cooking, so raw and cooked can be mixed together in warm salads. They have to be as appealing to the senses as anything else on the table, varied in color and texture as well as flavor.

KAJITCHIM

Steamed stuffed eggplant (Korea)

Traditionally, these eggplants have ground beef mixed into the stuffing. This recipe is a vegetarian version to be eaten with rice or noodles.

INGREDIENTS

4 purple eggplants, 5–6in (12–15cm) long
3 large onions, sliced
½ tsp salt
5 tbsp (75ml) warm water
3 tbsp vegetable oil
For the stuffing
2 garlic cloves, finely chopped
2 tsp sesame seed
½ tsp coarse sea salt
½ lb (250g) Chinese-style tofu
2 tbsp vegetable oil
1 tsp sesame oil
3 shallots, finely chopped
1 large fresh red chili, seeded and finely chopped
¼ lb (125g) fresh shiitake mushrooms, stems removed and caps thinly sliced
½ lb (250g) button mushrooms, thinly sliced
1 tsp very finely chopped fresh ginger
1 tbsp light soy sauce
2 tbsp chopped scallions
2 tbsp chopped fresh flat-leaf parsley or celery leaves
salt and freshly ground black pepper, to taste

PREPARATION

1 Cut 4 slits in each eggplant, as if cutting it in quarter lengthwise, but leaving the ends intact. Set aside while preparing the stuffing.

2 For the stuffing, crush the garlic, sesame seed, and salt to a paste, using a mortar and pestle. Put the tofu in a bowl and cover with boiling water. Let stand for 10 minutes.

3 Drain the tofu in a colander and let cool. When cool enough to handle, wrap it in a piece of cheesecloth or a clean dish towel and squeeze out all the excess water.

4 Heat the vegetable oil and sesame oil in a wok. Add the shallots and cook, stirring continuously, for 2 minutes. Stir in the garlic and sesame seed paste and the chopped chili. Add both types of mushrooms and the ginger and cook, stirring frequently, for 4 minutes.

5 Add the tofu, crushing it with the back of a spoon, and stir the mixture until everything is thoroughly blended. Stir in the soy sauce, scallions, and parsley and season to taste.

6 Spoon the stuffing into the slits in each eggplant. Spread the sliced onions in the bottom of a large pan. Sprinkle with the salt and pour the warm water over them. Arrange the stuffed eggplant on top of the onions in a single layer.

7 Cover the pan and cook over low heat for 1 hour. Check the pan regularly to make sure that the onions have not dried out and started to burn, adding more water if necessary. Alternatively, arrange all the ingredients in a large casserole dish and bake in an oven preheated to 325°F (160°C) for 1½ hours.

8 Transfer the eggplants to a warm serving platter. Add the vegetable oil to the onions in the pan or casserole and stir-fry for 3–4 minutes, or until browned. Spoon the onions over the eggplants and serve.

KCal 326 P 14g C 22g S 0.8g TF 21g SF 2g UF 16g (4)

YAM MAKHUA PHAO

Sweet and sour eggplant (Thailand)

For this dish, small round eggplants are normally used; they are available in Thai and some Chinese stores. Here, however, I have used large purple eggplants and have roasted them instead of the usual boiling or steaming.

INGREDIENTS

2 large purple eggplants
1oz (30g) dried shrimp (see page 31)
2 tbsp chopped fresh cilantro leaves
For the dressing
2 shallots, very finely sliced
1–2 bird's-eye chilies, finely chopped
3 tbsp fish sauce (nam pla) (see page 28)
3 tbsp lime or lemon juice
1 tbsp sugar
5 tbsp (75ml) water

PREPARATION

1 Roast the eggplants in an oven preheated to 375°F (190°C) for 35–40 minutes, then transfer to a heavy plastic bag and let stand until cool enough to handle.
2 Peel off the skin of the warm eggplants, then cut each one into large chunks and transfer to a salad bowl. Roast the dried shrimp for 2–3 minutes (see page 155), then let cool. Grind to a coarse powder with a mortar and pestle and set aside.
3 Put the dressing ingredients into a small pan and simmer for 2 minutes. Pour it over the eggplants, then sprinkle with the ground shrimp and the chopped cilantro. Toss the ingredients together to mix well and serve at room temperature.

KCal 73 P 7g C 10g S 1.2g TF 1g SF 0.2g UF 0.5g (4)

PHOOL GOBI AUR ALOO KI BHAJI

Cauliflower with potatoes (India)

In most Asian cuisines potatoes are considered a vegetable, not a staple. Serves 4–6.

INGREDIENTS

2 large boiling potatoes, about 10oz (300g) each
1 cauliflower, about 1½lb (750g), cut into small florets
2 tsp coriander seed
1–2 small dried red chilies
2 tsp cumin seed
5–6 tbsp (75–90ml) ghee (see page 29) or vegetable oil
1 tsp yellow mustard seed
1 large fresh green chili, seeded and finely chopped
½ tsp ground turmeric
1 tsp salt, plus extra to taste
¼ tsp freshly ground black pepper

PREPARATION

1 Boil the potatoes in their skins, then let cool. Peel and quarter and cut each into 2 or 3 pieces. Blanch the cauliflower in boiling water for 1 minute.
2 Roast the coriander seed, dried chilies, and half the cumin seed for 3–4 minutes (see page 155), then grind to a powder with a mortar and pestle.
3 Heat 5 tablespoons (75ml) of the ghee in a large, nonstick shallow pan or wok. Add the mustard seed and remaining cumin seed and stir until they start to pop. Add the green chili and turmeric.
4 Stir for a few seconds, then add the cauliflower and stir-fry for 2 minutes. Add the potatoes, the powdered spices, salt, and pepper and stir-fry for 2–3 minutes, until heated through. Add the rest of the ghee and more salt if necessary, then serve.

KCal 379 P 11g C 31g S 0.5g TF 25g SF 15g UF 8g (4)

ORAK-ARIK

Stir-fried cabbage with eggs (Indonesia)

I am not exaggerating if I say that virtually everybody in Java knows how to cook this very simple and homely dish, and everybody likes it. Serves 4–6 as a side dish.

INGREDIENTS

3–4 tbsp vegetable oil
4 shallots, finely sliced
2 garlic cloves, finely chopped
1 tsp finely chopped fresh ginger, optional
1–1½lb (500–750g) cabbage, finely shredded
1 tsp salt, plus extra to taste
5 tbsp (75ml) hot water
¼–½ tsp ground white pepper, plus extra to taste
2–3 eggs, lightly beaten

PREPARATION

1 Heat the oil in a wok. Add the shallots, garlic, and ginger and stir-fry for 2–3 minutes.
2 Add the shredded cabbage and salt and stir-fry for 3 minutes. Add the hot water and ground white pepper, stir again, then cover the wok and simmer for 2–3 minutes.
3 Uncover the wok, increase the heat, and stir the cabbage continuously for 1 minute. Add the beaten eggs and stir and turn them vigorously until they are scrambled and cooked through. Season to taste and serve immediately.

KCal 219 P 8g C 11g S 0.6g TF 16g SF 3g UF 12g (4)

Rebong Char

Bamboo shoots, shrimp, and pork in a spicy sauce (Singapore)

This dish is a very popular example of Nonya cooking: typically Chinese in origin, but with some Malaysian-influenced hot chili to give it an extra lift. Garnish with fresh cilantro and serve with boiled or fried rice.

INGREDIENTS

8–12 raw large shrimp, peeled and deveined (see page 82), halved lengthwise, shells reserved
2 cups (450ml) water
1 tsp all-purpose flour
1 tbsp light soy sauce
½lb (250g) boneless pork chops with a little fat, thinly sliced
3 tbsp pork fat or lard or vegetable oil
½in (1cm) piece of fresh ginger, finely chopped
2 large fresh red chilies, seeded and finely chopped
2 garlic cloves, finely chopped
2 star anise
1 tbsp yellow bean sauce (see page 28)
6–8oz (175–250g) canned whole bamboo shoots (drained weight), rinsed and thinly sliced
salt and freshly ground black pepper, to taste

PREPARATION

1 Rinse and wash the shrimp shells and place in a pan with the water. Bring to a boil, then cover and simmer for 20 minutes. Strain the stock through a fine sieve and discard the shells.

2 Blend the flour and the soy sauce together and rub into the pork slices. Set aside for a few minutes.

3 Heat the pork fat, lard, or oil in a wok. Add the ginger, chilies, and garlic. Stir-fry for 1–2 minutes. Add the pork and stir-fry rapidly for 2 minutes.

4 Add the star anise, yellow bean sauce, and the shrimp stock. Keep the wok over high heat and let the mixture bubble for 1 minute.

5 Add the shrimp and bamboo shoots and stir-fry for 2 minutes. Season to taste, stir again, and cook for 1 minute more, then serve immediately.

KCal 217 P 20g C 4g S 0.4g TF 14g SF 5g UF 7g (4)

Bandakka Curry

Okra curry (Sri Lanka)

Curries similar to this are made all over the Indian subcontinent as well as in Malaysia. This one tastes very good with Ikan Masak Molek (see page 36 for recipe), the classic Malaysian fish curry. If you eat them together, you do not need to make the sauce for the okra, because the fish curry has enough for both dishes. Serves 4 as a side dish or 2 as a main course with rice.

INGREDIENTS

1lb (500g) okra, trimmed and thinly sliced crosswise
½ tsp ground turmeric
½ tsp chili powder or paprika
½ tsp salt
½ cup (125ml) vegetable oil for frying
For the curry sauce
2 tbsp vegetable oil
1 small onion, finely sliced
2 large fresh green chilies, seeded and finely sliced
large pinch of ground turmeric
1 tsp ground coriander
½ tsp ground cumin
½ in (1cm) piece of cinnamon stick
4 fresh or dried curry leaves (see page 26), optional
1 tsp salt, plus extra to taste
¾ cup (175ml) coconut milk (see page 141)
freshly ground black pepper, to taste

PREPARATION

1 For the curry sauce, heat the oil in a pan. Add the onion and stir-fry for 4 minutes. Add all the remaining sauce ingredients, except the coconut milk, and stir-fry for 1 minute.
2 Add the coconut milk to the pan, bring to a boil, then lower the heat and simmer for 10 minutes. Season to taste and set aside.
3 In a bowl, toss the sliced okra with the ground turmeric, chili powder or paprika, and salt.
4 Heat the oil in a wok or skillet. Add the okra and cook, stirring frequently to prevent them from burning, for 3 minutes, or until crisp. (Cook the okra in two batches if necessary, to avoid overcrowding the pan.)
5 Remove the okra from the wok with a slotted spoon and drain on paper towels.
6 The okra can be served crisp, or soft, according to taste. If you prefer the latter, heat the sauce almost to boiling point and add the fried okra. Simmer for 1 minute and serve hot. For crisp okra, serve the sauce separately.

KCal 204 P 4g C 7g S 0.8g TF 18g SF 2g UF 14g (4)

Lo Han Chai

Buddha's delight (China)

This is adapted from a recipe by my friend Deh-ta Hsiung. The 18 principal ingredients of the original recipe represented the 18 disciples of Buddha, hence the name "Buddha's delight." Serves 4–6 as a side dish. See page 97 for illustration.

INGREDIENTS

½oz (15g) golden needles (see page 27), optional
½oz (15g) wood ears (see page 21), optional
2oz (60g) dried shiitake mushrooms
¼lb (125g) cellophane noodles (see page 25)
⅓lb (175g) snow peas
⅓lb (175g) baby corn, halved lengthwise
2 tbsp peanut oil
4 scallions, sliced on the diagonal
1 tbsp fresh peeled and chopped ginger
8oz (250g) canned straw mushrooms (drained weight), rinsed, or ½lb (250g) fresh small button mushrooms
1 tsp sugar
2 tbsp light soy sauce
½lb (250g) fried tofu (see page 24), sliced
3–4oz (90–125g) canned ginkgo nuts (see page 22), (drained weight), optional
½ tsp sesame oil
salt and freshly ground black pepper, to taste

PREPARATION

1 Soak the golden needles in boiling water for 10 minutes, then drain. Trim off the hard edges of the buds and cut each needle into 2 pieces.
2 Rehydrate the wood ears (see page 155), then cut into small pieces. Rehydrate the dried shiitake mushrooms for 30 minutes (see page 155), reserving the soaking liquid. Remove the stems and cut the caps in half.
3 Soak the cellophane noodles in hot water for 5 minutes. Drain. Then, with scissors, snip the noodles into short pieces. Blanch the snow peas and baby corn in boiling water for 1 minute, then refresh under cold running water and drain.
4 Heat the peanut oil in a wok or a casserole. Add the scallions and ginger and stir-fry for 20 seconds. Add all the mushrooms and the golden needles and stir-fry for 30 seconds.
5 Add the sugar and soy sauce, followed by the fried tofu, snow peas, and baby corn. Add ½ cup (125ml) of the mushroom soaking liquid, cover the pan, and simmer for 3 minutes.
6 Uncover the pan, and add the noodles, ginkgo nuts, if using, and the sesame oil. Stir-fry for 2 minutes longer, then season to taste and serve hot.

KCal 574 P 28g C 48g S 1.1g TF 30g SF 2g UF 26g (4)

Aloo Baigan Korma

Braised mixed vegetables with yogurt (India)

This is a vegetarian dish with potatoes and eggplant as the main ingredients, but with other vegetables added to make it a satisfying one-dish meal. Serve with rice or bread.

INGREDIENTS

3 tbsp vegetable oil
1 large onion, finely chopped
2 tbsp ground coriander
2 tbsp ground cumin
1 tsp ground turmeric
2 garlic cloves, finely chopped
2 tsp finely chopped fresh ginger
½ cup (120ml) plain yogurt, lightly whisked
2 tbsp ground almonds
4 ripe tomatoes, peeled, seeded, and roughly chopped
½ cup (120ml) hot water
6 medium new potatoes, scrubbed and quartered lengthwise
2 medium purple eggplants, halved across, then each half cut into 8 pieces
1 tsp salt, plus extra to taste
1–2 large fresh red chilies, seeded and finely chopped
10 whole baby carrots or 4–5 medium carrots, sliced on the diagonal
½lb (250g) yard-long beans (see page 21) or thin green beans, cut into 2in (5cm) lengths
4 tbsp chopped fresh cilantro leaves, to garnish

PREPARATION

1 Heat the oil in a large heavy skillet. Add the onion and stir-fry for 6 minutes.
2 Add the ground coriander, ground cumin, and turmeric and stir-fry for about 1 minute. Stir in the garlic and ginger.
3 Gradually add the yogurt to the pan and cook, stirring continuously, for 1–2 minutes. Add the ground almonds, half the chopped tomatoes, and the hot water. Stir again, then add the potatoes, eggplants, and salt. Lower the heat, cover the pan, and simmer for 7 minutes.
4 Add the chilies, the whole or sliced carrots, and the beans. Stir once, then cover the pan, and simmer very gently for about 15 minutes, or until all the vegetables are tender.
5 Add more salt, if desired, and stir in the remaining chopped tomatoes. Cook for 1 minute more, to heat the tomatoes through, then remove from the heat and sprinkle with the chopped fresh cilantro, to garnish.

KCal 299 P 10g C 34g S 0.6g TA 16g SF 2g UF 13g (4)

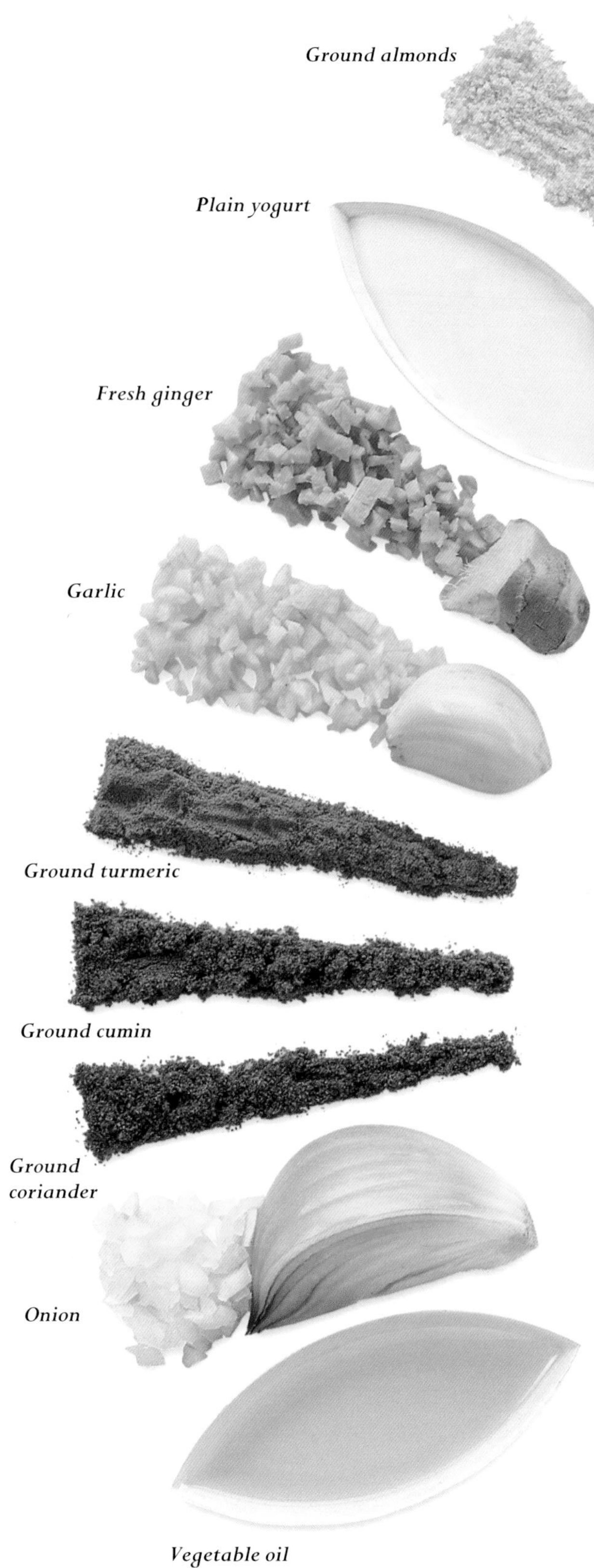

Tomatoes
New potatoes
Eggplants
Salt
Red chilies
Baby carrots
Yard-long beans
Fresh cilantro

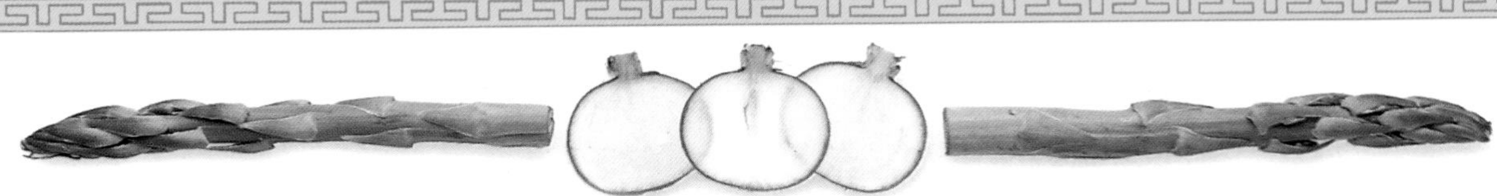

CHAI SIU NGO

Vegetarian goose (China)

This is a classic vegetarian dish; when cooked, the bean curd skin resembles that of roast goose or duck. If it has been deep-fried, the skin will also be crisp. Serves 4 as an appetizer or as part of a dim sum meal.

INGREDIENTS

8 dried shiitake mushrooms, rehydrated (see page 155), soaking liquid reserved, stems removed
1 tbsp light soy sauce
1 tsp sesame oil
3 bean curd sheets (see page 25)
2 carrots, cut into very fine julienne strips (see page 154)
2–3 celery stalks, cut into very fine julienne strips (see page 154)
1–2 tbsp dark soy sauce
1 tbsp sugar
about 1¼ cups (300ml) vegetable oil for deep-frying

PREPARATION

1 Strain the mushroom soaking liquid into a cup and add the soy sauce and sesame oil. Dice the mushroom caps.
2 Put the bean curd sheets on a plate, pour the liquid over them, and let soak for 5 minutes, to make them more pliable.
3 Spread out one bean curd sheet on a large tray. Place some carrot and celery julienne on the left half of the sheet. Sprinkle with a little of the dark soy sauce and the sugar. Fold the right half of the sheet over the filling and scatter over some of the diced mushrooms and a little more soy sauce.
4 Fold the whole sheet in half again, to form a roll 2–3in (5–7cm) wide. Repeat with the remaining bean curd sheets and vegetables. Brush or dab dark soy sauce on the outside of each roll. Do not seal.
5 Heat the oil for deep-frying in a wok or large pan to 300°F (150°C). To shallow-fry, heat about 2 tablespoons of oil in a skillet. Add one roll to the wok or skillet and fry for 2–3 minutes, turning it several times, until the outside of the roll is atractively crisp and golden.
6 Remove the roll from the pan with a slotted spoon and drain on paper towels. Keep hot in a warm oven while the remaining rolls are fried. Cut each roll crosswise into sections 2–3in (5–7cm) long. Serve immediately, because the bean curd will toughen once cold.

KCal 247 P 1g C 15g S 0.8g TF 12g SF 1g UF 10g (4)

SHIRA AE

Mixed vegetable salad with sesame dressing (Japan)

Serve this traditional Japanese dressing with any seasonal vegetables – cooked, raw, or a mixture of both. It also makes an excellent dip for crudités. Serves 4–6 as a side dish or an appetizer.

INGREDIENTS

4–8 asparagus spears, trimmed and thinly sliced on the diagonal
¼lb (125g) cauliflower, cut into small florets
1 medium yellow zucchini, cut into very fine julienne strips (see page 154)
4 red radishes, cut into very fine julienne strips (see page 154) and soaked in cold water
1 small red pepper, seeded and cut into very fine julienne strips (see page 154)
For the dressing
4 tbsp sesame seed
1 tbsp sugar
1 tsp salt
2 tsp light soy sauce
2 tbsp rice vinegar
3 tbsp bonito stock (see page 30) or other stock
1 tbsp mirin (see page 29)
¼ tsp freshly ground white pepper, optional
¾lb (375g) silken tofu

PREPARATION

1 For the dressing, put all the ingredients, except the silken tofu, in a blender and blend until as smooth as possible.
2 Add the tofu and blend until well mixed with the paste. Season to taste, then transfer to a glass bowl and refrigerate.
3 Cook the sliced asparagus in boiling water for 4 minutes, then refresh under cold running water. Blanch the cauliflower florets for 3 minutes and refresh, then blanch the zucchini strips for 1 minute and refresh. Drain the radishes.
4 Divide all the vegetables among 4 or 6 serving plates, arranging each vegetable separately around the edge. Spoon some dressing into the center of each plate and serve.

KCal 200 P 13g C 11g S 0.7g TF 12g SF 2g UF 9g (4)

YAM WOON SEN

Spicy salad of cellophane noodles, shrimp, and pork (Thailand)

Similar salads are also popular in Vietnam and Korea. This makes a refreshing cold lunch or appetizer. Serves 4–6 as a lunch by itself, or 6–8 as an appetizer. *See page 110 for illustration.*

INGREDIENTS

¼oz (7g) wood ears (see page 21), optional
7oz (200g) cellophane noodles (see page 25)
3 tbsp vegetable oil
1oz (30g) dried shrimp (see page 31)
½oz (15g) dried sliced garlic
¾lb (350g) lean pork, coarsely ground or hand-chopped
salt and freshly ground black pepper, to taste
3 large shallots, sliced
2oz (60g) small onions, thinly sliced into rings
2 scallions, thinly sliced on the diagonal
fresh celery leaves (the tender inner leaves)
4 tbsp fish sauce (nam pla) (see page 28)
4 tbsp lemon juice
2 tbsp sugar
4–6 small fresh red chilies, seeded and finely chopped
16 cooked peeled jumbo shrimp
4 cups (125g) fresh cilantro leaves, about half chopped
red chili flowers (see page 155), to garnish

PREPARATION

1 Rehydrate the wood ears in 2 cups (450ml) of warm water (see page 155). Rinse, then slice into thin strips and set aside.
2 Pour hot water over the noodles, let stand for 5 minutes, and drain. Using scissors, cut the noodles into 3–4in (7–10cm) lengths.
3 Heat 2 tablespoons of the oil in a pan. Add the dried shrimp and cook until just crisp. Remove from the pan with a slotted spoon and drain on paper towels.
4 Reheat the oil, add the garlic and cook for 1–2 minutes, until golden and crisp. Drain on paper towels. Heat the remaining oil in another pan and stir-fry the pork over high heat for 3–4 minutes, or until cooked through. Season to taste.
5 In a glass bowl, mix together the shallots, onions, scallion, celery leaves, and wood ears, if using. Add the fish sauce, lemon juice, sugar, and chilies.
6 About 10 minutes before serving, toss the noodles, mushroom mixture, pork, jumbo shrimp, and cilantro together in a large bowl. Arrange the noodle mixture on a serving plate and sprinkle with the crisp-fried shrimp and garlic. Garnish with the chili flowers and serve at room temperature.
KCal 313 P 24g C 35g S 1.2g TF 9g SF 1g UF 6g (8)

YAM PLA MUEK MAMUANG

Green mango and squid salad (Thailand)

Some green, unripe mangoes may be too sour for this salad, but unfortunately you will not know until you taste them. Those that are too sour need salting and sugaring before using, as described below. Serves 4–6 as an appetizer. *See page 111 for illustration.*

INGREDIENTS

2 small green, unripe mangoes (see page 23), peeled, flesh cut into thin slices or small matchsticks
1½lb (750g) small squid, cleaned and cut into rings (see page 150), tentacles discarded
handful of fresh cilantro leaves
handful of fresh Thai basil leaves (see page 26)
lettuce leaves, to serve, optional

For the dressing

juice of 2 limes
1 tbsp sugar
2 tbsp fish sauce (nam pla) (see page 28)
1–3 fresh red bird's-eye chilies, finely chopped
½in (1cm) piece of fresh lemongrass, center only, finely chopped
1 shallot, finely chopped
2 tbsp warm water
1 garlic clove, finely chopped, optional
1 tbsp finely chopped fresh cilantro leaves

PREPARATION

1 Taste the sliced mango; if it is too sour, put it in a colander and sprinkle with 1 tablespoon each of salt and sugar. Let stand for 1–2 hours, then rinse thoroughly under running water and drain well.
2 Cook the squid rings in lightly salted boiling water for 4 minutes. Drain in a colander and let cool. Mix all the ingredients for the dressing in a glass bowl.
3 About 1 hour before serving, add the squid, mango, cilantro, and basil to the dressing. Mix well and let stand at room temperature. To serve, arrange a layer of lettuce leaves, if using, on a plate, spoon the salad on top and serve immediately.
KCal 215 P 31g C 16g S 0.8g TF 4g SF 1g UF 2g (4)

NOODLES & RICE

Without noodles, without rice, Asia would be an inconceivably different place. Not every Asian lives on them; other staples – corn, sago, and cassava – are still supreme in some less-populated areas. But anyone who was brought up on rice will confirm that it is the most versatile and satisfying of all foods. Only noodles come close to it, but noodles are a product of city life; rice, however refined and polished, is always a reminder of the countryside.

UDON SUKI

Hot pot with udon noodles (Japan)

This is a kind of Japanese version of fondue, with the broth simmering in a heated pot or fondue pot or electric pan in the center of the table. Alternatively, the hotpot can be heated in a casserole and served in individual bowls at the table.

INGREDIENTS

¾ lb (375g) dried udon noodles (see page 24)
2 medium carrots, cut into thin rounds
12–16 snow peas
¾ lb (375g) spinach leaves or broccoli florets
8 leaves of napa cabbage or bok choy
4 fresh shiitake mushrooms or chestnut mushrooms, stems removed and caps halved
8–12 raw jumbo shrimp, peeled and deveined (see page 82)
½–¾ lb (250–375g) lean chicken, thinly sliced
½ tsp salt
2 tsp lemon juice

For the broth

6¼ cups (1.5 liters) bonito stock (see page 30) or chicken stock
4–6 tbsp (60–90ml) light soy sauce
2 tbsp mirin (see page 29)

For the condiments

4 scallions, finely chopped
1 tbsp finely chopped or grated fresh ginger
1 lemon, cut into 4 wedges

PREPARATION

1 Cook the noodles in plenty of boiling water for 18 minutes. Drain in a colander, then rinse under cold running water and let drain.

2 Blanch the carrots in lightly salted boiling water for 3 minutes. Refresh in cold water. Blanch the snow peas for 2 minutes, then refresh and drain.

3 Boil the spinach or broccoli for 2 minutes, then refresh in cold water and drain well. Compress the spinach in the palm of your hand and squeeze out any remaining excess water. Cut the dry spinach into 4 portions.

4 Blanch the napa cabbage leaves for 2 minutes and refresh in cold water. Drain well, then roll the leaves up inside a bamboo rolling mat or dish towel (see page 149) and cut each roll into 4 sections.

5 Arrange the prepared vegetables, mushrooms, and cooked noodles on a large serving platter. Cook the shrimp in boiling water for 2 minutes, then drain and arrange on a smaller plate. Sprinkle the chicken slices with the salt and lemon juice, then rub gently to coat evenly. Arrange with the shrimp.

6 To serve in a heated pot or electric pan, arrange the vegetables and noodle platter, the shrimp and chicken, and all the prepared condiments at the table. Place a deep soup bowl and chopsticks in front of each diner.

7 Mix the ingredients for the broth in a pan, bring to a rolling boil, then transfer it to the heated pot.

8 Let diners help themselves to the vegetables, noodles, shrimp, and chicken and cook them in the central pot. The mushrooms and chicken should be cooked for 3 minutes, the rest of the ingredients are simply reheated for 2 minutes.

9 Diners transfer what they have cooked to their own bowls, ladle over some broth, and help themselves to condiments. In Japanese households, where only chopsticks are used, the broth is drunk from the bowls, like tea.

10 Alternatively, heat the broth in a large casserole. Add the chicken, cook for 3 minutes, then add the raw shrimp and simmer for 1 minute. Add the vegetables and noodles and cook for 2 minutes longer. Bring the dish to the table and serve the hot pot in the individual bowls.

KCal 556 P 45g C 81g S 2.3g TF 8g SF 2g UF 6g (4)

Char Kwee Teow

Rice stick noodles with pork and shrimp (Singapore)

Chinese in origin, this dish long ago became popular street food in Singapore and Malaysia.

INGREDIENTS

8 cups (2 liters) cold water
1 tsp salt
½ lb (250g) rice stick noodles (see page 25), ¼–½ in (5–10mm) wide
5 tbsp (75ml) vegetable oil
3 shallots, finely sliced
2 tbsp yellow bean sauce (see page 28)
1 tsp ground coriander
½ tsp ground cumin
large pinch of ground turmeric
¼ tsp chili powder
2 tbsp hot water
2 tbsp lard or vegetable oil
¼ lb (125g) pork tenderloin, thinly sliced crosswise
8–12 jumbo shrimp, peeled and deveined (see page 82)
3 garlic cloves, finely sliced
1 tsp finely chopped fresh ginger
1 large fresh red chili, seeded and thinly sliced on the diagonal
½ cup (60g) fresh bean sprouts, rinsed and trimmed
1 tbsp dark soy sauce
1 tbsp light soy sauce
3 tbsp hot water or stock
5 scallions, cut into 1 in (2cm) lengths
salt and freshly ground black pepper, to taste

PREPARATION

1 Boil the water with the salt in a large pan. Add the noodles, stir well, and boil for 2–3 minutes. Drain in a colander, then rinse under cold running water until cold and drain.

2 Heat 2 tablespoons of the oil in a wok. Add the shallots and cook for 2 minutes. Stir in the yellow bean sauce, all the spices, and the hot water and stir-fry for 1–2 minutes.

3 Add the noodles, stirring and tossing them until heated through. Transfer the mixture to a platter, cover with foil, and keep hot in a warm oven.

4 Wipe the wok clean with paper towels. Heat the lard and remaining oil in the wok. Add the pork and cook, stirring frequently, for 3 minutes. Remove the pork with a slotted spoon and drain on paper towels.

5 Reheat the oil, add the shrimp and stir-fry for 3 minutes. Remove the shrimp with the slotted spoon and drain on paper towels.

6 Add the garlic and ginger to the wok and stir-fry for a few seconds. Add the chili, bean sprouts, the dark soy sauce and light soy sauce, and the hot water or stock and simmer for 2 minutes.

7 Return the pork and shrimp to the wok and add the scallions. Stir-fry for 1 minute, then season to taste. Remove the noodles from the oven, uncover, and spoon the pork and shrimp mixture over the top.

KCal 484 P 16g C 56g S 1.2g TF 21g SF 3g UF 18g (4)

Pancit Guisado

Fried noodles with mixed meat (Philippines)

Pancit Guisado differs from other Asian fried noodles mainly in its use of chorizo, the Spanish sausage. Ideal as a one-dish meal. Serves 6–8.

INGREDIENTS

10 cups (2.5 liters) water
½ tsp salt, plus extra to taste
¾–1 lb (375–500g) egg noodles or rice noodles
3 tbsp lard or olive oil
1 medium red onion, chopped
3 cloves garlic, chopped
½ in (1cm) piece of fresh ginger, finely chopped
1 large fresh red chili, seeded and finely chopped
¼–½ lb (125–250g) pork tenderloin, thinly sliced crosswise
1 large chicken breast, thinly sliced crosswise
½–¾ lb (250–375g) uncooked spicy chorizo sausage, sliced about ½ in (1cm) thick
¼ lb (125g) green cabbage or napa cabbage, thickly sliced
2 medium carrots, sliced into thin rounds
5 tbsp (75ml) hot water or chicken stock
1 tsp dried shrimp paste (see page 31), optional
2 tbsp light soy sauce
2oz (60g) Chinese chives (see page 26), cut into ¾ in (2cm) lengths
3 scallions, cut into ¾ in (2cm) lengths
freshly ground black pepper, to taste

PREPARATION

1 Boil the water with the salt in a large pan. Add the noodles, stir well, and cook for 3 minutes. Drain the noodles in a colander, then rinse under cold running water until cold and let drain.

2 Heat the lard in a wok. Add the onion, garlic, ginger, and chili and stir-fry for 2 minutes. Add the pork and stir-fry over high heat for 2 minutes. Add the chicken and chorizo and stir-fry for 2–3 minutes.

3 Add the cabbage and carrots, stir, and add the water or stock, the shrimp paste, and soy sauce. Cook for 3 minutes, stirring frequently.

4 Add the noodles, chives, and scallions. Stir and toss the noodles until they are heated through. Season to taste and serve immediately.

KCal 595 P 30g C 52g S 1.4g TF 31g SF 9g UF 21g (6)

Chapchae

Warm rice noodles with vegetables (Korea)

This was originally a noodle dish with beef, vegetables, and mushrooms, but, as so often in Asia, the meat was used very sparingly and cut, like the vegetables, into tiny strips. The result is that meat and mushrooms are almost indistinguishable. My vegetarian version, here, keeps the textures and flavors of the original dish without using any meat at all. Serves 4 as an appetizer, or 2 as a light lunch.

INGREDIENTS

½ lb (250g) rice noodles (see page 25)
2 tbsp light soy sauce
1 tsp sesame oil
2 tbsp peanut or vegetable oil
2 shallots, finely sliced
2–4 small dried red chilies, chopped, or salt and freshly ground black pepper, to taste
2 medium carrots, cut into fine julienne strips, (see page 154)
1–2 leeks, rinsed thoroughly, cut into fine julienne strips, (see page 154)
¼ lb (125g) fresh shiitake mushrooms or 2oz (60g) dried shiitake, rehydrated (see page 155), stems removed and caps thinly sliced

For the garnish

½ lb (250g) baby spinach leaves, rinsed and drained, or large spinach leaves, blanched
2 eggs, beaten, made into 1 thin omelet, cut into strips
2 tsp sesame seeds, roasted (see page 155)

PREPARATION

1 Cover the rice noodles with warm water and let stand for 20 minutes. Drain well in a colander.
2 Heat the soy sauce and sesame oil in a wok. Add the drained noodles, stir-fry for 2 minutes, then transfer to a large bowl. Wipe the wok clean with paper towels.
3 Heat the peanut oil in the wok. Add the shallots and dried chilies, if using, and stir-fry for 2 minutes. Add the carrots and leeks and stir-fry for 2 minutes more. Add the mushrooms and cook, stirring frequently, for 2–3 minutes more.
4 Season with salt and pepper, if not using the dried chilies, and remove the wok from the heat. Add the vegetables to the warm noodles and toss all the ingredients together to mix well.
5 Line individual serving plates with the raw baby spinach or the blanched large spinach and arrange portions of the noodles and vegetables on top. Garnish with the omelet and sprinkle over the roasted sesame seeds. Serve warm or cold.

KCal 346 P 13g C 47g S 0.7g TF 12g SF 3g UF 9g (4)

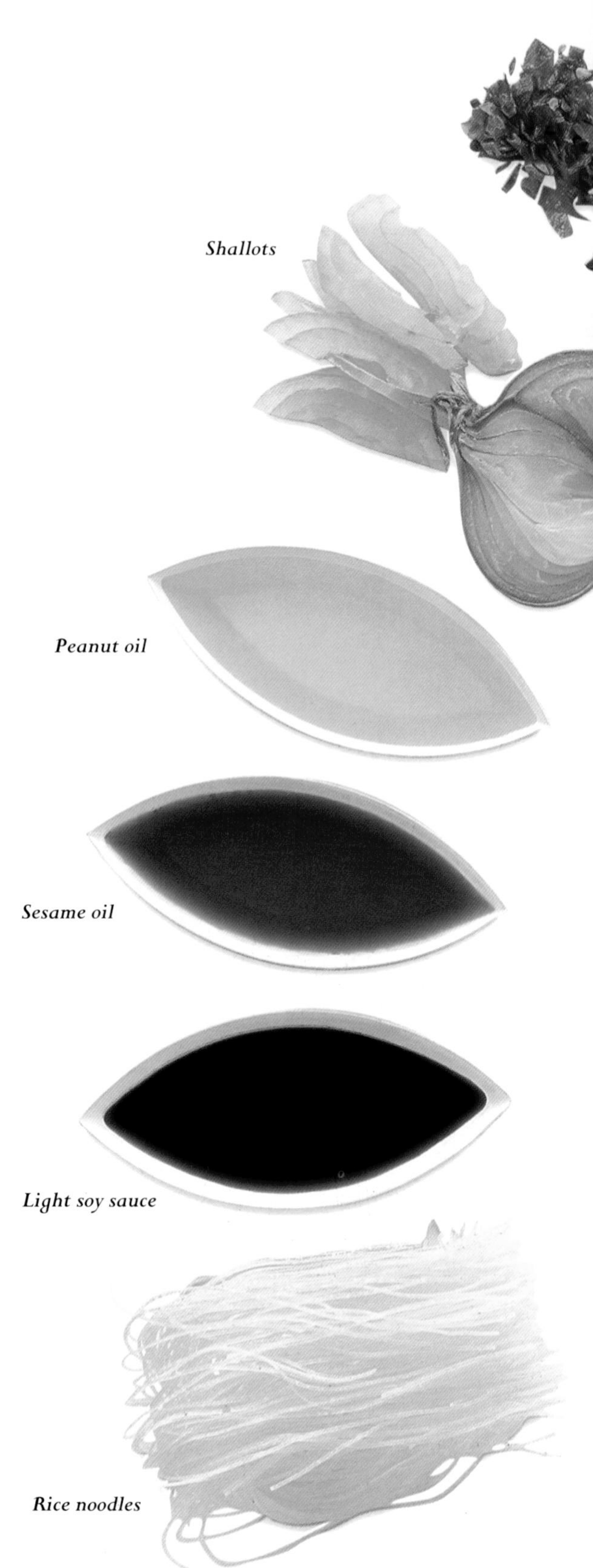

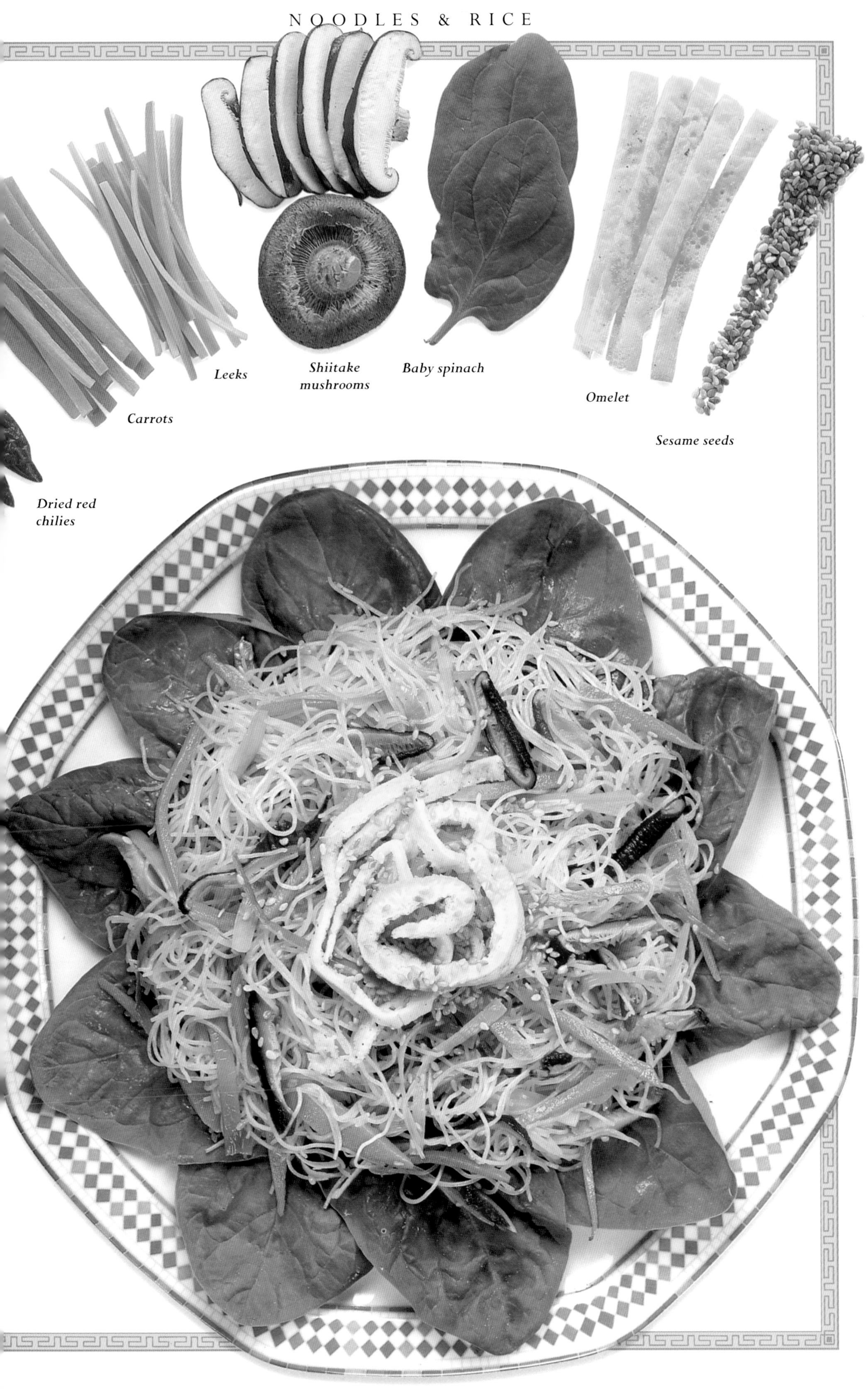
Leeks
Shiitake mushrooms
Baby spinach
Omelet
Carrots
Sesame seeds
Dried red chilies

HAI JO MAH JI MEE

Yifu noodles with crabmeat sauce (China)

The combination of powdered dried fish, crabmeat, and straw mushrooms is typical of southern China. Fresh egg noodles can be used instead of dried yifu noodles, but they need to be deep-fried for a few minutes before they are softened in the hot stock.

INGREDIENTS

2oz (60g) dried anchovies (see page 30)
or dried shrimp (see page 31)
¾–1lb (375–500g) dried yifu noodles (see page 24) or
1lb (500g) fresh egg noodles
about 1¼ cups (300ml) vegetable oil for deep-frying
(only if using fresh egg noodles)
2½ cups (600ml) boiling chicken stock, or boiling water
mixed with 1 tbsp ginger juice (see page 155)
4 tbsp chicken stock
1 tbsp oyster sauce
½ tsp freshly ground black pepper
1 tbsp dark soy sauce
¼lb (125g) fresh crabmeat, white meat only
½ tsp sesame oil
¼lb (125g) canned straw mushrooms (drained weight),
rinsed and halved, or 6oz (175g) fresh oyster mushrooms,
blanched in hot stock for 1 minute, sliced
4–6 scallions, thinly sliced on the diagonal
salt, to taste

PREPARATION

1 Place the dried anchovies or dried shrimp on a baking sheet and bake in an oven preheated to 325°F (160°C) for 6–8 minutes, or until crisp. Let cool, then grind to a powder in a blender or with a mortar and pestle.
2 Put the dried yifu noodles in a bowl. If using fresh egg noodles, heat the oil in a wok or deep-fat fryer, add the noodles, and fry for 2–3 minutes, or until crisp. Remove the noodles from the oil with a slotted spoon and transfer them to a bowl.
3 Pour the boiling stock or ginger-flavored water over the yifu noodles or the fried noodles, let stand for 2–3 minutes, then drain in a colander.
4 Heat a dry wok for 2 minutes, then add the ground fish or shrimp, followed immediately by the 4 tablespoons of stock. Swirl the stock around, then stir in the oyster sauce, black pepper, soy sauce, crabmeat, and sesame oil.
5 Add the mushrooms and noodles. Stir and toss the noodles with chopsticks until all the ingredients are thoroughly mixed and heated through. Add the scallions and some salt, if necessary. Stir and toss again for 1 minute, then serve immediately.

KCal 270 P 19g C 18g S 1.2g TF 14g SF 2g UF 11g (4)

KHAO PAD KHAI HORAPHA

Fried rice with chicken and basil (Thailand)

The basil in this classic fried rice dish is deep-fried for a few minutes, so that it becomes crisp when cold.

INGREDIENTS

½ cup (125ml) vegetable oil
handful of fresh Thai basil leaves (see page 26)
3 shallots, finely sliced
2 garlic cloves, finely sliced
1 large fresh red chili, seeded and finely chopped
¾lb (375g) chicken, thinly sliced into small pieces
2 cups (500g) jasmine rice, cooked (see page 156) and
left until cold
1 tbsp chopped scallions
2 tsp fish sauce (nam pla) (see page 28)
salt, to taste

PREPARATION

1 Heat the oil in a wok, add the basil leaves, and cook for 1–2 minutes. Remove from the wok with a slotted spoon and drain on paper towels.
2 Add the shallots to the wok and cook, stirring continuously, for 2–3 minutes, or until just beginning to brown. Remove from the wok with the slotted spoon and drain well on paper towels.
3 Drain all but 2 tablespoons of the oil from the wok. Reheat the wok, add the garlic and chili, and stir-fry for 1 minute. Add the chicken and stir-fry for 3 minutes. Add the rice and scallions and stir until heated. Add the fish sauce and salt, if necessary.
4 Stir half the fried basil into the rice and arrange on a serving dish. Sprinkle with the remaining basil and the fried shallots, then serve immediately.

KCal 425 P 33g C 40g S 0.3g TF 16g SF 2g UF 12g (4)

Nasi Kebuli

Savory rice with fried chicken (Indonesia)

This was originally a Middle Eastern pilaf that, over the centuries, has traveled far. Serves 6.

INGREDIENTS

about 1¼ cups (300ml) vegetable oil for deep-frying
2 cups (500g) basmati rice, soaked in cold water for 1 hour, then drained

For the stock

1 chicken, 3½–4lb (1.75–2kg), cut into 8–10 pieces (see page 153)
3 shallots or 1 medium onion, chopped
2 garlic cloves, chopped
1 tbsp ground coriander
1 tsp ground cumin
½in (1cm) piece of fresh galangal (see page 27)
2in (5cm) piece of fresh lemongrass
1 small cinnamon stick
2 cloves
¼ tsp grated nutmeg
2 tsp salt
8 cups (2 liters) cold water

For the garnish

2 tbsp Crisp-Fried Onions (see page 132 for recipe)
handful of fresh flat-leaf parsley
½ cucumber, sliced

PREPARATION

1 Put all the stock ingredients in a large pot. Bring to a boil and cook for 50 minutes. Remove the chicken and drain in a colander. Simmer the stock for 10 minutes more, then strain it into a bowl. Reserve 3¾ cups (900ml) of the stock and skim well.
2 Put 2 tablespoons of the oil in a pan. Heat the rest in a wok or deep-fat fryer to 350°F (180°C). Add half the chicken pieces to the hot oil and fry for 10–15 minutes, moving them around with a slotted spoon, until the skin is evenly brown and crisp.
3 Remove the chicken from the oil and drain on paper towels. Fry the rest of the chicken.
4 While the chicken is cooking, heat the reserved oil. Add the rice and stir until coated. Add the stock, then stir and cook over medium heat for 8–10 minutes, until the stock is absorbed.
5 Cover the pan, reduce the heat to very low, and cook undisturbed for 10–12 minutes. Remove the pan from the heat and set it, still covered, on a wet dish towel. Let stand for 5 minutes.
6 Pile the rice in the center of a large serving platter and place the chicken around it. Arrange the sliced cucumber over the rice and sprinkle the Crisp-Fried Onions and parsley over all.

KCal 766 P 43g C 69g S 0.8g TF 35g SF 8g UF 25g (6)

Brinjal Pullao

Spicy pilaf with eggplant (Southern India)

This dish has been a favorite of mine since I learned how to make it years ago from a charming south Indian chef working in New Delhi. It is easy to make, spicy, and chili-hot. Serves 2.

INGREDIENTS

2 tbsp split mung beans (see page 31), roasted for 5 minutes (see page 155)
2–4 small dried red chilies, roasted for 5 minutes, (see page 155)
about 1¼ cups (300ml) vegetable oil for frying
8 whole baby eggplants or 1 medium purple eggplant, cut into large cubes
2 tbsp ghee (see page 29) or peanut oil
½ tsp yellow mustard seed
1 tsp chopped fresh ginger
¼ tsp ground turmeric
¾ cup (175g) basmati rice, cooked (see page 156) and left until cold
1 tsp lemon juice
salt and freshly ground black pepper, to taste

PREPARATION

1 Crush the roasted mung beans and chilies to a coarse powder with a mortar and pestle.
2 Heat the oil in a wok or skillet. Add the eggplants and cook for 5–6 minutes. Remove from the wok with a slotted spoon and drain on paper towels.
3 If using whole baby eggplants, cut each one in half lengthwise, leaving the halves joined at the stalk end. Carefully drain the oil from the wok.
4 Heat the ghee or oil in the wok. Add the mustard seed and cook, stirring continuously, for 1–2 minutes. Stir in the ginger and turmeric. Add the rice and stir until it is heated through.
5 Add the lemon juice and the cooked eggplant to the wok and stir and turn the rice with a large spoon. Season to taste, then stir in the crushed mung bean and chili mixture before serving.

KCal 651 P 10g C 68g S 0.02g TF 41g SF 13g UF 25g (2)

NAVRATAN PULLAO

Mixed vegetable pilaf (India)

The name of this dish is sometimes translated as the "nine jewels" pilaf. The nine jewels, or navratan, symbolize nine brilliant ministers at the court of the great Mogul emperor Akbar in the sixteenth century. Here the "jewels" are represented by nine different vegetables. Serves 6–8 as a one-dish meal, or more as part of a buffet. *See page 134 for illustration.*

INGREDIENTS

3oz (90g) each of carrot, turnip, pumpkin, mushrooms, thin green beans, cauliflower, broccoli, fava beans, peas
3 tbsp vegetable ghee or vegetable oil
1 large onion, very finely sliced
½ tsp black cumin seed (see page 27)
3 green cardamom pods
2 cloves
1in (2.5cm) piece of cinnamon stick
¼–½ tsp chili powder
3 fresh or dried curry leaves (see page 26) or bay leaves
salt and freshly ground black pepper, to taste
2 cups (500g) basmati rice, rinsed, soaked in cold water for 30 minutes, then drained
3¾ cups (900ml) water

PREPARATION

1 To prepare the whole vegetables, cut the carrot, turnip, and pumpkin into small cubes. Slice the mushrooms, cut the beans into short lengths, and divide the cauliflower and broccoli into small florets.
2 Heat the ghee or oil in a large pan. Add the onion and cook, stirring frequently, for 5 minutes. Add all the spices and curry leaves or bay leaves and cook, stirring frequently, for 30 seconds.
3 Add the vegetables, stir for a few seconds, then cover the pan and cook the vegetables in their own juices for 4 minutes. Season to taste.
4 Add the rice and stir for 10 seconds. Stir in the water and bring to a rolling boil. Stir again, then immediately lower the heat. Cover the pan and simmer undisturbed for 20 minutes.
5 Remove the pan from the heat and set it, still covered, on a wet dish towel. Let stand for 5 minutes. Transfer the pilaf to a platter and serve.

KCal 430 P 11g C 76g S 0.01g TF 9g SF 4g UF 4g (6)

NASI KUNING

Savory yellow rice (Indonesia and Malaysia)

In many parts of Asia, yellow is considered a lucky or even a royal color – after all, it is the color of gold. This dish is served at any celebration, small or large: the birth of a baby, the building of a new house, success in an exam. *See page 73 for illustration.*

INGREDIENTS

3 tbsp vegetable oil
3 shallots, finely sliced
2 cups (500g) basmati rice, rinsed, soaked in cold water for 1 hour, then drained
1 tsp ground turmeric
1 tsp ground coriander
1 tsp ground cumin
1 cinnamon stick
2 cloves
2 fresh kaffir lime leaves (see page 26) or bay leaves
1 tsp salt
3¾ cups (900ml) coconut milk (see page 141) or chicken stock

PREPARATION

1 Heat the oil in a large pan. Add the shallots and cook, stirring frequently, until they are beginning to brown. Add the rice and stir until all the grains are well coated.
2 Add the spices, lime leaves, and salt and stir again. Add the coconut milk or stock and bring to a boil. Reduce the heat a little and cook, uncovered, until all the liquid is absorbed.
3 Cover the pan tightly and reduce the heat to minimum. Cook undisturbed for 10–12 minutes. Remove the pan from the heat and set it, still covered, on a wet dish towel. Let stand for 5 minutes. Transfer the rice to a warmed serving bowl. Remove the cinnamon, cloves, and lime or bay leaves, and serve.

KCal 575 P 10g C 111g S 0.7g TF 10g SF 1g UF 8g (4)

Nasi Goreng

Fried rice (Indonesia)

For good Nasi Goreng, the rice should be cooked 2–3 hours before it is fried, so that it has time to become cold. Serves 4–6 as an accompaniment.

INGREDIENTS

2 cups (500g) long-grain rice, washed in 2 changes of cold water, drained
2½ cups (600ml) cold water
3 tbsp peanut oil
3 shallots or 1 small onion, very finely chopped
1–3 large fresh red chilies, seeded and cut into thin rounds, or ½ tsp chili powder
1 tsp chopped fresh ginger
2 medium carrots, finely diced
2oz (60g) cabbage, finely shredded
¼lb (125g) button mushrooms, quartered
1 tsp paprika
2 tsp tomato paste or tomato ketchup
1 tbsp light soy sauce
salt, to taste

For the garnish

½ cucumber, sliced
2 tbsp Crisp-Fried Onions (see page 132 for recipe)
few sprigs of watercress

PREPARATION

1 Place the drained rice and cold water in a large pan. Bring to a boil, uncovered, then simmer for 10–12 minutes, until all the water is absorbed.

2 Stir once with a wooden spoon, then reduce the heat to low. Cover the pan and let cook undisturbed for 10–12 minutes. Remove the pan from the heat and set it, still covered, on a wet dish towel. Let stand for 5 minutes.

3 Spoon the rice into a bowl, cover with a damp dish towel, and let stand for 2–3 hours, or until cold.

4 Heat the oil in a wok. Add the shallots or onion, the fresh chilies or chili powder, and the ginger and stir-fry for 1–2 minutes. Add the carrots and cabbage and stir-fry 2 minutes longer.

5 Add all the remaining ingredients, except the rice and garnishes, and stir-fry for 6 minutes, or until all the vegetables are cooked through.

6 Add the cold rice and mix it thoroughly with the vegetables over low heat, until it is heated through and takes on the reddish tinge of the paprika and tomato paste. Do not allow the rice to burn. Transfer the mixture to a heated serving dish and arrange the garnishes on top and around the dish.

KCal 399 P 7g C 76g S 0.2g TF 9g SF 2g UF 7g (6)

SAUCES & ACCOMPANIMENTS

Dinnertime in an Asian household has always been the domestic equivalent of the rush hour, even if no guests are expected. In my childhood home in Sumatra, up to 20 family members were catered for each day. Among a large number of people there will always be differences in appetite and taste, so everyone is expected to help themselves to what he or she wants from all the dishes and accompaniments the cook has provided. In this way, the flavor of each dish is matched to each person's taste.

SAMBAL ULEK

Basic chili sauce (Indonesia)

This plain chili sauce will keep refrigerated for several weeks and saves you seeding and chopping fresh chilies every time you need one or two for a recipe. One teaspoon of this sauce is the equivalent of 1 large chili. Makes 1¼ cups (300ml).

INGREDIENTS

½ lb (250g) large fresh red chilies
1 tsp salt
3 tbsp vegetable oil
1 tbsp tamarind water (see page 101) or distilled white vinegar
2 tbsp hot water

PREPARATION

1 Put the chilies in a large pan of boiling water and cook for 2 minutes. Remove from the heat and drain well in a sieve.
2 Put the chilies in a blender, add the remaining ingredients, and blend until as smooth as possible. Transfer the sauce to a pan. Cook over low heat, stirring frequently, for 8 minutes.
3 Remove the pan from the heat and let the sauce cool. Can be kept refrigerated in an airtight jar for up to 4 weeks.

KCal 18 P 0.2g C 0.5g S 0.1g TF 2g SF 0.2g UF 1.4g (per 1 tbsp)

NUOC CHAM

Dipping sauce (Vietnam/Laos)

Almost every appetizer and savory snack in Vietnam is served with this sauce. It is supposed to be salty, chili-hot, garlicky, sweet, and sour. Feel free to adjust the quantity of each ingredient to suit your own taste and the food you are going to eat with it. The carrots, apart from adding color, are very useful for those who do not like their dip too hot or too salty.

INGREDIENTS

4 tbsp fish sauce (nuoc mam) (see page 28)
2 tbsp lime juice or lemon juice
2 tsp sugar
2–5 small fresh red chilies, finely chopped
1–2 garlic cloves, crushed
1 carrot, finely shredded
1–2 tsp finely chopped fresh cilantro leaves

PREPARATION

1 Combine the fish sauce, lime juice, sugar, chilies, and garlic in a glass bowl. Stir to mix well, then cover and refrigerate.
2 About 2 hours before serving, stir in the carrot and cilantro leaves. Keep refrigerated until serving time. Use the day it is made.

KCal 119 P 10g C 20g S 4.9g TF 2g SF 0.1g UF 0.3g (total)

Ajad

Namjeem

NAMJEEM

Sweet chili sauce (Laos/Thailand)

A delicious dipping sauce for spring rolls. The consistency can be adjusted by adding more water to thin it down, or it can be cooked longer until thickened.

INGREDIENTS

¾ cup (175ml) water
12 large fresh red chilies, chopped
4 garlic cloves
2 tsp sugar
½ tsp salt, plus extra to taste
1 tbsp fish sauce (nam pla) (see page 28)
1 tbsp distilled white vinegar or rice vinegar
1 tbsp peanut or vegetable oil
1 tsp sesame oil, optional

PREPARATION

1 Put all the ingredients in a pan. Bring to a boil, then cover and simmer for 15 minutes. Transfer to a blender and blend until fairly smooth.

2 Return the sauce to the pan and simmer for 2–3 minutes. Add more salt, if needed. Serve at once, or keep refrigerated in an airtight jar for up to 7 days.

KCal 248 P 8g C 22g S 2.2g TF 15g SF 3g UF 11g (total)

AJAD

Cucumber relish (Thailand)

Ajad is usually very hot as well as sour and sweet. It is used as a relish for spring rolls or satay, for those who do not like, or are allergic to, peanut sauce.

INGREDIENTS

1 medium cucumber, peeled and halved lengthwise
2–6 fresh red bird's-eye chilies, finely chopped
2 tbsp fish sauce (nam pla) (see page 28)
2 tbsp distilled white vinegar
1 tbsp sugar
¼ tsp salt
1 tbsp chopped fresh chives or scallions
1 tbsp chopped fresh cilantro leaves

PREPARATION

1 Remove the seeds from the cucumber with a teaspoon, then thinly slice the cucumber into half-moon shapes.

2 Transfer the cucumber slices to a glass serving bowl and stir in all the remaining ingredients. Serve the relish at once, or keep refrigerated in an airtight jar for up to 2 days.

KCal 161 P 8g C 31g S 2.9g TF 0.7g SF 0.01g UF 0.1g (total)

Sambal Kacang

Peanut sauce (Malaysia / Indonesia / Singapore)

Most satays, except for the Japanese Yakitori, are eaten with peanut sauce. It should be deep brown in color, so do not peel off the peanut skins before they are fried. Serve the sauce hot or warm. Makes about 2½ cups (600ml).

INGREDIENTS

¾ cup (175ml) vegetable oil
¾ lb (375g) shelled peanuts
5 cups (1.25 liters) cold water
2 tbsp dark soy sauce
1 tbsp lemon juice
salt and freshly ground black pepper, to taste
For the paste
4 shallots, chopped
4 garlic cloves, chopped
4 large fresh red chilies, seeded and chopped
1in (2.5cm) piece of fresh ginger, peeled and chopped
2 tsp ground coriander
3 candlenuts (see page 22) or 6 blanched almonds, chopped
1 tsp paprika
2 tbsp tamarind water (see page 101)
2 tbsp peanut oil
1 fresh kaffir lime leaf (see page 26), optional
2in (5cm) piece of fresh lemongrass, outer leaves removed, center chopped

PREPARATION

1 Heat the oil in a wok. Add the peanuts and deep-fry, stirring frequently, for 3–4 minutes, or until golden. Remove from the wok with a wire scoop and let drain on paper towels.
2 Put all the paste ingredients in a blender and blend until as smooth as possible. Transfer the paste mixture to a pan and bring to a boil. Boil, stirring continuously, for 2 minutes, then add the cold water. Return the mixture to a boil, then simmer for 10 minutes.
3 Grind the fried peanuts in an electric spice mill or a food processor to a fairly fine powder. Add to the sauce and stir until evenly incorporated.
4 Add the dark soy sauce and lemon juice to the sauce and season to taste. Simmer, stirring frequently, until it has reduced and thickened to the consistency you require. The sauce should be quite thick but still pourable.
5 The sauce can be frozen for up to 2 months. Defrost completely, then reheat, adding a cup or so of hot water. (The sauce usually becomes very thick after freezing.) Simmer the sauce until it has reduced to the consistency you require.
KCal 73 P 3g C 2g S 0.05g TF 6g SF 1g UF 5g (per 1 tbsp)

Mangai Achar

Mango pickle (India)

The unripe green mangoes used to make this pickle are available in Indian and some other Asian shops. They are small and the skin is thin, so they do not need to be peeled. Serve as an accompaniment to curries or with cold meat. Makes about 1¾ cups (425g).
See page 135 for illustration.

INGREDIENTS

12 small unripe green mangoes (see page 23)
2 tbsp salt, plus extra to taste
4 tbsp corn or vegetable oil
2–8 hot fresh green chilies, seeded and chopped
2 tbsp brown mustard seed
½ tsp ground turmeric
large pinch of asafetida powder (see page 30), optional
2 tsp sugar
2 tsp distilled white vinegar

PREPARATION

1 Wash the mangoes well, then cut off the flesh from either side of the large central pit in two sections. Cut each piece into quarters. Trim the remaining flesh from the sides of the pit.
2 Put the mango pieces in a colander and rub with the salt. Let stand for 1 hour, then rinse well under cold running water and let drain.
3 Heat the oil in a noncorrosive pan. Add the chilies and stir-fry for about 2 minutes. Add the mustard seed and stir-fry, about 1 minute. Stir in the mango slices, then cover the pan and simmer for 6–8 minutes.
4 Add all the remaining ingredients and simmer, uncovered, for 4–5 minutes, stirring occasionally. Add more salt, if necessary. Remove the pan from the heat and let the mixture stand until cold.
5 Transfer the pickle to an airtight jar. Let age at least 5 days. Can be kept refrigerated up to 4 weeks.
KCal 23 P 0.3g C 2g S 0.4g TF 2g SF 0.2g UF 1.4g (per 1 tbsp)

ACAR KUNING

Mixed vegetable pickle (Malaysia / Indonesia)

Acar Kuning can be bought ready-made. However, the commercial products often contain more cabbage than other vegetables. So, in the summer, I like to preserve my own vegetables this way. Serve cold as an accompaniment to curry and rice, or serve hot or warm as a vegetable, with grilled meat or fish. Makes 4 cups (1kg).

INGREDIENTS

¾ cup (175ml) water
10–12 small onions, peeled
½ lb (250g) thin green beans, cut into 2–3 pieces
½ lb (250g) carrots, cut into thin sticks ¾ in (2cm) long
½ lb (250g) cauliflower, cut into small florets
2–8 small dried red chilies
1 tsp dry mustard
1 tsp sugar
1 tsp salt, plus extra to taste
freshly ground black pepper, to taste

For the paste
3 shallots, chopped
2 garlic cloves, chopped
2 large fresh red chilies, seeded and chopped
3 candlenuts (see page 22) or 5 blanched almonds, chopped
1 tsp ground turmeric
3 tbsp distilled white vinegar
2 tbsp olive or vegetable oil

PREPARATION

1 Put all the paste ingredients in a blender and blend until as smooth as possible. Transfer the paste mixture to a noncorrosive pan. Bring to a boil, then simmer, stirring frequently, for 2 minutes. Add the water and simmer for 3 minutes.

2 Add the onions to the pan, cover, and cook for 3 minutes. Add the beans and carrots and cook, covered, for 3 minutes. Add all the remaining ingredients. Stir once or twice, then simmer, uncovered, for 4 minutes, or until the vegetables are tender and have absorbed most of the sauce.

3 Season to taste and remove from the heat. Serve hot, warm, or cold. Can be kept refrigerated in airtight jars for up to 4 weeks.

KCal 182 P 1g C 2g S 0.06g TF 1g SF 0.1g UF 0.8g (per 1oz)

VAMBOTU PAHI

Eggplant pickle (Sri Lanka)

Like the Indian Mango Pickle (see opposite), this pickle can be made mild or very hot by simply adjusting the amount of chilies added. I like to make this with good olive oil, though I know it is not the oil used in Sri Lanka. Besides serving this pickle as an accompaniment to curry, I like it as a sandwich filling, either by itself or with ham or bacon. Makes 4 cups (1kg).

INGREDIENTS

3–4 medium purple eggplants, about 2lb (1kg) in total
1 tbsp salt, plus extra to taste
¾ cup (175ml) virgin olive or vegetable oil
3 shallots, finely chopped
2 garlic cloves, chopped
2–8 fresh hot green chilies, finely sliced
2 tsp yellow mustard seed, crushed
1 tsp ground turmeric, optional
2 tsp ground coriander
1 tsp ground cumin
1 tsp ground fennel seed
¼ tsp chili powder
2 tsp sugar
½ cup (125ml) water
4 tbsp tamarind water (see page 101) or distilled white vinegar

PREPARATION

1 Halve the eggplants lengthwise, then cut each half across into ¼ in (5mm) slices. Put the slices in a colander, rub with the salt, and let stand for about 1 hour. Rinse the slices under running water, then pat dry with paper towels.

2 Heat the oil in a nonstick skillet. Add the sliced eggplant in batches and cook for 3–4 minutes per batch. Remove the eggplant from the pan with a slotted spoon and transfer to a plate. Repeat with the remaining batches.

3 Pour the oil remaining in the skillet into a noncorrosive pan and reheat it. Add the shallots, garlic, and chilies and cook, stirring continuously, for 2 minutes. Add the mustard seed, all the ground spices, and the sugar, and cook, stirring frequently, for 1–2 minutes. Add the water and tamarind water and simmer for 5 minutes.

4 Add some more salt, if necessary, then add the sliced eggplant and all the cooking juices from the plate. Stir once, then simmer for 5–8 minutes. Remove the pan from the heat and let cool.

5 Transfer the cold pickle to airtight jars. Top off with a little more olive oil, if desired. Can be kept refrigerated for up to 4 weeks.

KCal 52 P 0.6g C 2g S 0.2g TF 5g SF 0.8g UF 4g (per 1oz)

Kimchi

Pickled cabbage (Korea)

Kimchi is widely available in Asian supermarkets. But if you cannot buy it and if you like preserving, here is how to make it at home. It takes several days to "cure," so make it well in advance. Makes 4 cups (1kg).

INGREDIENTS

1oz (30g) small dried red chilies
1 tsp dried shrimp (see page 31)
2lb (1kg) napa or bok choy
1½ tbsp salt
3 garlic cloves, crushed
1 bunch scallions, green part only, chopped
2 tsp sugar

PREPARATION

1 Soak the dried chilies and dried shrimp separately in warm water for 10 minutes, then drain well in a sieve.
2 Shred the napa roughly, then place in a colander and mix with the salt. Let stand for 1 hour, then rinse well under cold running water and let drain.
3 In a large bowl, mix the napa with all the remaining ingredients. Cover with a clean cloth and let "cure" for 3–4 days, in a cool, dark place.
4 Pack the pickle into airtight jars. Can be kept refrigerated for up to 4 weeks.

KCal 10 P 1.4g C 1.4g S 0.2g TF 0.2g SF 0g UF 0.2g (per 1oz)

Goreng Bawang

Crisp-fried onions (Malaysia/Indonesia)

Most Southeast Asian soups, salads, or fried rice dishes call for a sprinkling of Crisp-Fried Onions. To make them at home, I suggest you use Asian red onions or shallots. They become crisp more quickly than ordinary onions and do not need to be floured before frying. If you do not want to make your own, you can buy them at Asian supermarkets.

INGREDIENTS

½ cup (125ml) vegetable oil
1lb (500g) Asian red onions (see page 21) or shallots, finely sliced

PREPARATION

1 Heat the oil in a wok. Add the onions in 2 batches and stir-fry for 6–8 minutes, until golden. Remove with a slotted spoon and drain on paper towels.
2 Transfer the cold, crisp onions to an airtight container. Store in a cool place for up to 4 weeks.

KCal 30 P 0.2g C 0.4g S 0.001g TF 3g SF 0.3g UF 2.6g (per ½ oz)

Balachaung

Chili and dried shrimp relish (Myanmar)

This relish can be eaten with raw or steamed vegetables as an accompaniment to rice. I also use it in Chicken Curry with Limes (see page 87 for recipe). Balachaung is available in most Asian supermarkets; it is usually chili-hot and garlicky. Makes about 1¼ cups (300g).

INGREDIENTS

8oz (250g) dried shrimp (see page 31)
3 tbsp peanut or vegetable oil
2 onions, very finely chopped
8 garlic cloves, finely sliced
2 tsp sesame oil
3–8 large fresh red chilies, seeded and chopped
2 tsp finely chopped fresh ginger
½ tsp ground turmeric
1 tbsp fish sauce (nam pla) (see page 28)
½ tsp salt, plus extra to taste
1 tsp sugar, optional
juice of 2 limes or lemons

PREPARATION

1 Put the dried shrimp in a bowl and cover with warm water. Let stand for 10 minutes, then drain in a sieve. Chop them fine, or grind with a mortar and pestle, or process in a food processor.
2 Heat the oil in a wok, add the onions and garlic and cook, stirring continuously, for 5–8 minutes. Remove from the wok with a slotted spoon and transfer to a bowl.
3 Add the sesame oil, chilies, ginger, turmeric, fish sauce, salt, and sugar, if using, to the wok. Stir-fry, for 3 minutes. Add the ground shrimp and stir-fry for 4 minutes.
4 If the mixture becomes too dry, add about 4 tablespoons of water and stir-fry for 2–3 minutes. Return the onions and garlic to the wok, stir once, and add more salt, if necessary.
5 Stir-fry for 1–2 minutes, then add the lime juice and stir for a few seconds. Remove from the heat and let stand until cold. Transfer the relish to an airtight jar. Can be kept refrigerated for up to 4 weeks.

KCal 116 P 16g C 4g S 1.4g TF 4g SF 0.8g UF 3.2g (per 1oz)

SERUNDENG

Roasted grated coconut (Indonesia)

Several Asian countries use roasted coconut as a garnish. In Indonesia, however, it is something more: Serundeng contains ingredients that make the grated coconut tastier, more savory, and aromatic. It is often mixed with fried peanuts or small pieces of fried or grilled steak and served as a buffet dish.

INGREDIENTS

2½ cups (250g) freshly grated coconut (see steps below) or
2½ cups (250g) dried coconut soaked in
½ cup (125ml) cold water for 5 minutes
5 fresh kaffir lime leaves (see page 26)

For the paste

5 shallots, chopped
3 garlic cloves, chopped
2 tsp ground coriander
1 tsp ground cumin
1–2 small dried red chilies
1 tsp dried shrimp paste (see page 31), optional
2 tbsp tamarind water (see page 101)
3 tbsp vegetable oil
1 tsp salt, plus extra to taste

PREPARATION

1 Put all the paste ingredients in a blender and blend until as smooth as possible. Transfer the paste mixture to a wok and simmer, stirring frequently, for 3 minutes.

2 Add the grated fresh coconut or soaked dried coconut and the lime leaves. Cook over medium heat, stirring continuously, until the coconut is golden brown. Add more salt, to taste, and remove the pan from the heat.

3 Use the Serundeng immediately, or transfer to an airtight container and store in a cool place for up to 2 weeks.

KCal 50 P 0.6g C 1g S 0.09g TF 5g SF 3g UF 1.4g (½ oz)

GRATING FRESH COCONUT

1 Wrap the coconut in a plastic bag, then tap it sharply around the middle with the back of a heavy knife until it breaks in half. Cut the meat into sections and pry it away from the shell.

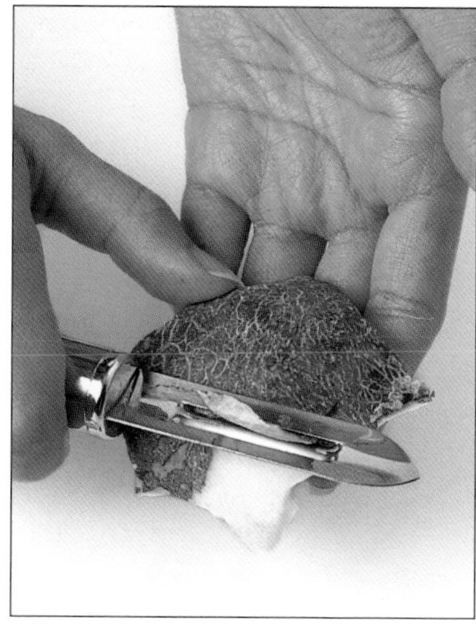

2 Pare off the brown skin from the coconut meat using a small vegetable knife or a peeler. If making coconut milk (see page 141), the brown skin does not need to be removed.

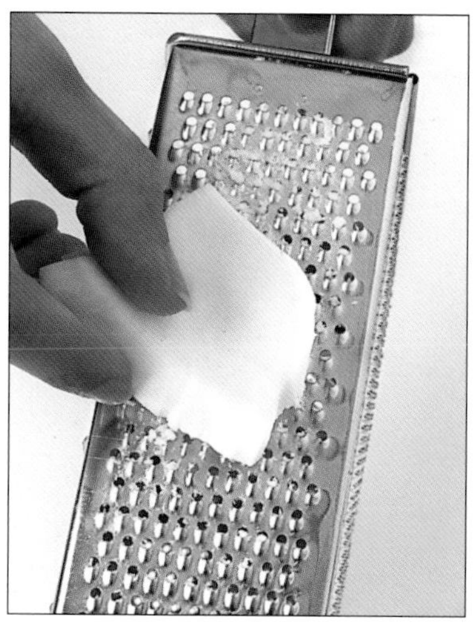

3 Grate the coconut on the fine side of a hand grater. Use immediately or, if necessary, transfer to an airtight container, and keep refrigerated for up to 24 hours.

INDIA

Rich, almost earthy, spice pastes and the fragrance of food cooked in ghee or coconut milk mark the endless variety of Indian dishes. This is a warm and welcoming cuisine, which turns the simplest meal into an occasion, yet lends an informal atmosphere to the grandest dinner.

NAVRATAN PULLAO
Mixed vegetable pilaf.
(See page 126 for recipe.)

PATRANI MACHCHI
Baked fish wrapped in banana leaves.
(See page 75 for recipe.)

MANGAI ACHAR
Mango pickle, center (see page 130 for recipe), with sliced raw onion, cucumber, and pappadoms.

VINDALOO
Pork cooked in hot and sour sauce. (See page 101 for recipe.)

DESSERTS

Every country has its own way of concluding a meal. In most parts of Southeast Asia, dessert is simply fresh seasonal fruit; its sweetness and acidity cleanse the palate and aid digestion. Dishes such as sticky rice cakes and rice porridge, or spiced fruit salads and custards, are considered snacks to be eaten at any time. India and China, on the other hand, have created all sorts of magnificent desserts, most so elaborate that only a wealthy family has the resources to make them. I believe that desserts should be simple and should use local ingredients to their best advantage; that has led me to this selection.

KULFI

Ice cream (India)

This is adapted from a recipe by Camellia Panjabi. It is the best recipe I have found for this Indian dessert, and the easiest to make. In India, kulfi is usually made by professionals and served at grand occasions. It is formed in cone-shaped molds and decorated with chopped nuts and edible silver leaf.

INGREDIENTS

2 x 14oz (410g) cans evaporated milk
4 tbsp sugar
3 green cardamom pods
about 12 strands of saffron
3 tbsp heavy cream

PREPARATION

1 Put the evaporated milk, sugar, and cardamoms into a heavy-based pan. Cook over low heat for 10 minutes, stirring and scraping the sides and bottom of the pan continuously.
2 Remove the pan from the heat and discard the cardamoms. Add the saffron, mix well, and let cool.
3 Stir the heavy cream into the kulfi, then spoon it into individual molds. Alternatively, pour the kulfi into ice-cube trays or a shallow freezer-proof baking dish. Transfer the kulfi to the freezer and freeze for a minimum of 4 hours, or until solid.
4 To serve, dip each mold quickly into hot water, to loosen the ice cream, then invert onto a serving plate and press out the kulfi.
5 Alternatively, press the kulfi out of the ice-cube trays or, if using a baking dish, cut the kulfi into 1½in (4cm) squares. Pile up several squares on each plate and serve immediately.

KCal 439 P 17g C 39g S 0.4g TF 25g SF 15g UF 8g (4)

BUBUR KETAN HITAM

Black glutinous rice porridge (Indonesia)

I have eaten this since I was a little girl. It is delicious served hot or cold for breakfast, or as a dessert after any meal. I was not at all surprised to learn, during a recent trip to Bali, that this has become a popular breakfast dish in big hotels with visitors from all over the world.

INGREDIENTS

8 cups (2 liters) coconut milk (see page 141)
½ cup (125g) black glutinous rice (see page 24), soaked in cold water overnight, drained
½ tsp salt, plus extra to taste
1 cinnamon stick
2 tbsp grated jaggery (see page 30) or dark brown sugar
2 tbsp superfine sugar

PREPARATION

1 Reserve 1 cup (250ml) of the coconut milk and pour the remainder into a large pan. Add the drained black rice, salt, and cinnamon stick. Bring to a boil, then reduce the heat and simmer slowly for 10 minutes.
2 Add the jaggery and superfine sugar to the pan and simmer, stirring frequently, for about 1 hour, or until the porridge is thick. Remove from the heat.
3 Discard the cinnamon stick, and pour the rice into a serving bowl. Let the porridge cool slightly. Serve warm, or transfer to the refrigerator when cold and chill until required.
4 To serve, put the reserved coconut milk and a large pinch of salt in a small pan. Heat gently for 1–2 minutes and serve with the rice. Alternatively, serve the porridge with light or heavy cream.

KCal 298 P 4g C 69g S 0.8g TF 2g SF 1g UF 0.3g (4)

RUJAK

Hot, spicy fruit salad (Indonesia)

This is another classic Indonesian dish that has made its way to Malaysia. There it is known as "rojak" and ingenious chefs serve meat dishes with rojak sauce. But this original Indonesian version is still a favorite, especially with women, who eat it as a snack at almost any time of the day. Eat it like a fruit salad, or serve instead of a vegetable salad with satay or any other grilled meat. See page 73 for illustration.

INGREDIENTS

1 pomelo, segmented
1 firm medium mango, peeled, flesh removed from either side of the central pit, halved, and sliced
1 green apple, quartered and cored, cut into chunks
2 firm pears, peeled, quartered, and cored, cut into chunks
1 small pineapple, peeled, quartered, and cored, cut into chunks
½ cucumber, halved lengthwise, seeded, and sliced

For the sauce
1–3 fresh red bird's-eye chilies
1 slice dried shrimp paste, grilled (see page 31), optional
¾ cup (175g) jaggery (see page 30), chopped
½ tsp salt
2 tbsp tamarind water (see page 101) or lemon juice

PREPARATION

1 For the sauce, crush the chilies and shrimp paste, if using, with a mortar and pestle.

2 Add the jaggery and salt and pound until everything is blended together. Add the tamarind water or lemon juice and stir well with a spoon.

3 Transfer the sauce to a serving bowl, add all the prepared fruit and cucumber, and mix well. Serve immediately or chill lightly.

KCal 293 P 3g C 76g S 0.3g TF 0.6g SF 0.04g UF 0.2g (4)

HAHNG YAHN DAUH FUH

Almond float (China)

This recipe, similar to Gulaman (see page 138 for recipe), is an almond gelatin served on a fruit sauce. See page 97 for illustration.

INGREDIENTS

For the gelatin
2 cups (450ml) water
4 tsp powdered gelatin
2 cups (450ml) milk
3 tbsp superfine sugar
1 tsp almond extract

For the fruit sauce
2 cups (450ml) fresh orange juice
½ cup (100g) sugar
14oz–1lb (425–500g) fresh fruit, such as cubed pears, peaches, and melon and whole blueberries

PREPARATION

1 For the gelatin, pour ½ cup (125ml) of the water into a small pan. Sprinkle the gelatin over it and let stand. Put the remaining water, the milk, and sugar in another pan. Bring almost to a boil, stirring frequently, then remove from the heat.

2 Warm the gelatin over low heat until dissolved. Stir into the milk and add the almond extract. Stir for 1–2 minutes, then pour into a container about 8in (20cm) square. Let cool, then refrigerate.

3 For the sauce, put the orange juice and sugar in a pan. Bring to a boil and boil for 4–5 minutes, until syrupy. Add the fruit and simmer for 2 minutes. Transfer the sauce to a bowl and let stand until cold.

4 Remove the gelatin from the refrigerator and cut into diamond shapes or triangles. Arrange on top of the sauce and serve cold or lightly chilled.

KCal 317 P 7g C 65g S 0.09g TF 5g SF 3g UF 1g (4)

VATALAPAN

Spiced coconut custard (Sri Lanka)

My Sri Lankan friend Thana Srikantha gave me this recipe. She uses kitul treacle, which is available only in Sri Lankan shops, but jaggery will also work well.

INGREDIENTS

4 eggs
scant 1 cup (200ml) kitul treacle or melted jaggery (see page 30) or brown sugar syrup (see page 156)
scant ½ cup (100ml) water
scant 1 cup (200ml) thick coconut milk (see page 141)
1¼ tsp mixed spice (see page 156)

PREPARATION

1 Put the eggs and treacle in a large bowl and beat thoroughly until quite pale in color. Add the water, coconut milk, and mixed spice. Continue beating until all the ingredients are well mixed.

2 Pour the mixture into a 5 cup (1.25 liter) soufflé dish. Put a circle of waxed paper across the top of the mold, then tie a piece of cheesecloth over it.

3 Stand the mold in a large pan. Pour enough hot water around it to come halfway up the sides. Cover the pan and steam for 25 minutes.

4 Remove the mold from the pan and take off the cheesecloth and waxed paper. Unmold the custard onto a serving plate and serve hot or cold.

KCal 272 P 8g C 41g S 0.1g TF 11g SF 6g UF 4g (4)

Gulaman

Fresh fruit mold (Philippines)

Fruit gelatin molds are typical of Southeast Asia. They are set with agar-agar, made from a type of seaweed, which can jell without being chilled. The Filipino version is usually made creamy with evaporated milk, but here I suggest coconut cream and eggs. Though mango is a favorite fruit, almost any fruit in season can be used, and the strawberries make this a delicious summer dessert for temperate climates.

INGREDIENTS

For the mold

5 cups (1.25 liters) cold water
½ oz (15g) agar agar strands (see page 31), soaked in cold water for 1 hour, then drained
1 pint (500g) fresh strawberries
2 tbsp superfine sugar
2 eggs, beaten
½ cup (120ml) coconut cream (see page 141)
pinch of salt

To decorate

fresh fruit, such as raspberries, redcurrants, and blueberries

Egg

Superfine sugar

Strawberries

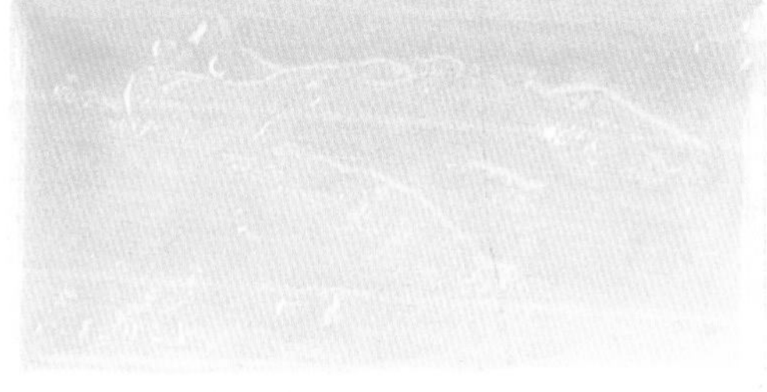

Agar agar

PREPARATION

1 For the gelatin, put the water and the drained agar-agar strands into a pan. Bring to a boil, then simmer, stirring occasionally, until the agar-agar has dissolved. Remove the pan from the heat.
2 Strain the liquid through a sieve into a measuring cup, then pour half of it into a bowl.
3 Reserve a few of the strawberries for decoration and put the remainder in a blender with the sugar. Blend the mixture for a few seconds, then pass the resulting pulp through a fine sieve into a bowl.
4 Pour the strawberry juice into one quantity of the agar-agar mixture, stirring vigorously with a wooden spoon.
5 Pour the strawberry gelatin mixture into a flat-based container, such as a baking pan, about 9in (23cm) square. Let set in a cool place, or refrigerate for about 30 minutes.
6 Pour the remaining agar-agar mixture into a pan and add the beaten eggs, coconut cream, and salt. Heat very gently for about 5 minutes, stirring continuously, until the mixture thickens enough to coat the back of the spoon. Do not overheat the mixture or the eggs will curdle.
7 Pour the coconut mixture into a second flat-based container, preferably the same size as the one used for the strawberry gelatin. Let stand in a cool place or refrigerate until set.
8 To serve, cut the gelatin into equal-sized diamond shapes, about 2½ in (6cm) long. Arrange the gelatin in a decorative pattern on a large serving platter or individual plates. Decorate with the reserved strawberries and the other fresh fruit.

KCal 221 P 6g C 20g S 0.2g TF 14g SF 10g UF 3g (4)

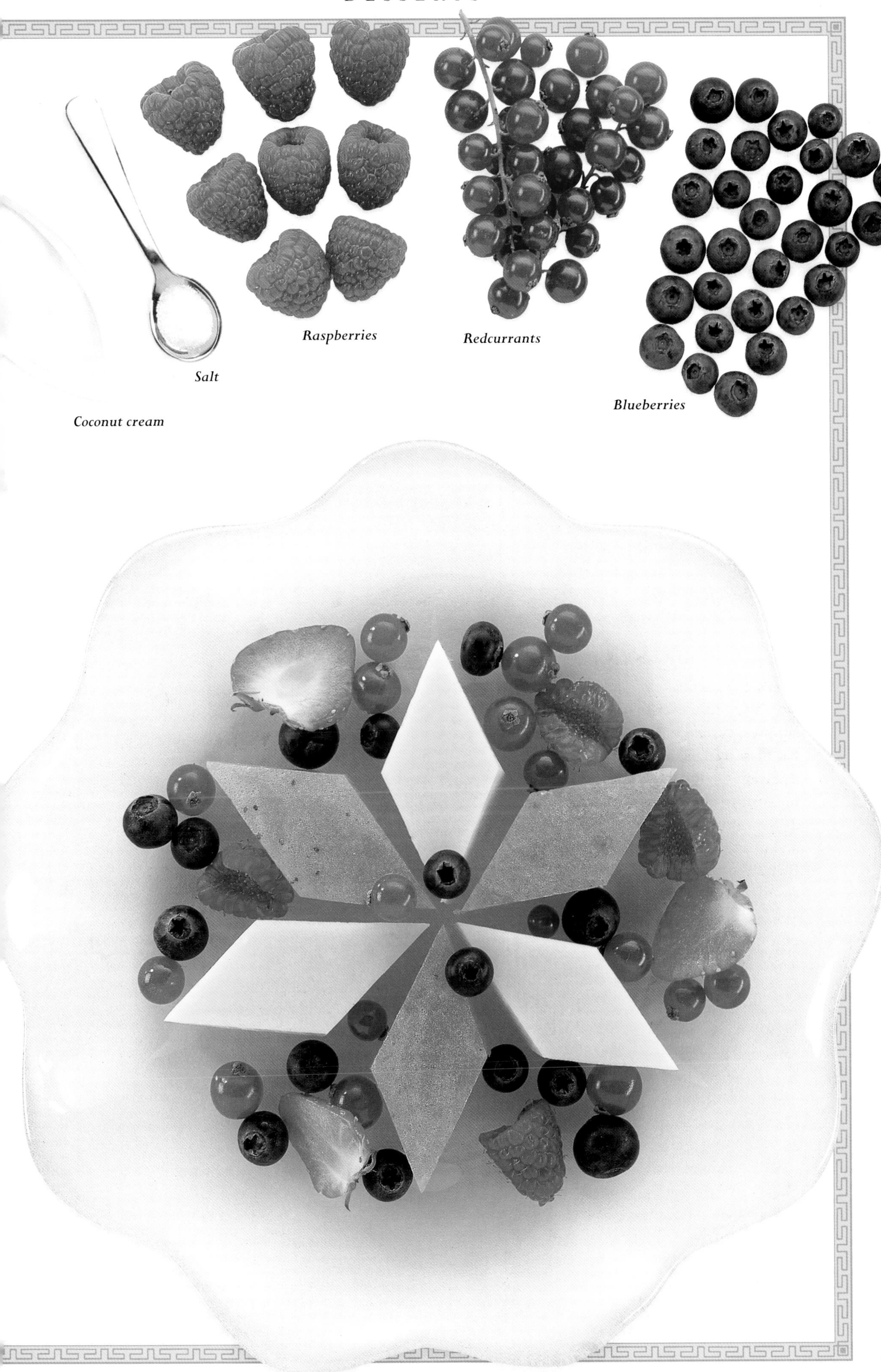
Raspberries
Redcurrants
Salt
Blueberries
Coconut cream

Pisang Goreng

Fried bananas (Indonesia / Malaysia)

These are very easy to make. In the tropics we have many varieties of banana that are suitable for frying, each with its own distinctive flavor. Ordinary bananas are perfectly good, but even better are ripe yellow plantains, which fry with a firmer and better texture. Serves 4–6.

INGREDIENTS

¾ cup (90g) rice flour (see page 31)
¼ cup (30g) all-purpose flour
pinch of salt
2 tbsp butter, melted
¾ cup (175ml) coconut milk (see steps opposite)
3 yellow plantains (see page 20) or 4 fairly ripe bananas
peanut oil or clarified butter for frying

PREPARATION

1 Sift both the flours and salt into a bowl. Mix the melted butter with the coconut milk and gradually stir into the dry ingredients until the mixture forms a smooth batter.
2 Cut the plantains lengthwise down the middle, then cut each half across into 3 pieces. For bananas, cut each in half and then across into 2 pieces.
3 Heat some oil in a skillet or a deep-fat fryer. Dip several pieces of banana into the batter and coat well. Add to the oil and shallow- or deep-fry for 3–4 minutes per batch, or until golden brown.
4 Remove from the pan with a slotted spoon and drain on paper towels. Keep warm while frying the remaining batches and serve hot or cold.

KCal 389 P 3g C 55g S 0.2g TF 18g SF 7g UF 10g (4)

Kolak Labu Kuning

Pumpkin in coconut syrup (Malaysia)

You can find this dish in most Southeast Asian countries, with various names. The pumpkin can be replaced with sweet potatoes or bananas. Serve by itself or as an accompaniment to sweet glutinous rice (see below) instead of the mango. Serves 4–6.

INGREDIENTS

1 lb (500g) peeled pumpkin, cut into ½ in (1cm) cubes
2½ cups (600ml) boiling water
scant ½ cup (90g) grated jaggery (see page 30) or light brown sugar
2½ cups (600ml) thick coconut milk (see steps opposite)
pinch of salt

PREPARATION

1 Put the pumpkin in a large pan with the boiling water and boil for 5 minutes. Drain and set aside.
2 Put the sugar in another pan and melt over medium heat. When the sugar is liquid and bubbling, pour in the coconut milk, a little at a time, stirring continuously. Add the salt and simmer for 2 minutes.
3 Add the pumpkin and cook over low heat, stirring occasionally, for 5–8 minutes. Remove from the heat and serve hot or cold.

KCal 254 P 3g C 33g S 0.3g TF 14g SF 12g UF 1g (4)

Mamuang Kuo Nieo

Mango with sweet glutinous rice (Thailand)

Although this is considered a classic Thai dessert, it is equally popular in Malaysia, Indonesia, and the Philippines. Mango is the favorite fruit, with durian a close second, followed by jackfruit. Pumpkin in Coconut Syrup (see above) also goes well with this rice. Serves 6–8.

INGREDIENTS

1 lb (500g) white glutinous rice (see page 24), soaked in cold water for 1 hour and drained
2½ cups (600ml) coconut milk (see steps opposite)
pinch of salt
3 tbsp superfine sugar
4 small or 2 large ripe mangoes, peeled, flesh removed from either side of the central pit, and sliced or cubed

PREPARATION

1 Put the rice, coconut milk, salt, and sugar in a pan. Stir and bring to a boil. Stir again and simmer, uncovered, until all the liquid is absorbed by the rice. Remove the pan from the heat, cover, and let stand for 5 minutes.
2 Transfer the rice to a bamboo steamer (see page 149) lined with cheesecloth, or the top of a double boiler. Cover and steam for 15–20 minutes.
3 Line 6 or 8 ramekins or individual soufflé dishes with plastic wrap and press the rice into them. Alternatively, press the rice onto a tray lined with plastic wrap to make a cake about ½ in (1cm) thick, then cut into diamond-shaped pieces.
4 Place one unmolded rice cake, or a few diamond shapes in the center of each plate. Arrange some mango around the rice and serve immediately.

KCal 399 P 8g C 87g S 0.2g TF 2g SF 0.6g UF 1g (6)

Making Coconut Milk & Cream

1 Put 2 cups (175g) dried coconut or freshly grated coconut (see page 133) in a blender and pour in 2½ cups (600ml) warm water. Blend the two together for about 4 seconds, until evenly mixed.

2 Pour the mixture into a sieve over a bowl and squeeze it to extract the milk. This produces **thick milk**. For **thin milk**, return the coconut to the blender and add 2½ cups (600ml) warm water. Repeat the blending and squeezing.

3 To make **cream** or **very thick milk**, refrigerate the first extraction for 1–2 hours. The **cream** or **very thick milk** will rise to the surface and **thin milk** will be left underneath. For **standard milk**, mix the first and second extractions together.

Mamuang Kuo Nieo

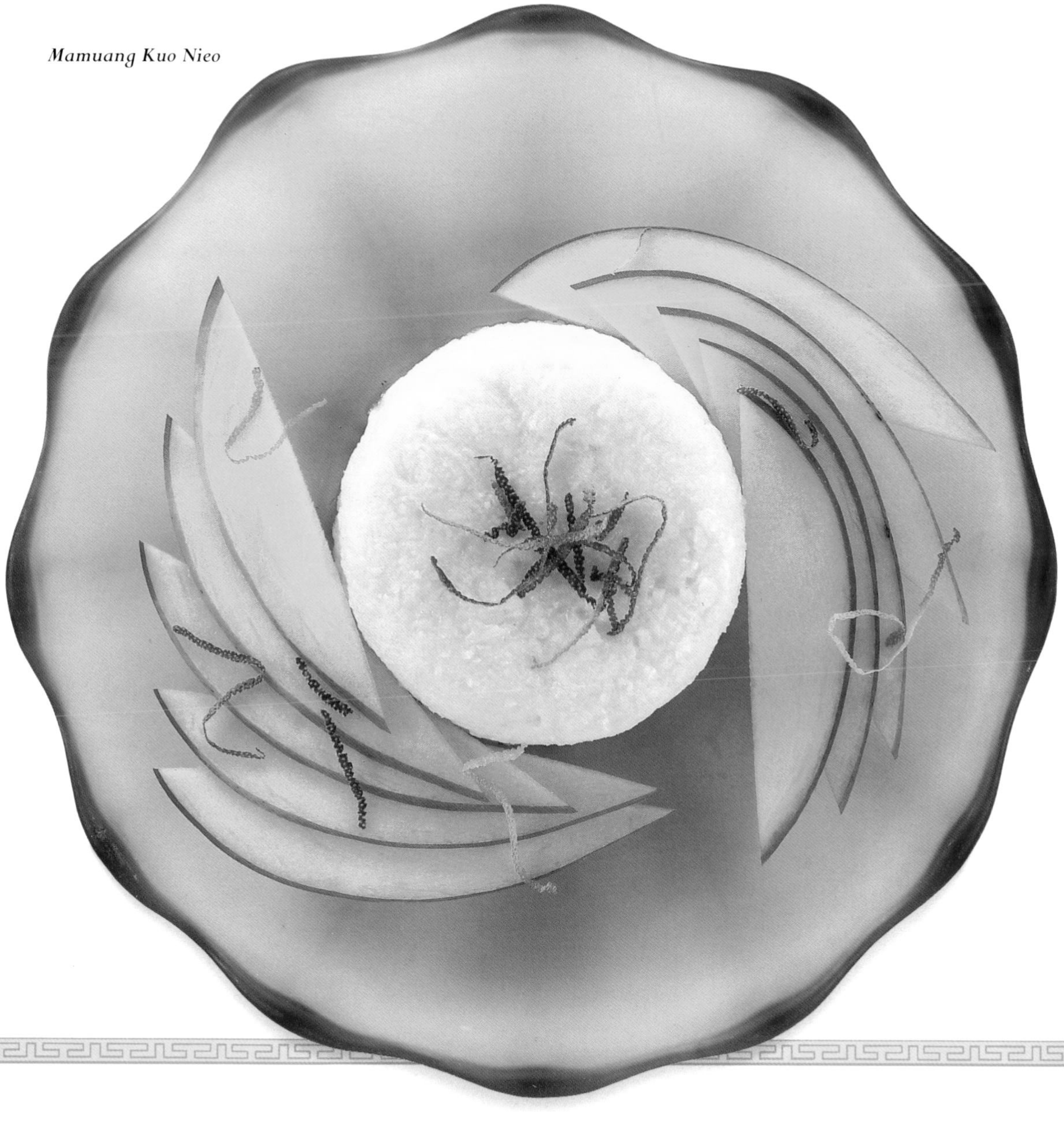

MENU PLANNER

When planning a meal, it is unusual to think, "I want a soup from China and some Thai fish..." Like any art, cooking starts from the resources that are available. But for most people the recipes in this book will be more or less exotic, and some of the ingredients will need to be bought from stores you do not visit every day. So the chances are that you will be driven by a sense of adventure or curiosity, or perhaps a desire to re-create the flavor of a dish sampled during a vacation in Asia or at a rather good local restaurant. These menus are intended as an introduction to the rich and diverse cuisines of Asia. The meals are more or less Western-style in plan, divided into courses (which is not how meals are actually served in many Asian countries). The selection of dishes, too, is not necessarily typical of the traditions from which the recipes originated. I have simply tried to make each menu reflect the food that people in Delhi, Jakarta, or Beijing now like to eat for lunch or dinner. There are no suggestions for desserts, except for the vegetarian menus, because most Asians prefer to end a meal with fresh seasonal fruit.

CHINA

LUNCH

Daan Far Tong (see page 60)
Egg drop soup

•

Sze Chuan Jar Gai (see page 90)
Fried chicken Szechwan style

Steamed rice

LUNCH

Shuen Guen (see page 64)
Spring rolls

•

Hai Jo Mah Ji Mee (see page 124)
Yifu noodles with crabmeat sauce

DINNER

Hojan Hsin Taiji (see page 79)
Stir-fried scallops in oyster sauce

Hak Tjin Tjan Nah Hiu (see page 93)
Stir-fried duck with black pepper

Huhng Siu Ngauh (see page 104)
Red-cooked beef with broccoli

Lo Han Chai (see page 115)
Buddha's delight

Steamed rice

Huhng Siu Ngauh

INDIA

LUNCH
Rasam (see page 60)
Vegetarian soup
•
Jingha Kari (see page 83)
Shrimp curry

Brinjal Pullao (see page 125)
Spicy pilaf with eggplant

LUNCH
Samosa (see page 65)
Pastries with vegetable filling
•
Vindaloo (see page 101)
Pork cooked in hot and sour sauce

Plain boiled basmati rice

SUPPER
Navratan Pullao (see page 126)
Mixed vegetable pilaf

Rogan Josh (see page 48)
Lamb in rich chili sauce with yogurt
with *Mangai Achar (see page 130)*
Mango pickle

SUPPER
Jingha Kari (see page 83)
Shrimp curry

Dhansak (see page 89)
Chicken cooked with lentils and vegetables

Plain boiled basmati rice

Rogan Josh

INDONESIA/MALAYSIA

LUNCH
Pergedel Jagung (see page 64)
Corn fritters
•
Oseng Oseng Ayam Dengan Sayuran (see page 86)
Stir-fried chicken with vegetables

Nasi Goreng (see page 127)
Fried rice

LUNCH
Laksa Lemak (see page 61)
Hot noodle soup with coconut milk
•
Rujak (see page 137)
Hot, spicy fruit salad

DINNER PARTY
Gado-Gado (see page 52)
Cooked vegetable salad with peanut sauce

Rempah-Rempah (see page 70)
Shrimp and bean sprout fritters
•
Ikan Masak Molek (see page 36)
Fish curry

Bandakka Curry (see page 115)
Okra curry

Nasi Kuning (see page 126)
Savory yellow rice

Gado-Gado

Thailand

Lunch
Kai Tom Ka (see page 61)
Chicken and galangal soup
•
Yam Woon Sen (see page 119)
Spicy salad of cellophane noodles, shrimp, and pork

Lunch
Hoy Lai Phad Nam Prik Phao (see page 85)
Braised clams with basil
•
Moo Wan (see page 98)
Sweet pork with marigold

Plain boiled rice

Dinner
Kung Thord (see page 63)
Marinated and fried shrimp
•
Kai Tom Ka (see page 61)
Chicken and galangal soup
•
Massaman (see page 103)
Beef curry

Yam Makhua Phao (see page 113)
Sweet and sour eggplant

Khao Pad Khai Horapha (see page 124)
Fried rice with chicken and basil

Kung Thord

Japan

Lunch
Udon Suki (see page 120)
Hot pot with udon noodles
•
Japanese green tea

Lunch
Bara-Zushi (see page 50)
Sushi rice with julienne of omelet
•
Japanese green tea

Dinner
Satsumajiru (see page 57)
Miso soup with mixed vegetables
•
Suzuki Sashimi (see page 78)
Raw sea bass with vegetables and dipping sauce
•
Fish Teriyaki (see page 77)
Glazed grilled fish

Shira Ae (see page 118)
Mixed vegetable salad with sesame dressing

Plain boiled Japanese rice
•
Fresh fruit
•
Japanese green tea

Bara-Zushi

Buffet (for 10–12)

Menu 1

Muc Don Thit (see page 38), Vietnam
Stuffed squid

Kajitchim (see page 112), Korea
Steamed stuffed eggplant

Pad Som Sin Moo (see page 99), Laos
Pork in coconut milk with pickled onions

Chapchae (see page 122), Korea
Warm rice noodles with vegetables

Steamed glutinous rice

Namjeem (see page 129), Laos / Thailand
Sweet chili sauce

Menu 2

Mohinga (see page 56), Myanmar
Fish soup with rice noodles

Plea Tray (see page 76), Cambodia
Fish salad

Kyet Thar Hin (see page 87), Myanmar
Chicken curry with limes

Adobong Baboy (see page 100), Philippines
Red stew of pork

Gado-gado (see page 52), Indonesia
Cooked vegetable salad with peanut sauce

Steamed white rice

Muc Don Thit

Vegetarian

Menu 1

Gado-gado (see page 52), Indonesia
Cooked vegetable salad with peanut sauce

Pergedel Jagung (see page 64), Indonesia
Corn fritters

•

Navratan Pullao (see page 126), India
Mixed vegetable pilaf

Kajitchim (see page 112), Korea
Steamed stuffed eggplant

•

Pisang Goreng (see page 140), Indonesia / Malaysia
Fried bananas

Menu 2

Chai Siu Ngo (see page 118), China
Vegetarian goose

•

Shira Ae (see page 118), Japan
Mixed vegetable salad with sesame dressing

Chapchae (see page 122), Korea
Warm rice noodles with vegetables

Phool Gobi Aur Aloo Ki Bhaji (see page 113), India
Cauliflower with potatoes

•

Mamuang Kuo Nieo (see page 140), Thailand
Mango with sweet glutinous rice

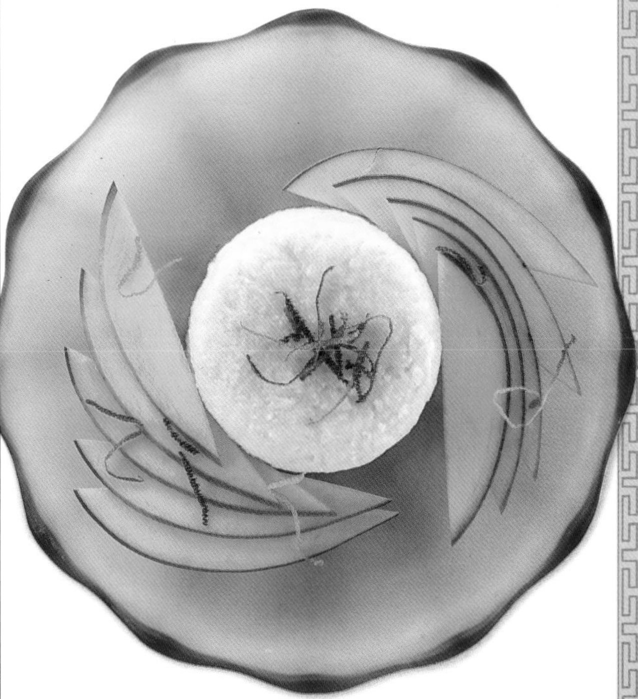

Mamuang Kuo Nieo

TECHNIQUES

Watching an experienced cook at work gives me great pleasure. Much as I love, and use, kitchen gadgets, for me the real joy of cooking comes from utilizing simple, elegant utensils, and from performing tasks made familiar through years of practice. This is especially true in Asian kitchens, where technology assists but has still not quite replaced clay cooking pots, the charcoal fire, and utensils made of bamboo and coconut shell.

EQUIPMENT

Many of the recipes in this book can be cooked to perfection without the need for special kitchen equipment, but the items described here will make some tasks easier to complete. As this in turn will increase your enjoyment of the preparation and cooking of food, the finished dishes will taste better still. Of all the items of equipment shown here, perhaps the most useful and versatile is the wok.

MORTAR AND PESTLE
Made of marble, stone, or wood, this is invaluable for grinding small quantities of spices that would be lost in a food processor. Add a little coarse salt to make grinding easier, or some chopped shallot, garlic, and ginger to make a paste.

CHINESE CLEAVER
This lethal-looking tool is a useful kitchen aid. It chops and slices efficiently, the blunt edge is useful for cracking open coconuts, and the broad blade flattens fillets of steak or fish.

CUTTING BOARD
A wooden cutting board is more hygienic than a plastic one, and knives stay sharp longer when used on a wooden surface. Clean after every use, particularly after cutting meat, scrubbing it well under hot running water.

DUCK HOOK
This is almost essential for Peking Duck (see page 46 for recipe). It consists of three hooks, loosely shackled together, two of which fit under the wings of the scalded and glazed duck. The duck is then hung for 12 hours or so, until the skin is dry and taut.

Cook's knife

Paring knife

KNIVES
Grip and balance are important, and of course knives must be sharp. You need a large knife for cutting up meat and one or two small ones for vegetables; other special knives are useful but not essential.

RICE COOKER

If you eat rice more than once a week, I suggest you invest in one of these. It is not too expensive, lasts a long time, and ensures perfectly cooked rice every time, provided you add the correct amount of water. It keeps cooked rice hot, but the rice quickly loses its texture and is best eaten soon after cooking. Leftover cooked rice should be kept refrigerated and eaten within 24 hours.

SUKIYAKI POT

In Japan, this pot is strictly for making sukiyaki, but it can be used on the stove like any other pan and then brought to the table to stand on a trivet or warming tray. For cooking at the table, it requires a powerful hotplate.

ROLLING MAT

This is ideal for rolling rice for sushi. It is also useful for pressing excess liquid from blanched bok choi. Always use a bamboo mat; plastic is not as good.

WOK

A wonderfully versatile pan – and not only for Chinese cooking. A wok is ideal for stir-frying and deep-frying; a large one, with a domed lid, is also useful for steaming. It can be made of carbon steel, stainless steel, or aluminum. The latter are often enameled, and I find these best because they do not corrode and are easier to clean. Some woks have one handle, others have two – this is a matter of personal choice.

BAMBOO STEAMER

Most people recognize this as the container in which dim sum are served in Chinese restaurants. Steamers are sold in many kitchen shops, but are least expensive in Chinese supermarkets. They are excellent for steaming fish and vegetables, inside a lidded wok or pan. After use, scrub the steamer under hot water and let air-dry.

WOK STIRRER

Once you are accustomed to using a wok you will find that a wok stirrer, also known as a wok scoop, is indispensable. It is by far the most efficient tool for turning and scooping food while stir-frying.

Preparing Fish & Seafood

Most of the fish recipes in this book use fish fillets or steaks. However, in some recipes the fish is cut into thin slices or julienne strips for stuffing and rolling, or using raw in salads. If you use whole fish that require scaling, it is easiest to ask the fish seller to descale them. Seafood must be cleaned thoroughly before cooking.

Slicing Thin Strips

***For best results**, use a skinned fillet about 1½in (4cm) thick in the center. Cut the fillet vertically into thin slices, using a sharp knife. The slices can then be cut into julienne strips, if required.*

Diagonal Slicing & Rolling

1 Take a skinned fillet and trim off any ragged edges. Lay the fillet sideways in front of you and cut it on the slant, horizontally (from head to tail), into four slices of equal thickness.

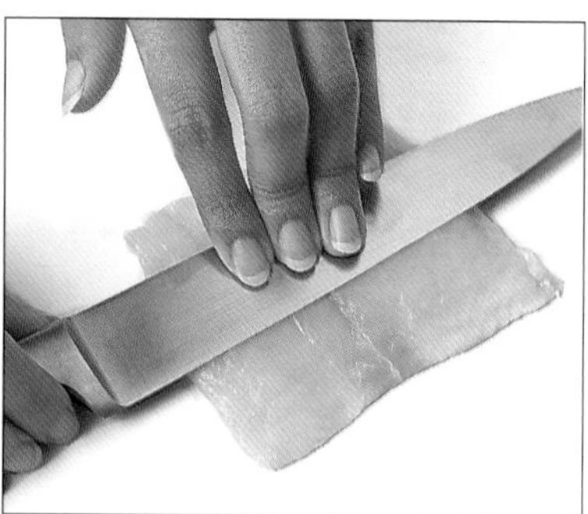

2 For rolling and stuffing, the slices must be flattened. Using the flat of a knife blade, press down on the fish, then drag it across the width of the slice to make it wider and thinner.

Preparing Squid

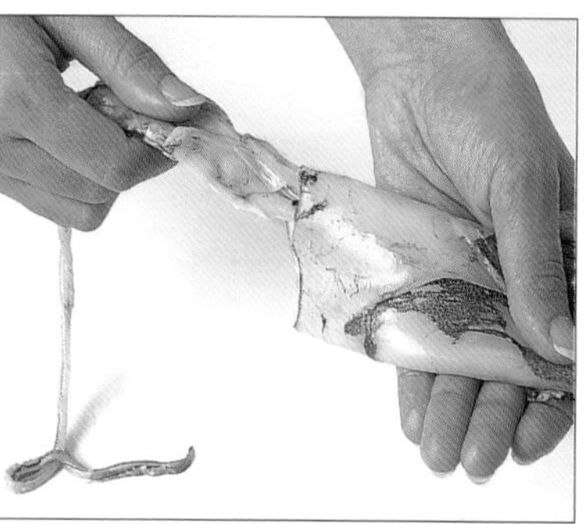

1 Pull the head of the squid away from the body, or pouch, to remove the contents, making sure you discard the transparent backbone, or pen. Rinse the pouch under cold running water.

2 Separate the crown of tentacles from the head of the squid, cutting it off just before the eyes. Rinse the tentacles under cold running water and discard the head and the intestines.

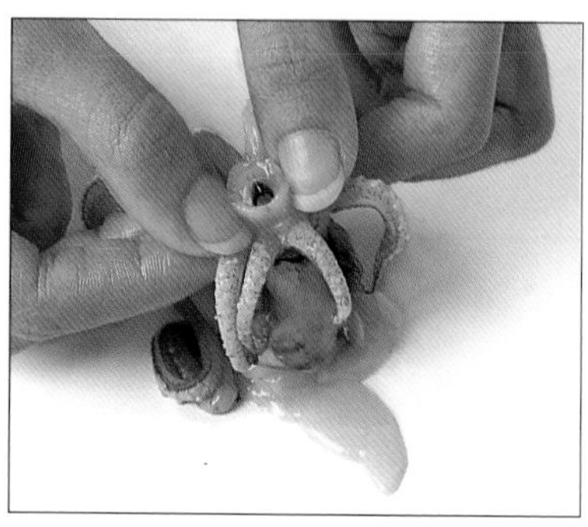

3 Open up the center of the crown and press out the mouth, or beak, with your fingers. Discard the beak and reserve the tentacles as one piece, or cut into sections.

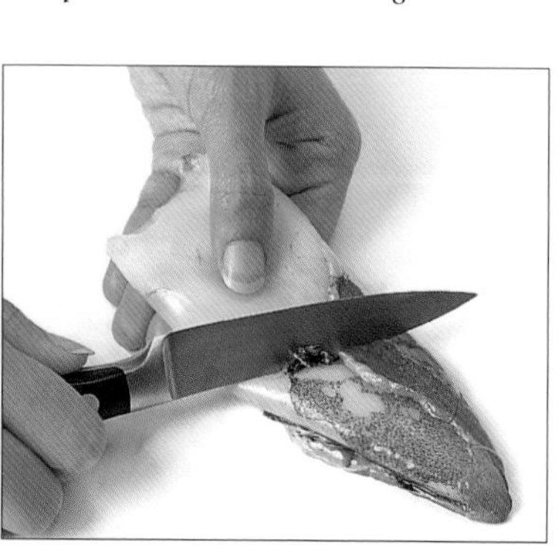

4 Remove the thin black skin covering the pouch by rubbing it with your fingers, or by scraping it off with a small knife. Rinse the pouch under cold running water and pat dry with paper towel.

5 Lay the pouch flat and, using a sharp knife, cut it into rings about ½in (1cm) wide. Alternatively, cut the pouch in half, lengthwise, then cut into diamond shapes or bite-sized pieces.

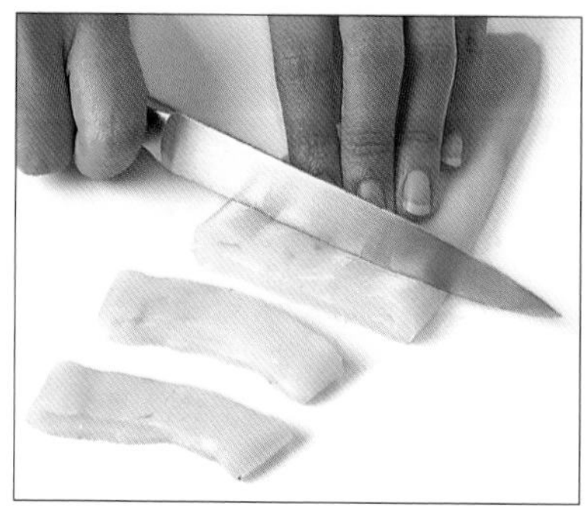

Preparing Cooked Crab

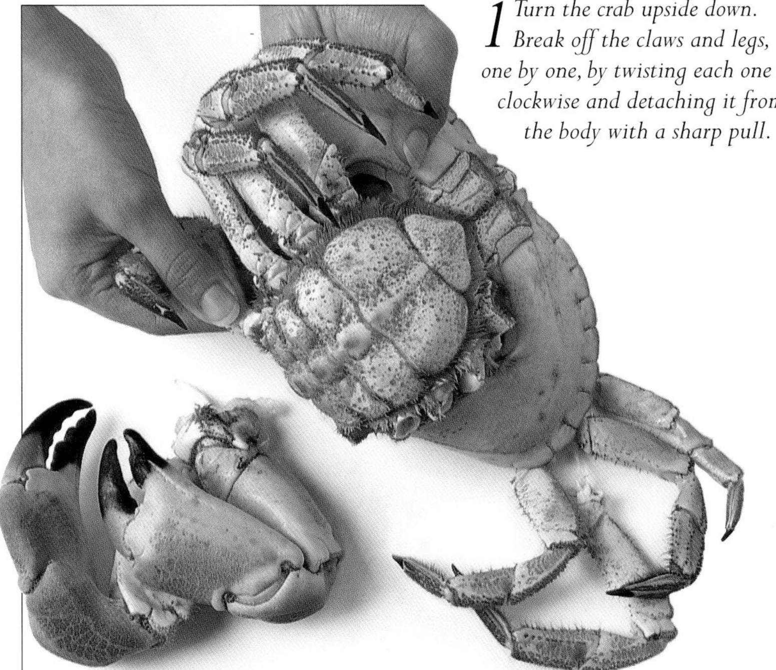

1 Turn the crab upside down. Break off the claws and legs, one by one, by twisting each one clockwise and detaching it from the body with a sharp pull.

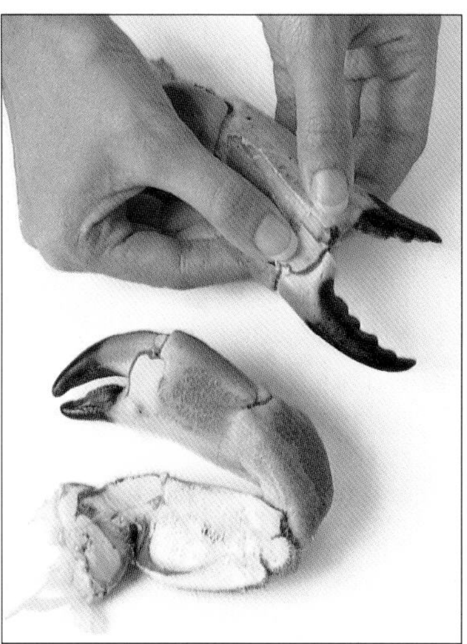

2 Crack the shell of each claw with a mallet or the back of a heavy knife. Extract the flesh and discard the central cartilage. Crack open the legs and pick out the meat with a crab pick or skewer.

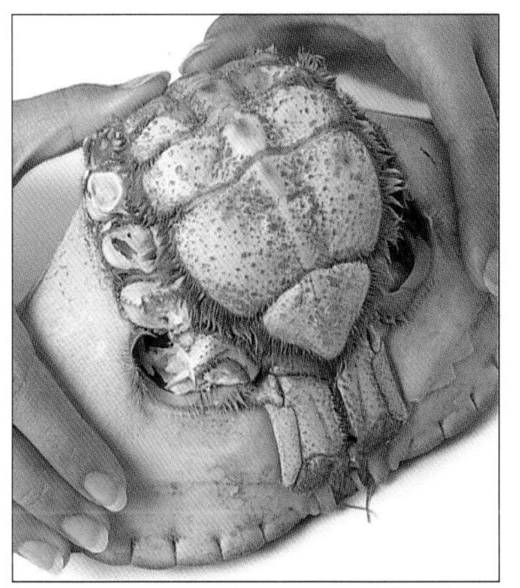

3 Slide a small knife into the join between the body and shell near the tail. Pry it apart, then, with both thumbs, push the body away from the shell.

4 Pull off the feathery gills, or dead man's fingers, from the body section and discard them. They are not edible.

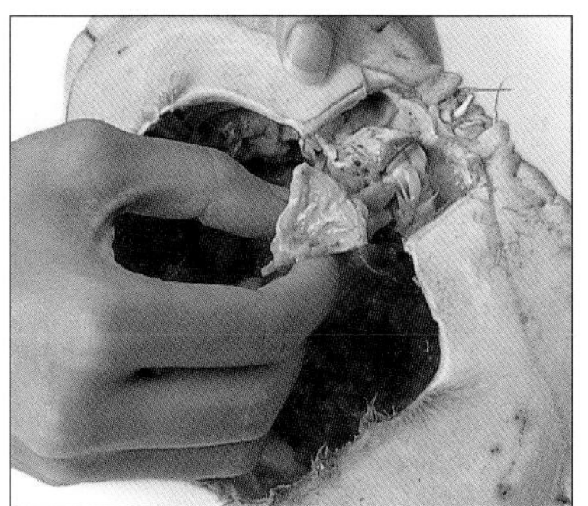

5 Locate the small, round stomach sac, or head sac, situated just behind the eyes in the main shell, then pull it out with your fingers and discard it. It is not edible.

6 Use a teaspoon to scrape out all the soft brown meat inside the main shell. In female crabs, you will also find some edible bright red roe, or coral. Spoon this into a separate bowl.

7 Cut the body section open and poke out all the white meat with a crab pick or skewer. To serve the meat in the shell, neatly break the shell along the line running around the underside.

Preparing Meat

For curries and stews, meat is usually cut into ½–¾ in (1.5–2cm) cubes. When stir-frying, meat or poultry should be thinly sliced or cut into julienne strips, but these must be big enough to be conveniently picked up with a pair of chopsticks, or a spoon or fork. A chicken or duck that is to be cooked on the bone is usually cut into 8 or 10 pieces, see steps opposite. If the bones are removed before cooking, they can be made into stock. The whole carcass of a duck or chicken that has been cooked and had the meat removed is also good for making stock – for example, Deep-Fried Crispy-Skin Chicken (see page 86 for recipe) or Peking Duck (see page 46 for recipe). For a very flavorful stock use a combination of chicken, beef, and pork bones.

Thinly Slicing Meat

***Freeze the meat** for 30 minutes to make it firm. Using a sharp knife, cut it into very thin slices across the grain. For julienne, cut the slices into thin strips.*

Boning Chicken Thighs & Drumsticks

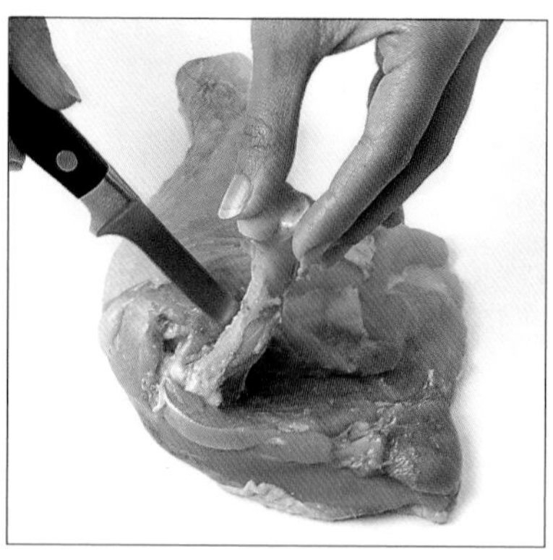

1 Using a small knife, scrape the meat from the thighbone down to the joint. Bend the joint backward, then cut through it and remove the thighbone.

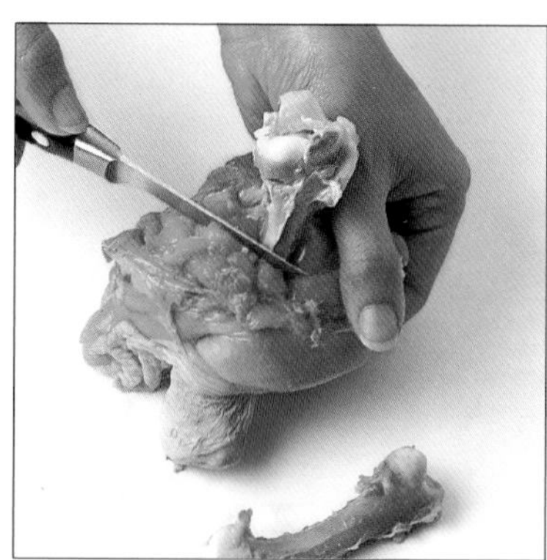

2 Scrape the meat from the drumstick, pulling the meat and skin downward. Pull the bone away, cutting through the cartilage at the bottom if necessary.

Scalding a Duck

1 Place the duck in a colander over a large pan in the sink. Take a tea kettle full of boiling water and pour half over the duck. Turn the duck over and pour the remaining water over the other side.

2 Remove the colander and duck from the pan and place in the sink. Ladle half the hot water from the pan over the duck. Turn the duck over and ladle the remaining water over the other side.

Hooking a Duck

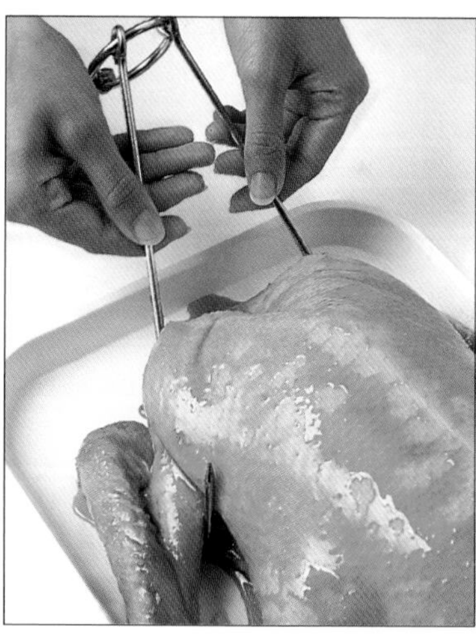

***Lay the glazed duck** on a baking tray. Place the two longer arms of the duck hook under the wings of the duck and make sure they are secure. The duck is now ready for hanging.*

CUTTING UP POULTRY

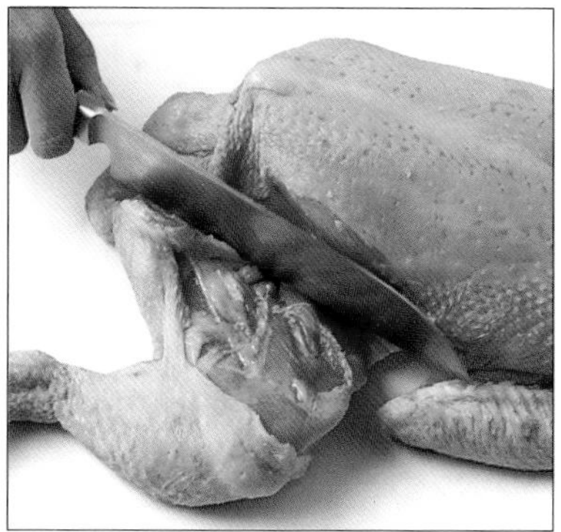

1 Pull one leg away from the body. Cut through the skin to reveal the joint, then cut through it to remove the leg. Repeat with the other leg.

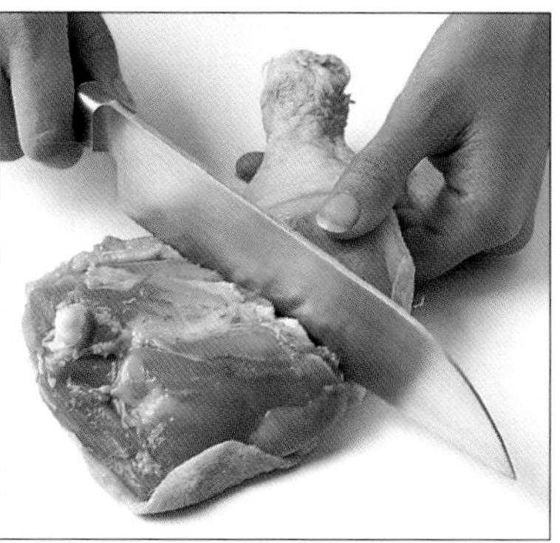

2 Place the legs skin side down. Cut through the joint to separate the drumsticks from the thighs. Cut off and discard the ends of the drumsticks.

3 Pull one wing away from the body until the joint is visible. Cut through it, leaving some breast meat attached to the wing. Repeat with the other wing.

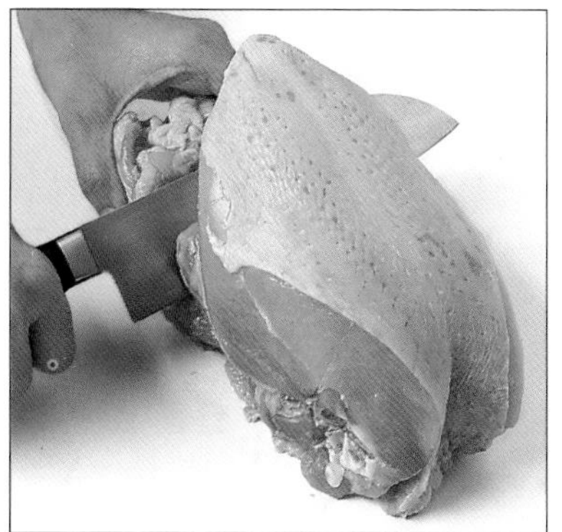

4 With a large, sharp knife, cut through the rib cage beneath the breast meat, until about halfway along. Bend back the underside of the rib cage and cut it off.

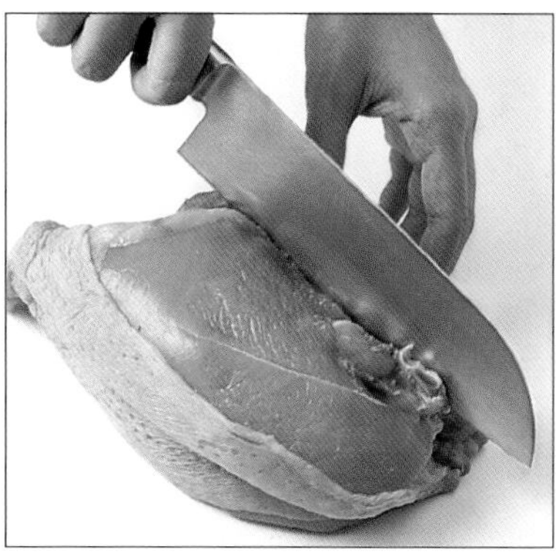

5 Turn the breast onto its side and cut through the shoulder-bone joints on either side to detach the breast section from the rest of the rib cage.

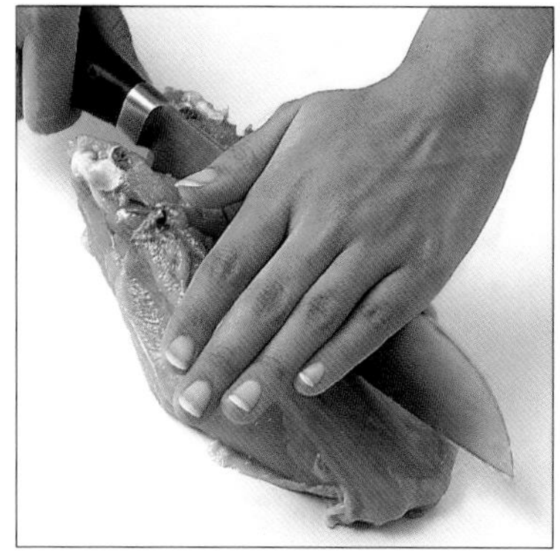

6 Turn the breast upside down. Using a large, heavy knife, and a mallet if necessary, chop through the breast bone to cut it in two down the center.

7 Cutting up a chicken or duck into 8 pieces is suitable for most curries and slow-cooked stews. If you require 10 portions, cut the two breast pieces across in half. The carcass bones and the wing tips can be used for stock.

Wings ***Breasts*** ***Thighs*** ***Drumsticks***

Preparing Vegetables

The preparation of vegetables should really be a matter of individual taste and preference. However, most of the recipes in this book specify that vegetables be cut into a particular size and shape – usually short sticks or julienne strips. In Asian cooking, nothing is cut too large because a knife and fork are not used at the table. Individual pieces of food are picked up with a spoon or fork, with chopsticks, or with fingers, so they must be the right size to be conveyed to the mouth gracefully. In dishes containing mixed vegetables – some curries and stir-fries, for example – I suggest that all the different vegetables be cut into similar-sized pieces. For the Chinese, Japanese, and Korean recipes, vegetables are usually cut into matchstick-sized julienne strips.

Cutting Short Sticks & Julienne Strips

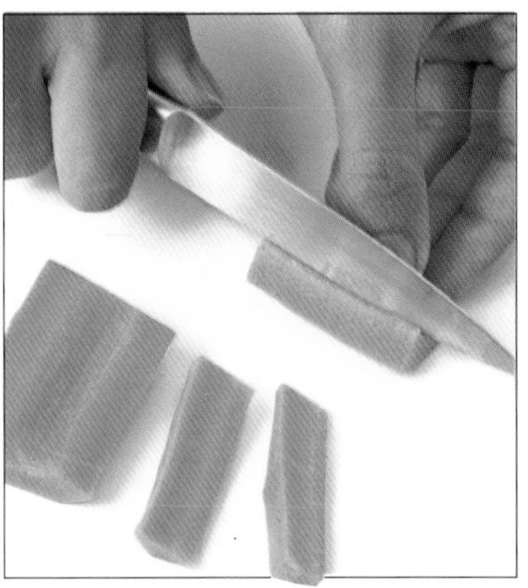

1 For short sticks, peel and trim the vegetable, then cut across into 1½–2in (4–5cm) sections. Cut each section in half, then cut again into 3–4 sticks.

2 For julienne strips, cut the sections lengthwise into thin slices. Stack a few slices together and cut lengthwise again, into very thin matchsticks.

Making Carrot Flowers

Peel and trim *the carrot. Using a sharp knife, cut 3 or 4 V-shaped channels lengthwise to form petals. Slice the carrot crosswise into rounds.*

Rolling Bok Choi Leaves

1 Place the blanched leaf flat. Shave off the thickest part of the stem at an angle, so that the whole leaf is, as near as possible, of uniform thickness.

2 Lay 2 leaves side by side, overlapping slightly, across the rolling mat. Roll them up tightly, without rolling the mat inside, to form a solid cylinder.

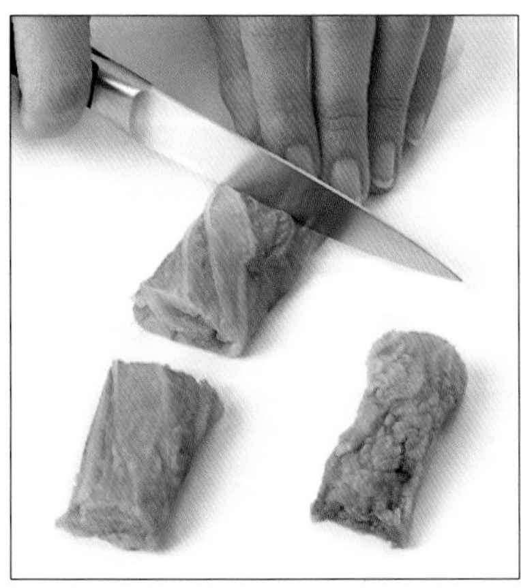

3 Repeat the shaving and rolling procedure until all the leaves are used, then cut each roll across into 4 equal-sized sections.

Making Scallion Brushes & Chili Flowers

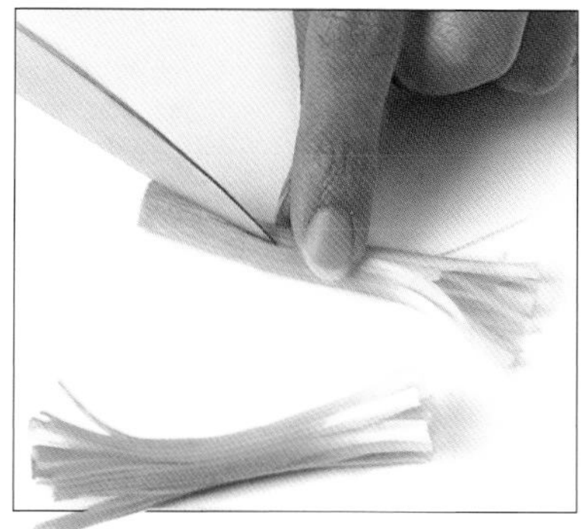

1 Trim the scallion into 2½–3in (6–7cm) lengths. Make repeated cuts lengthwise at both ends, leaving at least ½in (1cm) intact in the middle.

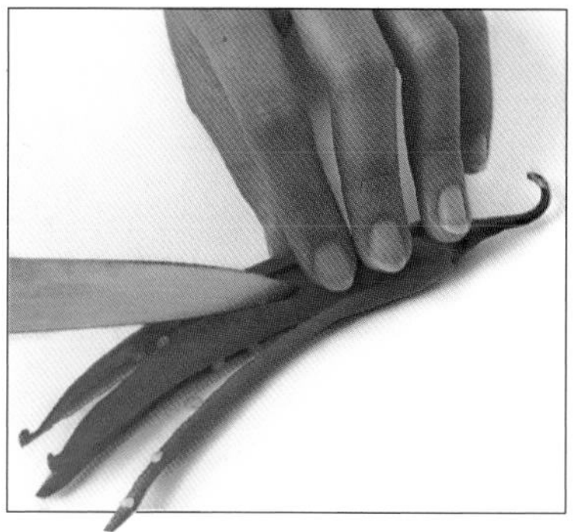

2 Using a medium-sized red chili, slit it in half from near the stem end to the tip. Cut these strips in half, and in half again to give eight petals.

3 Place the prepared scallions and chilies in iced water and refrigerate for 2–3 hours, or until curled into shape.

Cutting Ginger

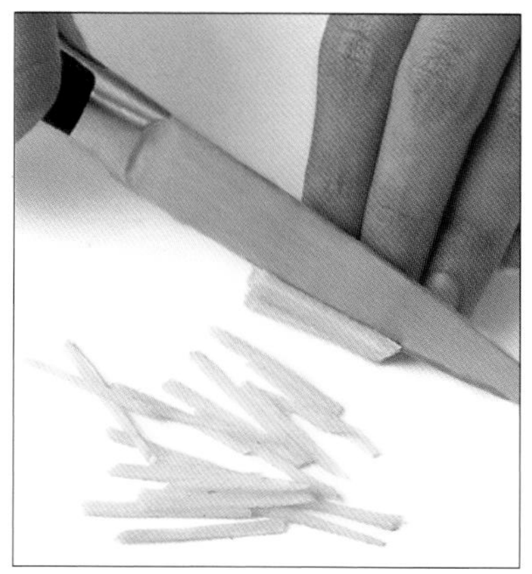

1 Cut a piece of ginger the required size, and peel it. Cut it into very thin slices, then stack up the slices and cut again into very thin slivers or needles.

2 To chop the ginger finely, cut the slivers crosswise into tiny dice. Add these to sauces or blend with other ingredients to make a curry paste.

Making Ginger Juice

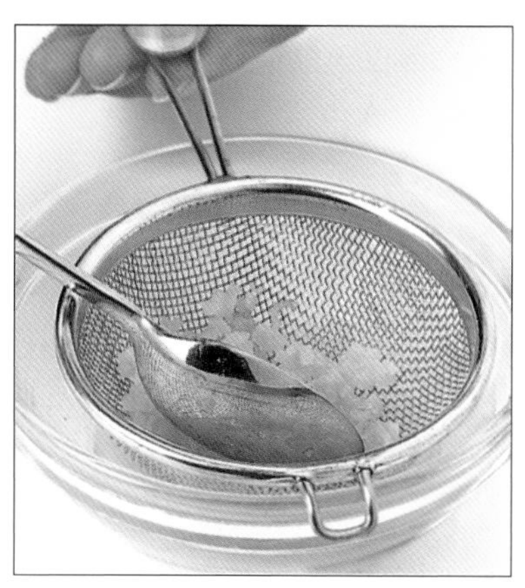

Mix 1 tablespoon *of finely chopped ginger with an equal amount of warm water. Mash with a spoon, then strain through a fine sieve or some cheesecloth.*

Rehydrating Dried Mushrooms

Cover dried shiitake *with boiling water. Place a plate over the bowl and let stand for 15–20 minutes. Remove the stems. Soak wood ears for 15 minutes, then trim.*

Dried shiitake

Rehydrated shiitake

Roasting Seeds & Nuts

Heat sesame seeds *in a dry skillet over low heat, stirring constantly, until pale brown. Allow 5 minutes for pine nuts; 6–8 for peanuts; 8–10 for cashew nuts.*

General Techniques

Cooking Rice

Long-Grain & Short-Grain Rice

The easiest way to cook rice is in an electric rice cooker (see page 149 for illustration), but just as good results can be achieved in an ordinary saucepan or a steamer.

1 Measure the rice into a heavy-based pan: 1 cup (about 250g) is sufficient for 2–4 people. Rinse the rice once or twice in cold water, and pour off all the water. Using the same cup, measure an equal amount of water and add it to the rice. If you like rice fairly moist, add a little more water. Do not add salt.

2 Bring to a boil over a moderate heat, stir once with a wooden spoon, then simmer, uncovered, for about 10 minutes, or until all the water has been absorbed.

3 To "finish" the rice, cover the pan tightly. If the lid is not tight-fitting, put a layer of foil or a dish towel between it and the pan. Turn the heat down to minimum and let the rice cook, undisturbed, for 10–12 minutes more.

4 Leave the lid on, but place the pan on a cold, wet cloth to rest for 5 minutes. (This will prevent the bottom layer of rice from sticking to the pan.) The rice is then ready to serve.

5 Alternatively, to "finish" the rice, put it in a steamer and steam over boiling water for 10 minutes. (If you do not have an ordinary stainless steel steamer, wrap the rice in cheesecloth and steam it in a Chinese bamboo steamer, inside a large pan or wok with a domed lid.) Serve immediately.

Jasmine rice

Glutinous rice

Glutinous Rice

Soak the glutinous rice for at least 30 minutes (2–3 hours is preferable) in cold water, then drain well in a sieve. Put the rice in an ordinary steamer or bamboo steamer, as step 5 above, and steam for 10–15 minutes.

Making Spice Mixes & Other Flavorings

Garam Masala

This is a traditional spice mixture from India and, as with all spice mixtures, the ingredients and proportions vary according to personal taste. You can buy garam masala premixed or make your own. The usual basic ingredients are 1–2 parts cloves, some cinnamon, 2 parts each black peppercorns and cumin seeds, 3–4 parts each coriander seeds and cardamom seeds, and a little grated nutmeg. Slightly crush the spices, then grind them using a mortar and pestle or an electric spice mill. The cumin and coriander can be lightly roasted before grinding, if preferred.

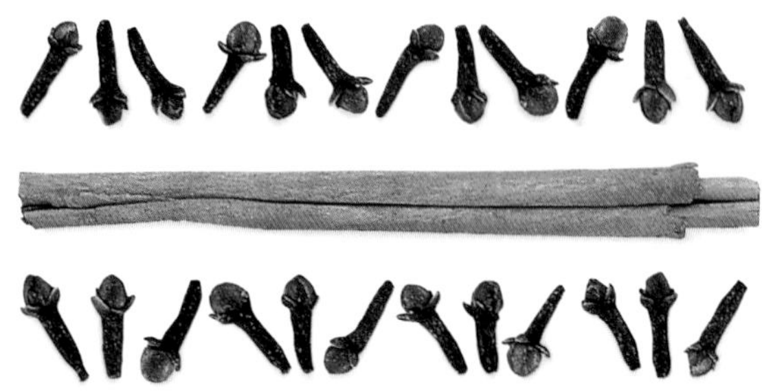

Mixed Spice (Pie Spice)

As with garam masala, the type of spices and proportions can vary, and a lot of commercial blends contain too many ingredients. I prefer to use equal quantities of freshly ground cinnamon, cardamom seeds, cloves, and nutmeg.

Brown Sugar Syrup

This is a reasonable substitute for kitul treacle (see page 31). Dissolve ½ cup (125g) coconut palm sugar (jaggery) or dark brown sugar in 1 cup (250ml) water, and simmer for 5 minutes.

Bonito Stock (Dashi)

Bonito stock can be bought ready-made in an instant form, although it is best to make your own. It is used as a stock or soup in Japan.

1 Put a length, about 18in (50cm), of kelp (kombu) into a pan with 4 cups (1 liter) water, and bring almost to a boil.

2 Remove the kelp, return the water to a boil, then add ½ cup (125ml) cold water and 2oz (60g) bonito flakes (katsuobushi).

3 Bring to a boil again, then remove from the heat, skim, and strain to clarify.

INDEX

Figures in **bold** type refer to pages with illustrations

A

B

C

D

E F

ACKNOWLEDGMENTS

AUTHOR'S APPRECIATION

Like my other books, this book involved a lot of travel and research. Many people helped me in all sorts of ways; I want particularly to mention the Regent Four Seasons group of hotels. I do not have space to name everyone, but I remember them with deep gratitude and send them my sincere thanks.

For this book, I must first thank Rosie Kindersley, who proposed my name to Daphne Razazan, editorial director at Dorling Kindersley. I am grateful to Daphne and to managing editor Susannah Marriott.

I learned much about India, not only from my travels, but also from Joyce P. Westrip, author of *Moghul Cooking*. On Sri Lanka, I was helped by Thana Srikantha and her mother, Mrs. Siwasambu, and on Burma/Myanmar by Kate Riley, who gave me recipes from her Burmese mother and aunt. Soun Vannithone and his wife, Keo, helped with Laotian recipes. On Japan, I am greatly indebted to my friend Hiroko Sugiyama in Seattle, and to Professor Richard Hosking of Hiroshima; on the Philippines to Professor Doreen Fernandez; and on Korea to David Wilkinson, formerly of the Seoul Hilton International. My teachers for Vietnamese cooking were Lan Anh Phung and her mother Mme. Kim, who for many years had a restaurant in Paris. Also in Paris I thank Rosine Ek for her Cambodian recipes, translated for me into English by my friend Suzy Benghiat. In Indonesia I was able to call on William Wongso, Anak Agung Gede Rai, and Ni Wayan Murni. Special thanks, too, to Chef Tam Kwok Fung of the China House Restaurant at the Oriental Hotel, Bangkok, who taught me how to make several Chinese dishes and devised a Chinese New Year menu so that I could watch him cook the food and then taste it. Most of the Chinese recipes in this book, however, are from Chef Simon Yung of the Oriental Restaurant at the Dorchester, Park Lane, London. My good friend Deh-ta Hsiung gave me his recipe for Buddha's Delight on page 115, and checked the names of the Chinese dishes.

I have had the pleasure of working with a great team at DK: Nicola Graimes, Kate Scott, Tracey Clarke, and Toni Kay; as well as designer Sue Storey, home economist Oona van den Berg, and photographers Clive Streeter and Patrick McLeavey.

Finally, I must say thank you to Sallie Morris for supplying Cherry Valley ducklings for photography, and to Roz Denny for Tilda rice; to my agent John McLaughlin; and, as ever, to my husband, Roger.

DK Publishing would like to thank Carole Ash for initial design work; Alexa Stace for initial editorial work; Hannah Atwell for design assistance; Sarah Ponder for the artworks; Anne Sheasby for nutritional analysis; Camellia Panjabi, author of *50 Great Curries of India*, published by Kyle Cathie, for her kulfi recipe on page 136. Roger Owen for the index; Patrick McLeavey for photography on pages 4; 10b,r;12b,r; 13r; 15b; 17b; 63b; 65–6; 70–1; 74; 76b; 77–9; 82t; 83–5; 88; 92–3; 95; 100–1; 103; 106; 109; 112; 114b; 118–19; 124–26; 128; 130–33; 140; 141t; 142l;143t; 145t; 150–55; Ian O'Leary for photography on pages 39b, 82b, 123b; home economists Sunil Vijayakar and Kara Hobday for additional food styling; Rahat Ara Siddique for hand modeling; and makeup artist Sue Sian.

Photography credits key: t = top, c = center, b = bottom, l = left, r = right